Former Naval Person

ALSO BY RICHARD HOUGH

Louis & Victoria : The Family History of the Mountbattens
Mountbatten : Hero of our Time
Edwina : Countess Mountbatten of Burma
(ed.) *Advice to a Grand-daughter : Letters from Queen Victoria to*
  Princess Victoria of Hesse

AND AMONG OTHERS :

The Fleet that had to Die
Admirals in Collision
The Potemkin Mutiny
The Hunting of Force Z
First Sea Lord
Captain Bligh & Mr Christian
One Boy's War (autobiography)
The Murder of Captain James Cook
The Great War at Sea 1914–18

Richard Hough

FORMER NAVAL PERSON

CHURCHILL
and the
Wars at Sea

Weidenfeld and Nicolson   London

For Peter

First published in Great Britain by
George Weidenfeld & Nicolson Limited
91 Clapham High Street, London SW4 7TA

ISBN 0 297 78706 3

Printed in Great Britain at The Bath Press, Avon

Contents

Illustrations

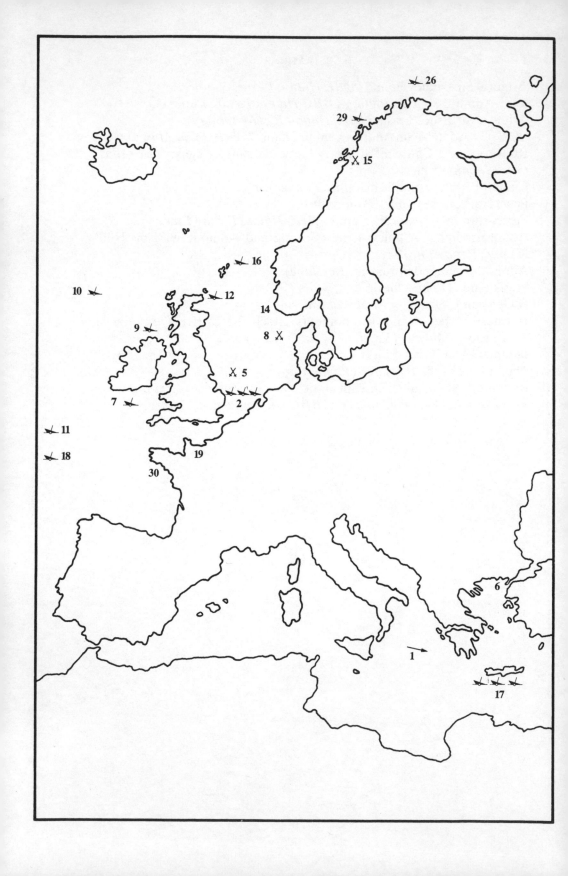

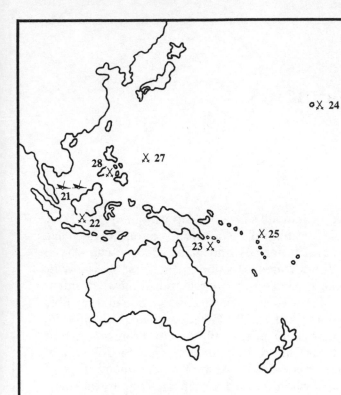

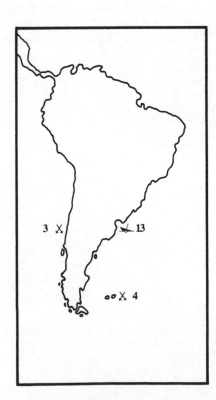

1 *Goeben* escapes to Turkey 10 Aug. 1914
2 *3 Bacchante*s sunk 22 Sept. 1914
3 Battle of Coronel 1 Nov. 1914
4 Battle of Falkland Islands 8 Dec. 1914
5 Battle of Dogger Bank 24 Jan. 1915
6 Dardanelles bombardment opens 19 Feb. 1915
7 *Lusitania* sunk 7 May 1915
8 Battle of Jutland 31 May 1916
9 *Audacious* sunk 27 Oct. 1917
10 *Athenia* sunk 3 Sept. 1939
11 *Courageous* sunk 17 Sept. 1939
12 *Royal Oak* sunk 14 Oct. 1939
13 *Graf Spee* sunk 17 Dec. 1939
14 *Altmark* apprehended 14 Feb. 1940
15 Battles of Narvik 10 and 13 April 1940
16 *Glorious* sunk 8 June 1940
17 Severe RN losses May 1941
18 *Bismarck* sunk 27 May 1941
19 D-Day landings 6 June 1941
20 Pearl Harbor attacked 7 Dec. 1941
21 *Prince of Wales* and *Repulse* sunk 10 Dec. 1941
22 Battle of Java Sea 27 Feb. 1942
23 Battle of Coral Sea 4-8 May 1942
24 Battle of Midway 8 May 1942
25 Battle of Santa Cruz 26 Oct. 1942
26 *Scharnhorst* sunk 26 Dec. 1943
27 Battle of Philippine Sea 19-20 June 1944
28 Battle of Leyte Gulf 25 Oct. 1944
29 *Tirpitz* sunk 12 Nov. 1944
30 German U-boat bases

Acknowledgements

The theme of this book – Churchill's relationship with the Royal Navy and, by association, with Franklin D. Roosevelt – is one that I have discussed with fellow naval historians and many officers who served at sea in the Second World War, and some in the First World War. Of them all I would like to single out for grateful acknowledgement Lieutenant-Commander Peter Kemp, whose contribution and tangible help are evident throughout ; Admiral Sir Guy Grantham, Captain John Litchfield, the late Captain Stephen Roskill, the late Professor Arthur Marder, Martin Gilbert, Sir Clifford Jarrett and the late Sir John Lang, who saw so much of the inside of the Admiralty, and many more of 'the silent service', some of whom wish to remain anonymous. In America the Historical Department of the Department of the Navy and the archivists and staff of the Franklin D. Roosevelt Library at Hyde Park have been particularly helpful, and I am most grateful to them.

RICHARD HOUGH

Foreword

Although essentially an army man, with a soldiering past and a military ancestry, it was the Admiralty rather than the War Office which first claimed Winston Churchill in 1911. 'It was', he remarked, 'the biggest thing that has come my way.' And, when offered a cup of tea by the Prime Minister's daughter, he exclaimed, 'I don't want tea – I don't want anything – anything in the world. Your father has just offered me the Admiralty.'

The regular army was a puny service by contrast with the mighty navy, and at the age of thirty-six Churchill, bursting with reforming zeal and with small concern for establishment feelings and opinions, began a relationship which lasted through peace and war almost until his death. It was never a quiet affair. It was marked by volatile extremes, from his rejection and ejection in May 1915 and his return, like the homecoming of a hero – 'Winston is back!' – in September 1939.

With his admirals, Churchill was, in his early days, impatient, intolerant and highly critical. There were only a handful he admired without qualification – Fisher, Beatty, Keyes among them – all positive, aggressive leaders.

Then, within days of his return to the Admiralty, Churchill received a letter from Franklin D. Roosevelt, welcoming him back to his old job and asking to be kept in touch with the course of events. It was the prelude to a relationship between the self-named 'Former Naval Person' and the President, whose own career had been as closely linked with the United States Navy as Churchill's with the Royal Navy. Thus were born a unique alliance and a personal friendship which were mountainous in their achievement.

It all began – as does this book – with a meeting at sea, appropriately aboard mighty men o'war.

The Fishing Party

On 4 August 1941 the battleship *Prince of Wales*, still carrying the scars of her recent fight with the German battleship *Bismarck*, steamed out of the bleak anchorage of Scapa Flow into the mist of the North Atlantic. Unlike her departure in May, her errand was a peaceful one. There were 14-inch and 5.5-inch shells in the ship's magazines, but there was also rare prime beef, grouse, caviar, champagne and brandy in the galley's stores. There were other refinements for the satisfaction of the battleship's principal passenger, including a number of full-length feature films for showing after dinner in the wardroom. One of them was *Lady Hamilton*, starring Laurence Olivier and his wife Vivien Leigh.

It was twenty-seven years to the day since this passenger, now the Prime Minister of Britain, had sent out the message to every ship of the Royal Navy : 'Commence hostilities against Germany.' As the Prime Minister signalled the President of the United States, reminding him of the anniversary, 'We must make a good job of it this time. Twice ought to be enough.'

And now this Second World War had been waged against the same adversary for almost two years, with Britain and the British Empire and Commonwealth fighting for much of the time alone against the fascist dictatorships of Germany and Italy.

The British people had been told nothing of this trip. A special train had steamed out of Marylebone station in London at noon the previous day with the Chiefs of Staff and their staffs and many others of the hierarchy of government and the war machine on board. An hour later the train stopped briefly at a small station where the Prime Minister awaited it. Winston Churchill was wearing a blue suit, a yachting cap as if heading for Cowes regatta, and he was, as always, smoking a large cigar. He smiled and waved to the crowd on the opposite platform, stepped into the train and, almost at once, settled down to a substantial lunch of tomato soup, sirloin of beef and raspberry and currant tart, washed down with champagne. He was in a jovial mood of youthful excitement for the adventure that lay ahead, an expedition that contained all the ingredients he relished – a secret journey, an historic first meeting at a secret rendezvous with Roosevelt, another man of supreme power and authority, with whom he had struck up a close friendship by letter, telegram and telephone. In addition, he would have a sight at least of the American continent which he loved, and all this with a generous dose of danger.

And now, as the *Prince of Wales* rose and fell with ponderous dignity on the swell, Churchill emerged to take a turn on the quarterdeck, pausing to be introduced to two writers who were part of the Premier's entourage, Howard Spring and H.V.Morton. 'I hope we shall have an interesting and enjoyable voyage,' he said with the faint lisp familiar to the whole civilized world through his recent broadcasts. Then after a brief pause and change of voice : 'And one not entirely without profit.'

The voyage was never without interest but was not always enjoyable, even for the Prime Minister, who evacuated himself from his admiral's quarters in the middle of a night storm and settled himself down in the admiral's sea cabin on the bridge instead. The destroyer escort could not maintain station in this storm and the battleship proceeded on its own at high speed as the best defence against U-boat attack. But there were calmer days later. Churchill conducted his affairs of state, sent and received numerous messages, talked, read one of C.S.Forester's 'Hornblower' books with great enjoyment, and attended a film show every night – his favourite form of relaxation.

The films were a mixed lot, Laurel and Hardy in the unfortunately titled *Saps at Sea* ('a gay but inconsequent entertainment' was the Prime Minister's comment), Paulette Goddard in *Ghost Breakers*, and *Lady Hamilton* which he had already seen four times but which made him cry again when Nelson, dying, begged his old friend and captain, 'Kiss me, Hardy.' When the lights went up Churchill stood, turned and addressed the audience in solemn tones. 'I thought this would interest you, gentlemen,' he said in reference to the *Bismarck* fight, 'who have been recently engaged with the enemy in matters of equal importance. Good night !'

Another pastime for the Premier was playing backgammon with Harry Hopkins. Hopkins, aide, close friend and confidant of President Roosevelt, had been in London and subsequently in Moscow to discuss with Stalin how best the United States could help Russia with war materials. Churchill had taken this frail-looking, shrewd and kindly American to his heart. Hopkins arrived by bomber from Russia in time to join the *Prince of Wales* for this crossing, and he provided welcome company for Churchill. H.V.Morton had first seen him 'standing in the shadow of a gun turret, holding a soft felt hat on his head, a loose American overcoat of brown tweed blowing about him'. He was, wrote Morton, 'a thin man of extraordinary pallor and fragility. He looked as I have seen men look when they come out of a nursing home.' Moscow had caused him to need a nursing home. 'Harry returned dead-beat from Russia,' Churchill signalled Roosevelt.

Hopkins fancied himself as a backgammon player and, it appears, usually beat Churchill. 'The Prime Minister's backgammon game is not of the best,' Hopkins wrote. 'He likes to play what is known to all backgammon addicts as a "back game". As a matter of fact, he won two or three very exciting games from me by these tactics. He approaches the game with great zest, doubling and redoubling freely.'

Destroyers from Iceland rendezvoused with the battleship on 6 August and provided a renewed escort for the remainder of the voyage, which offered no greater excitement than the showing of more films, *The High Sierras* and *The Devil and Miss Jones*, which Alexander Cadogan from the Foreign Office described respectively as 'bad' and 'awful bunk'. On the last day at sea there was a full-scale rehearsal of the reception for President Roosevelt, with Churchill in the leading role – dressed inadequately in the cold wind, considered his bodyguard, who hastened below to fetch the Prime Minister's overcoat.

At dawn on 9 August, a cold grey day with a calm sea, Churchill emerged on to the admiral's bridge, dressed in his one-piece 'siren' (for air raids) suit, his first cigar of the day alight. Only a scattering of sailors on watch were up, besides the eager Morton who was to report this occasion. Churchill was looking for the first sight of the American escort that was to lead them into their anchorage; 'his sandy hair still ruffled from the pillow, he stood watching the sea that stretched to the New World'.

The American destroyers came into sight at 7.30 a.m. and Churchill, now in his uniform of Warden of the Cinque Ports, stood at the salute as they passed by on either quarter, and then led the battleship – full war paint in striking contrast with the shining American men o'war – towards land.

The anchorage chosen for this historic meeting was Placentia Bay, the southernmost of two deep bays which almost cut off the south-eastern tip of Newfoundland. Placentia, the finest anchorage on the eastern coast of North America, is ninety miles deep and fifty-five miles wide at its entrance. 'This is all an iron-bound coast – cliffs against which the ocean swells perpetually dash, and with many harbour openings,' Samuel Eliot Morison has described it. 'The scenery is very fine,' Baedeker declares. Many of the *Prince of Wales*'s company compared it with the anchorage of Scapa Flow which they had left the previous Sunday, but Placentia is grander in scale and the forests rising above the indented shoreline offer a softer scene than the shoreline of Hoy or South Ronaldsay. Lieutenant James Cook, soon to open up the Pacific Ocean, served part of his navigating apprenticeship along this southern shore of Newfoundland as master of the *Northumberland* in 1762. He moored this ship at the entrance for a week, and later his 'Draughts and Observations', according to Rear-Admiral Lord Colville, were proof of 'Mr Cook's Genius and Capacity'.

The battleship rounded the 500-foot-high Cape St Mary's which John Cabot had first noted in 1497. Now, almost 500 years later, 'as the battleship steamed towards that wide inland sea perhaps no more eager voyagers have ever gazed towards the shores of Newfoundland than those who stood together on the morning of Saturday, August the ninth upon the bridge of the *Prince of Wales*'. It was a sight to move the heart of anyone who witnessed it, this powerful detachment of peace-time warships of the New World. With flags flying and bands playing, they greeted this single great battleship, camouflaged and rust-streaked from hawsepipe and bow flare, carrying the man who, more than any other, had defied the tyranny of Nazism.

One American has written :

As the sun burned through the morning fog, the mist broke, revealing a hill-rimmed harbor filled with United States ships of all sizes, their decks lined with seamen that were cheering and bands that were playing. Slowly and majestically the *Prince of Wales*, its band playing and a marine detachment standing at present arms, moved to its anchorage.

The cable ran out on the *Prince of Wales*'s fo'c'sle, the one note on the bugle – the 'G' – rang out mournfully, the booms swung out, gangways went down and the Jack was hoisted at the bows. Churchill and his party prepared to disembark. A message to King George VI was despatched to London : 'I have arrived safely and am visiting the President this morning.'

During the summer of 1941, as the German armies marched into Russia on a massive front, it became increasingly evident both in London and Washington that the two Western leaders must meet. The exchange of messages between Roosevelt and Churchill, becoming ever longer and more frequent, the exchange of officials and emissaries – Harry Hopkins was one of many – provided a stout link, and the flying-boat service across the Atlantic had led to a relatively swift passage for these officials. But Churchill especially was longing for the opportunity to talk personally with the President, and Roosevelt increasingly accepted the need for a long *tête à tête*. In the end, like a woman who proposes marriage, it was Roosevelt who suggested the meeting ; and the ardent suitor leapt at the idea. Harry Hopkins put it more celestially : 'You'd have thought', he wrote of Churchill during the voyage, 'he was being carried up into the heavens to meet God.'

Once the date and place of their meeting had been decided, it was agreed by both leaders that security must be total. For Roosevelt, it would have been politically damaging for the newspapers to learn beforehand that the President was off on a 'war parley'. United States neutrality was delicately poised, and any hint that the President was frogmarching the American people into another European war, however circuitously, must be highly damaging. As for Churchill, whose appreciation of the value of tight security went back to the First World War, he took every precaution to ensure that his whereabouts and his mission remained concealed for as long as possible, for safety rather than political reasons. The North Atlantic was thick with U-boats – a wall chart in the *Prince of Wales* daily noted the position, as far as it was known, of each one – and here was a torpedo's target like no other.

Security was tight, the myth-makers were busy, in Washington. The White House let it be known that the President would shortly embark on the little white presidential yacht, the 370-ton *Potomac*, for a summer fishing trip. *Time* magazine had it all pat for its readers :

Franklin Roosevelt ... glanced at his cluttered desk. There was the same old optimistic cast in his eye. It was still possible to hope, in spite of all, that the U.S. would not have to get into a shooting war. The President was still hopeful .... The heat was melting the tar on Massachusetts Avenue. Mr Roosevelt patted his moist forehead .... Then he fled from the White House, fled from Washington. A week or ten days on the yacht *Potomac* out on salt water would be fine, and, so far as he could see, it was a good time to take a vacation.

Roosevelt embarked at New London at 7 p.m. on 2 August, one day before Churchill left London, to 'cruise away from all newspapermen & photographers & I hope to be gone ten days', he told his mother. Among those he had with him were General Edwin M. ('Pa') Watson, his military aide-de-camp, Ross McIntyre, his physician, and his naval aide-de-camp Captain John R. Beardall. Out of sight of land off Martha's Vineyard, Roosevelt and his party transferred to the heavy cruiser *Augusta*. The *Potomac* then continued her shadow fishing trip, passing through the Cape Cod Canal with four figures impersonating Roosevelt and his party on the afterdeck, and later despatching telegrams *en clair* reporting their catches – 'Watson got the big fish today ...'.

On 6 August the US Navy Department made public a message which aroused a certain amount of curiosity : 'Cruise ship proceeding slowly

along coast with party fishing. Weather fair, sea smooth. Potomac River
sailors responding to New England air after Washington summer.'

The two leaders could not hope to stem all curiosity about their absence and speculation began to grow rapidly. Why was Churchill not
at the christening ceremony for his godson as expected? On 7 August
the *Augusta*'s newspaper, the *Morning Press*, aroused amusement
among the sailors with this report: 'Mystery still surrounded the absence
from London of Prime Minister Churchill as neither London nor Washington officials denied that he had left to fly across the Atlantic for
a rendez-vous with President Roosevelt.'

It may have been inspired guesswork, intelligent speculation or the
result of a leak. But even before the two men met, a Midwest American
newspaper printed the story that the President and Premier were about
to meet somewhere at sea, a Swiss radio station broadcast the same
message, and the Japanese Ambassador in Washington cabled Tokyo
that the meeting was about to take place. In London the Foreign Secretary, Anthony Eden, learned that the cat was out of the bag and suggested to John G. Winant, the American Ambassador, that a statement
be made in Parliament, without mentioning time or place. Winant
passed on the proposal to Roosevelt, who emphatically opposed any
such thing. Later, Roosevelt learned that, contrary to the agreement
that neither side should bring any members of the press, Churchill had
brought two writers, Morton and Spring, masquerading as Ministry
of Information officers. This was a misinterpretation of the role to be
played by the two writers, whose function was purely historical, but
the damage had been done. Fearing the outcry from American
reporters, Morton and Spring were excluded from all US men o'war.
All this did no lasting damage, and Roosevelt determined to make
no reference to upset a meeting to which he was looking forward as
keenly as Churchill, with whom he shared a fellow feeling for the great
historic occasion.

Escorted by destroyers, the *Augusta* entered Placentia Bay on 8
August and anchored close to the battleship *Arkansas*. There was much
naval activity in the anchorage unconnected with the imminent visit.
At the small town of Argentia the US Navy was swiftly building the
facilities for a full-scale naval base on land recently granted to it by
Britain.

The mist had cleared and the morning was turning bright as Roosevelt
came up on deck helped by his son Elliot, and waited under an awning
rigged up midships. The President was wearing a tan Palm Beach suit,
without hat, and for all his fine tall figure and familiar features might
from a distance have been mistaken for a disabled and elderly tourist
at that Florida resort. He watched the admiral's barge carrying the

Prime Minister and his party swing away from the gangway of the battle-ship, which dwarfed all the American men o'war, and cut through the calm water separating the two ships. The side of the *Augusta*'s hull obstructed Roosevelt's view of Churchill momentarily; the Marines' band striking up 'God Save the King' indicated that the Prime Minister had stepped on to the gangway and was making his way up the steps. 'The Star-Spangled Banner' followed the British anthem, the last notes died, Churchill stepped forward with a letter in his hand, bowed almost imperceptibly, smiled and handed to the taller man the sealed envelope. It was a letter from the King.*

The proceedings began with a small awkwardness which, like the security episode, irritated the President. Churchill remarked on how happy he was to meet at last the man whom he had corresponded with and talked to on the transatlantic telephone so often. Roosevelt told him in reply that indeed they had met before, in the summer of 1918 on a day when he had also met the King's father, George v. It was at a dinner at Gray's Inn and Roosevelt as Assistant Secretary of the Navy had made a speech which Churchill, as a member of the British War Cabinet, had listened to. Churchill covered up the gaffe skilfully, but it was clear that he did not remember the occasion. Later, however, in his war memoirs he wrote warmly of Roosevelt at this first meeting at the close of another war before Roosevelt was struck down with polio and Churchill had suffered his many years in the political wilderness. Roosevelt, for his part it became clear later, made no reference to the 1918 meeting in his extensive diaries and letters at that time. It might never have happened.

Churchill was now taken on a brief tour of the American cruiser and rejoined Roosevelt and his party in the *Augusta*'s wardroom, where, thankfully, the US Navy's alcohol prohibition was lifted for the preliminaries but not for the disappointing fork lunch that followed for all but the two chiefs. The British and American officials mingled and then paired off, the American Under-Secretary of State Sumner Welles with Cadogan; General George C. Marshall, Chief of Staff of the US Army with General Sir John Dill; Admiral Harold Stark, Chief of US Naval Operations, with Admiral Sir Dudley Pound; and General Henry Arnold, Vice Chief of US Air Staff, with Air Chief Marshal Sir Wilfrid Freeman.

Roosevelt and Churchill had lunch (*not* dry) at which they spoke freely and easily, rapidly getting to know one another. Averell Harriman, Roosevelt's 'Special Representative', wrote of Churchill being 'in his best form'; and 'the President liked him enormously'. So all

* See Appendix A

Churchill's anxieties, expressed earlier to Hopkins – 'I wonder if he will like me' – were laid to rest.

While the staff talks continued, on subjects from high strategy to some of the more mundane aspects of waging a war in which only one partner was yet fighting, the Churchill–Roosevelt relationship rapidly flowered. Both men had guided their navies through difficult times, loved to talk naval history and naval affairs generally, and now discussed, like old shipmates, the present difficulties in the North Atlantic where U-boats were again proving so destructive and the US Navy was already becoming more deeply involved in the Battle of the Atlantic. And what more appropriately nautical venue could these two sailor-statesmen have than a fine 8-inch-gunned heavy cruiser and a battleship that had so damaged the mighty *Bismarck* that she was soon hounded down to her destruction ?

Churchill returned to the *Augusta* to dine on that first evening together, a lengthy and bonhomous occasion, at which Premier and President as well as the British Chiefs of Staff made speeches. They ate vegetable soup, broiled chicken, spinach omelette, lettuce and tomato salad and chocolate ice cream. Later, conversation deviated from the war and high policy, and, according to Cadogan who was sitting on his left, Roosevelt 'conversed charmingly about his country estate at Hyde Park, where he hoped to grow Christmas trees for the market'.

But Churchill did most of the informal talking and the rest of the company were content to listen. 'Winston Churchill held every one of us that night – and was conscious every second of the time he was holding us,' Elliot Roosevelt recalled later. 'All that Father did was to throw in an occasional question – just drawing him on, drawing him out . . . . Churchill rared back in his chair, he slewed his cigar around from cheek to cheek and always at a jaunty angle, he hunched his shoulders forward like a bull, his hands slashed the air expressively, his eyes flashed. He held the floor that evening . . .'

The emotional culmination of the Newfoundland meeting was the combined service on Sunday 10 August on the quarterdeck of the *Prince of Wales*. It was the sort of occasion that Churchill relished and for which he prepared with loving attention, including the choice of the hymns 'Onward Christian Soldiers', 'O God, our Help in Ages Past', 'Eternal Father' and the sailors' hymn, 'For Those in Peril on the Sea'.

To transport the crippled President from the *Augusta* to the *Prince of Wales* with the least inconvenience required a complex process with the destroyer *McDougal* coming alongside the cruiser's main deck on the same level as the destroyer's bow. The *McDougal* then steamed across to the *Prince of Wales* and made a Chinese landing – bow to stern – on the battleship, again on the same level. The official American naval historian, S.E. (Sam) Morison, described how

the British crew were drawn up at attention along the rail, Mr Churchill alone being on the fantail to receive the President. A chief boatswain's mate of *McDougal* hailed the Premier with 'Hey! Will you take a line ?' Mr Churchill replied 'Certainly!' and not only caught the line but hauled it most of the way in before British tars came to his assistance.

Roosevelt arrived on board dressed in a dark blue suit with an ivory-handled stick, leaning heavily on the arm of his son Elliot, and took his seat next to Churchill facing the four 14-inch guns of 'Y' turret. The congregation, half American and half British, mixed freely and were given only 250 hymn books for the 500 congregation, so that all had to share.

The lesson was from the first chapter of Joshua : 'There shall not any man be able to stand before thee all the days of thy life: as I was with Moses, so will I be with thee : I will not fail thee, nor forsake thee. Be strong and of good courage . . .' The first prayer was for the President: 'Oh Lord, High and Mighty, Ruler of the Universe, look with favour, we beseech thee, upon the President of the United States of America and all others in authority . . .' Prayers followed for the king and his ministers and admirals, generals and air marshals ; prayers for the invaded countries, the wounded, the prisoners, the sick and exiled, the homeless, the anxious, the bereaved ; and a prayer that 'we may be preserved from hatred, bitterness, and all spirit of revenge'.

No one was more moved than Churchill himself. He wrote :

This service was felt by us all to be a deeply moving expression of the unity of faith of our two peoples, and none who took part in it will forget the spectacle presented that sunlit morning on the crowded quarterdeck – the symbolism of the Union Jack and the Stars and Stripes draped side by side on the pulpit ; the American and British chaplains sharing in the reading of the prayers . . .

Roosevelt wanted to see as much as possible of the battleship and her company. He 'was having a fine time', wrote Robert E. Sherwood, 'and so was the Former Naval Person. Here, on the decks of a mighty battleship, these two old seafaring men were on common ground.'

The diplomatic culmination of this meeting lay in the signature of a joint Anglo–American declaration of principles. 'President Roosevelt told me at one of our first conversations that he thought it would be well if we could draw up a joint declaration laying down certain broad principles which should guide our policies along the same road,' Churchill wrote later. On the issue of United States entry into the war, it was evident from the first that Churchill would get nowhere, as he had been warned by Hopkins on the voyage over. But the joint signature of a document of the kind proposed by Roosevelt, powerfully worded for all the world to read, could clearly have an enormous moral effect and proclaim clearly how close were the two Western nations.

Churchill took on the task of drawing up 'the substance and spirit' of what was to be called the Atlantic Charter;* and with encouraging ease and speed the two leaders, with a little compromise on both sides, agreed a draft to put up to their governments. It was, in essence, an idealistic proclamation of freedom and peace at a time when half the world was enslaved or at war, committing the two nations to 'seek no aggrandisement', and 'no territorial changes' without the express wishes of the people; to respect the right of all to choose their own form of government, with freedom of speech and thought; to strive to bring about greater equality of production in the world, and to seek a peace 'which will cast down for ever the Nazi tyranny'.

Roosevelt added two further clauses, committing the two nations to establish peace for all on the high seas and oceans, and to use every endeavour to further peace in the world and abandon the use of force.

This Atlantic Charter, it was agreed between Premier and President, should be proclaimed simultaneously to the world on 14 August, together with a statement that they had held conversations at sea, along with members of their respective staffs; but, striking a cautious political note for the sake of the Americans, there was no reference to naval or military commitments of any kind 'other than as authorised by Act of Congress'.

Churchill and Roosevelt left well satisfied with the meeting, both leaders feeling that future communication must benefit from the intimacy of their long talks. Just as Hopkins from his visit to Stalin had brought into focus the needs and plight of the Russians facing the onslaught of Germany from the west, so Churchill had succeeded in itemizing realistically and graphically the needs of Britain. For his part, Churchill recognized more clearly the political problems Roosevelt had to face while governing a nation that had unbounded sympathy and admiration for the British people but was still hard in its opposition to direct involvement.

American newsmen, who had been waiting at Swampscott, Massachusetts, for the return of the President from his fishing trip for almost two weeks, were furious at being misled and hoodwinked and upstaged

* See Appendix B

by the British newsmen when they had been muzzled. They were advised to move to Rockland, Maine; and there, after two further days of waiting, they got their story. At Penobscot Bay, at 3 p.m. on 15 August 1941, the mist cleared and the blue-grey hull of the *Potomac* came into sight, escorted by a coast-guard cutter. A few minutes later Roosevelt gave them the news of the meeting and the signature of the Atlantic Charter. He did not say where, but *Time* magazine guessed correctly that it was Placentia Bay. 'President Roosevelt was back from the most momentous journey of all his 200,000 miles of White House travel.' And the *New York Times*, recalling the German Deputy Führer's recent sensational flight to Britain, commented: 'Franklin Roosevelt and Winston Churchill, no men to let a beetle-browed Nazi named Hess run off with the title of Mystery Man of World War Two, last week presented the world with the deepest, juiciest, most momentous mystery since the war began.'

The *Prince of Wales* sailed out of Placentia Bay at 5 p.m. on 12 August, the ship's company suddenly rich in the little luxuries that had for long been scarce or unobtainable in Britain – chocolate and razor blades, canned food, stockings for their wives and girls, glossy magazines. The presence of American destroyers as escort as far as Iceland – one of them with the President's son Franklin D. Roosevelt Jr serving on board – emphasized on the one hand the newly reinforced accord between the two nations and the dangers that lay ahead on the return crossing of the Atlantic. They were back at war. This was emphasized on the following morning when the voice of the battleship's captain, John Leach, blared out from every loudspeaker throughout the ship. The captain told the ship's company, and the passengers, that the historic meeting had become known in Germany, and that it was also known there that it had taken place off Newfoundland. U-boat attack, therefore, was likely, and there might also be attack from the air when nearer to Britain. 'If ever there was a time when the utmost vigilance is required, it is upon this voyage,' Captain Leach concluded.

The journey home was completed safely. But within fifteen weeks, the *Prince of Wales* had been sent to the bottom of the South China Sea. Captain Leach was drowned and some 300 officers and men perished with him. When Churchill had been asked in the battleship's gunroom if the Japanese were likely to come into the war, he had replied, 'No, I don't think so.' No loss at sea saddened Churchill more than this.

The USS *Augusta* had a longer war, escorting convoys to Murmansk and bombarding the D-Day beaches in June 1944. Churchill saw more of her proud silhouette when she escorted the *Queen Mary* in which he was a passenger to New York. And in her final exalted role the cruiser carried another president, President Harry Truman, on a more extended 'fishing trip' to and from the Potsdam Conference in 1945.

I
'Kitchener the blackguard . . .'

Churchill had first crossed the Atlantic in 1895. He was twenty and intent on military action, preferably with a touch of glory and a medal. As he wrote later to his mother, he was 'more ambitious for a reputation for personal courage than for anything else in the world'. And three weeks after that he wrote to her again, as 'a philosopher', that bullets were not worth considering. 'Besides I am so conceited I do not believe the Gods would create so potent a being as myself for so prosaic an ending.'

Churchill was a young soldier destined later to impose as great an influence on the Royal Navy as any sailor, but at this age, glowing with the heat of limitless ambition, with no thought of war at sea. Like his great ancestor, the First Duke of Marlborough (Blenheim in 1704, Ramillies, Oudenarde, and Malplaquet), it was the evolutions of great armies, the thunder of artillery, the rattle of musketry and the pounding hooves of the cavalry that set the heart of this ardent lieutenant beating faster.

Years earlier, the young Winston wrote from the ancestral home of Blenheim Palace to thank his mother for his eighth birthday present, 'Soldiers and Flags and Castle they are so nice it was so kind of you . . .' The toy-soldier army grew mightier at every Christmas and birthday until it numbered over 1,400 troops, just as the real-life navy was to increase under his overall leadership when he grew up. He and his younger brother Jack played battles against one another for hours on end. Jack always commanded the enemy and was not allowed artillery. One day, Churchill recalled, his father visited the nursery, which was a very rare event. He had come to make a formal inspection of Winston's army arranged in the correct formation of attack. When all had been approved his father asked him if he would like to go into the army. 'I thought it would be splendid to command an Army, so I said "Yes" at once ; and immediately I was taken at my word.'

He studied the tapestries at Blenheim which depicted the victories of the first Duke of Marlborough, and read of them, carved in stone, on the great column at the palace. Fifty years later he wrote a massive

and adulatory four-volume life of his illustrious ancestor. His early letters were often decorated with military scenes, cannon firing, soldiers
with bayonets fixed. At Harrow school when he was thirteen he enrolled
in the School Rifle Corps. After a large-scale mock battle against
another school, he sent his mother a map. 'It was most exciting you
could see through the smoke the enemy getting nearer & nearer . . .'

The Corps turned Winston into a good shot and Public Schools Fenc-
ing Champion. The school magazine expressed its pride, praising his
unorthodoxy. Churchill's success 'was chiefly due to his quick and dashing attack which quite took his opponents by surprise'.

The young Churchill gravitated towards a career in the army with
the inevitability that brought so many of those who were later to serve
under him into the navy: Admirals Fisher and Jellicoe, Prince Louis
of Battenberg, Arthur Wilson and many others. Churchill was fourteen
when he joined the army class at Harrow, and from that time his education contained a strong element of the military to prepare him for Sandhurst. To the distress of his father and mother he did not find it easy
to qualify and 'was relegated as a forlorn hope to a "crammer"'. At
length all obstacles were overcome and he was accepted by the military
college.

Churchill was installed at Sandhurst in early September 1893 at the
age of eighteen. Writing to his father he described the austere conditions: 'No such thing as unpunctuality or untidiness is tolerated. Still
there is something very exhilarating in the military manner in which
everything works; and I think that I shall like my life here during the
next 18 months very much.'

Churchill's early letters to his father and mother, who were rarely
together, reflect his strong affection and admiration, and he suffered
their rebukes and neglect with remarkable stoicism. While making due
allowance for the relatively wide gulf between parents and children
of affluent families in Victorian England, with compensating surrogate
links with the downstairs world and the nursery staff, Lord and Lady
Randolph Churchill (or so Churchill would have us believe) neglected
and ignored their first-born to a cruel degree. Some members of the
family, however, are not prepared to believe that things were as bad
as all that and feel that from an early age he complained of cruelty
and neglect when he did not get his way in every respect all the time.
Be that as it may, it was, we must believe, not a happy childhood;
and it is on record that, in spite of his pleas ('I should like you to
come and see me very much'), they very rarely, if ever, visited him
when he was at Harrow.

Lord Randolph, the second son of the seventh Duke of Marlborough, was not a great credit to the noble family, for all his charm, sprightliness and political courage when he was a young man. Profligate, like so many of his ancestors, he was also insensitive and utterly selfish. When he was twenty-four he met and instantly fell in love with an American girl, Jennie Jerome, at a royal reception and dance on board the frigate HMS *Ariadne* at Cowes. Amongst the numerous beauties on this fashionable occasion, Jennie stood out as the ultimate beauty of them all. Lord Randolph Churchill, son of a great English duke: what more wonderful match could there be? 'I must say I have been very happy all day,' commented Jennie's father, Mr Leonard Jerome, when he heard of the engagement. The Duke was less certain and wanted the couple to wait for a year to consider 'the unwisdom of your proceedings'.

Jennie's father was a successful financier and stockbroker, a politician, a patron of the turf and of the arts. Jerome Park in the New York Bronx was built by him as a race track. He founded the American Jockey Club and supported opera. His origins were Huguenot. Jennie was the second of four daughters by his wife Clarissa. Randolph and Jennie were married in Paris on 15 April 1874. Their first child, a son, was born at Blenheim on 30 November in the same year, two months prematurely because the dashing Jennie refused to give up riding. He was christened Winston Leonard Spencer Churchill. Like many children of his social class and life-style, Winston saw little of his mother and even less of his father, but he loved inordinately his beguiling, feckless, extravagant and lively-minded mother and admired and loved equally his brilliant, intemperate and undisciplined father.

In Parliament Lord Randolph was regarded as one of the most promising young politicians of his day, 'a great elemental force in British politics', but his career was as brief as the passage of a comet. With sensational speed he rose to be Chancellor of the Exchequer, but his impulsiveness led to a damaging social quarrel with the Prince of Wales, and politically to his resignation over the failure of the army and the navy to cut expenditure. The events surrounding the end of Lord Randolph's political career reflected his instinctive loyalty to a principle and what he judged to be the disloyalty of his colleagues. His father's fall from grace and office made a deep and lasting impression on his elder son. It was, no less, the fall of his God. To Winston, his father was right in all things, good in all things, a brilliant orator, compassionate towards the less privileged, at fault only in his failure to comprehend the wicked chicanery and treachery of his enemies.

The spur to right this great wrong, to rehabilitate the name of Churchill in politics, to rise himself to the uttermost peaks, was dug deep into the flanks of Winston's ambition when his father died, a syphilitic wreck, in 1895. 'There remained for me only to pursue his aims and vindicate his memory,' Churchill recalled. He was twenty years old; and on this 24 January, seventy years to the day before his own death, his military-political career was released, like a long-distance runner at the starting-line. It was to be a dangerous and varied course which sometimes brought him almost to his knees; but with his courage and ruthlessness, his perceptive eye and judgement, the priceless combination of brains and good luck, his sentimentality and patriotism, he could not fail to become the greatest Briton of the century.

Churchill once wrote that 'a boy deprived of his father's care often develops, if he escapes the perils of youth, an independence and a vigour of thought which may restore in after life the heavy loss of early days'. This was manifested in the summer of 1895, within months of his father's death. As a newly appointed subaltern in the 4th Hussars he was due for nine years' service in India, but faced a period of leave. Most of his contemporaries would be content with riding to hounds and other autumnal sports. Churchill determined to find military action, a rare experience at that time, and to combine it with war despatches for the *Daily Graphic*. There was a revolt against the Spanish Government in Cuba, and supported by the privileges his name inspired and accompanied by a fellow subaltern, Churchill sailed first to New York with the intention of joining the Cuban government troops being despatched against the revolutionaries.

In New York Churchill stayed at the apartment of a well-known lawyer and Democrat Congressman, Bourke Cockran, who saw to it that his guests were richly entertained and amused for their brief stay. Churchill's lifelong love of America stemmed from this visit. 'They really make rather a fuss over us here and extend the most lavish hospitality.' He warmed to the freshness and the egalitarianism, the transportation system 'accessible alike to the richest and poorest', the affluence acquired 'not by confiscation of the property of the rich or by arbitrary taxation but simply by business enterprise'.

The city to which he was to return again and again to nourish his own American roots also on this first visit offered him an introduction to the United States Navy, if only a brief one. The 8,000-ton belted cruiser *New York*, armed with 8-inch and 5-inch guns, was in port and Churchill was invited on board. 'I was much struck by the sailors: their intelligence, their good looks and civility and their general businesslike appearance,' he wrote. His opinion of the US Navy never changed.

Churchill found American journalism was 'vulgarity divested of truth'. But, as he wrote to his young brother, 'vulgarity is a sign of strength. A great, crude, strong, young people are the Americans.'

After a week in New York, Churchill and his friend took the train to Key West in Florida and thence travelled by steamer to Havana where they made contact with the C-in-C of the Spanish expeditionary force. Journeying hazardously inland by train, Churchill achieved his ambition on his twenty-first birthday when 'for the first time I heard shots fired in anger and heard bullets strike flesh or whistle through the air'. There was no time to taste more than a sample of close and dangerous action before he had to return. But he was now initiated into professional writing and war, two of the greatest preoccupations of his life.

Another first experience awaited him on his return, and like his experience of war, the Cuban expedition provided only a foretaste of the lifelong ordeal against which he had to harden himself. The influence of his pen through his few despatches to the *Daily Graphic* was small indeed in 1895, but with the by-line 'Winston S.Churchill' it gave him a whiff of the smoke and fire that lay ahead.

The Spanish Government's cause was not a popular one either in Britain or in the USA, where there was widespread support for the rebels. 'Spending a holiday in fighting other people's battles is rather an extraordinary proceeding even for a Churchill,' was one press comment, and other British newspapers thought it was time he was brought home. When he returned to New York, Churchill gave a press interview to defend himself: 'I have not even fired a revolver.' At the same time he let it be known that he hoped that the USA would not annexe Cuba as a solution to the intermittent civil war on the island – 'I hold it a monstrous thing if you are going to merely procure the establishment of another South American Republic . . .'

Two years later, the USA declared war on Spain, and within three more months American forces had captured Manila, an exercise in imperial acquisition warmly applauded by the ten-year-old kinsman of the American President, Franklin D.Roosevelt, but not by Churchill. By an odd chronological coincidence, two weeks later Churchill was in action again in a British imperial campaign; and this time he fired his revolver many times and missed death by a hair's-breadth.

With a reluctant acceptance that there would be little adventure and opportunity for proving himself in India, Churchill sailed with his regiment in the late summer of 1896. 'Life out here is stupid dull & uninteresting,' he complained to his mother, who appeared unwilling to use her influence to have him transferred to Egypt. Here an expeditionary force was being assembled to recover Khartoum and the Sudan and avenge the death of General Charles Gordon at the hands of the Dervishes and their leader, the Mahdi.

Churchill had been following this Egyptian river campaign with envious fascination. In one letter to his mother (10 January 1898) he wrote, 'Oh how I wish I could work you up over Egypt! I know you could do it with all your influence – and all the people you know. It is a pushing age and we must shove with the best . . .'

In the event, Churchill succeeded in joining another punitive expedition to the North-West Frontier, from which he sent back despatches to the *Daily Telegraph* describing skirmishes with the tribesmen and his own brushes with death. He was furious when several of these appeared without his name, but he succeeded in finding a publisher for a book about the expedition. This was the first of his numerous books and he entitled it *The Story of the Malakand Field Force*.

The book attracted the attention of a number of people, including the Prime Minister, Lord Salisbury, who summoned him to his office when Churchill was on leave in London. The interview concluded with Salisbury making an offer: 'If there is anything at any time that I can do which would be of assistance to you, pray do not fail to let me know.' These were sweet words to Churchill's ears, and words that were soon acted upon.

'I am vy anxious to go to Egypt and to proceed to Khartoum with the Expedition . . .', Churchill wrote to Salisbury on 18 July 1898. Almost three years since he had visited the United States and observed the fighting in Cuba, his fortunes were about to change. From this time sword and pen together were to keep his name in the public eye, from which he never disappeared for long until a seat in Parliament launched him from battlefield to the cut and thrust of politics. On the way he was to acquire many other admirers than Lord Salisbury, and many enemies, none so damaging as one of the most famous soldiers of his day, General Sir Horatio Herbert Kitchener.

Years before Churchill's birth, Kitchener had been a fighting soldier about the world, most notably as a volunteer with the French against the Germans in the Franco–Prussian War. He later served in the Sudan Campaign of 1882–5 and the expedition up the Nile intended to relieve the besieged General Gordon in Khartoum. Since 1892 he had been C-in-C ('Sirdar') of the Anglo–Egyptian Army and was now engaged in the long-drawn-out Sudan campaign. He was an austere, unmarried, devout man, unusually tall, with piercing eyes which did not invite debate, and a full moustache that was already becoming a national military insignia.

It was Churchill's faith in 'shoving' as a boost to progress, his 'scribbling' as a journalist and book writer, and his aristocratic lineage and the brash self-confidence this engendered, that led to the suspicion and distaste Kitchener felt for Churchill long before he met him. Kitchener's origins were relatively humble, stemming from East Anglian farming on a small scale. His grandfather had bettered himself as a tea merchant, his father had a brief and disappointing career in the army, selling his commission and buying a property in Ireland when land was almost given away after the potato famine. Kitchener was born there in 1850.

Churchill was always quick to recognize an enemy and he knew that he had to overcome the opposition of this notable soldier before he could fulfil his immediate ambitions: 'Quite early in the process of making my arrangements to take part in the Sudan campaign, I became conscious of the unconcealed disapproval and hostility of the Sirdar of the Egyptian Army, Sir Herbert Kitchener,' Churchill wrote of his early army life. 'My application to join that army, although favoured by the War Office, was refused, while several other officers of my service and rank were accepted. The enquiries which I made through various channels made it clear to me that the refusal came from the highest quarter.'

But shoving, together with the good luck which rarely forsook him, brought Churchill success none the less. A crack cavalry regiment, the 21st Lancers, was due to join Kitchener's expedition, and the death of a young officer created a vacancy which Churchill eagerly filled, making his own way to Alexandria, then up the Nile to Luxor. Before leaving England he had taken two important steps. The first, and more prosaic, was to secure a contract with the *Morning Post* to write despatches; and second, he made a political speech at Bradford which was a brilliant success and attracted the interest and admiration of a number of influential politicians. As he had told Lord Salisbury, it was not his intention to make his career in the army, and his political ambitions were now widely known.

These ambitions, and Churchill's intention of leaving the army, were also known to Kitchener before he arrived, and were deplored. He was 'only making a convenience of it', Kitchener commented bitterly. Churchill was now well aware of the hostility of the C-in-C. '. . . whatever his knowledge of war may be his acquaintance with truth is rudimentary,' Churchill wrote to his mother. 'He may be a general – but never a gentleman.'

In the last days of August 1898, Kitchener's Anglo–Egyptian Army of some 26,000 mixed British, Egyptian and Sudanese troops, supported by a vast supply train and numbers of Nile river gunboats, had arrived at a point twenty miles from Omdurman. They faced an army of 60,000 well-armed and fanatical Dervishes, and an action, large in scale and decisive in its result, had become inevitable.

On his return from a reconnaissance Churchill reported direct to Kitchener himself, the first meeting face to face between the twenty-three-year-old cavalry lieutenant and the famous forty-eight-year-old general. Churchill found him calm, prepared for any eventuality, indifferent as to whether the Khalifa – the Mahdi's successor – attacked that day or the next. 'The heavy moustaches, the queer rolling look of the eyes, the sunburnt and almost purple cheeks and jowl made a vivid manifestation upon the senses,' Churchill wrote.

Another first meeting which Churchill was to remember for the rest of his life, and which was to lead later to a happier relationship, took place before the two armies clashed. Later that day Churchill and a brother officer were strolling in the heat beside the Nile awaiting the call to battle when they were hailed by a naval officer commanding one of the gunboats. 'How are you off for drinks?' he asked. 'We have got everything in the world on board here. Can you catch?'

A bottle of champagne was slung like a howitzer shell from the vessel, falling short of its target. Churchill waded in and retrieved it. The name of the benefactor, he learned, was David Beatty. Some forty-eight years later Churchill calculated that he had averaged half a bottle of champagne a day throughout his adult life. On this one day at least of campaigning in the desert he was thus able to keep up his average.

The following day, 2 September 1898, the two great armies met, and the 21st Lancers were called upon to make a classic cavalry charge. Churchill relied on his Mauser pistol as his first weapon, and was thankful that he did so. 'The charge ... passed like a dream and some part I cannot quite recall,' he wrote home to his mother.

The Dervishes showed no fear of cavalry and would not move unless you knocked them over with the horse. They tried to hamstring the horses, to cut the bridles – reins – slashed and stabbed in all directions and fired rifles at a few feet range. Nothing touched me. I destroyed those who molested me and so passed out without any disturbance of body or mind.

In spite of the reputation he was later to acquire as a belligerent man of war, Churchill learned during the few minutes of danger and exhilaration of this charge and the aftermath of mourning for lost friends 'the shoddiness of war'. 'You cannot gild it,' he told his mother. 'The raw comes through.' The blend of excitement and disgust which he experienced at Omdurman remained with him for long. A number more of his friends had been wounded. They were well cared for, unlike the Khalifa's wounded. Kitchener's orders to finish off the Dervish wounded as they lay on the desert disgusted Churchill and hardened his hatred of the general. 'I shall merely say that the victory of Omdurman was disgraced by the inhuman slaughter of the wounded and that Kitchener was responsible for this,' he wrote.

Churchill also spread the scandal of the desecration of the Mahdi's tomb and the treatment of his bones. As a gesture of vengeance for the Mahdi's murder of General Gordon in Khartoum, Kitchener entrusted Gordon's nephew, a major in his army, with the razing to the ground of the Mahdi's tomb and the casting into the River Nile of his bones. The fine large skull was, however, retained and presented to Kitchener as a trophy. This resulted in some rare ribaldry among Kitchener and his staff as they – and Kitchener himself – played with the skull and discussed what to do with it. Kitchener was reported to have unwisely suggested various uses for it, as his inkwell or drinking cup, or that it should be sent to the Royal College of Surgeons in London.

Churchill reported this first in his articles for the *Morning Post* and later and more damagingly in his book, *The River War*. 'Being now free from military discipline, I was able to write what I thought about Lord Kitchener without fear, favour or affection,' Churchill wrote of his second book. 'And I certainly did so. I had been scandalized by his desecration of the Mahdi's tomb and the barbarous manner in which he had carried off the Mahdi's skull in a kerosene-can as a trophy.'

In this book, which attracted a great deal of attention, Churchill wrote of Kitchener that he

treated all men like machines – from the private soldiers whose salutes he disdained, to the superior officers he rigidly controlled. The comrade who had served with him and under him for many years in peace and peril was flung aside incontinently as soon as he ceased to be of use . . . . The stern and unpitying spirit of the commander was communicated to his troops, and the victories which marked the progress of the River War were accompanied by acts of barbarity not always justified even by the harsh customs of savage conflicts.

Churchill's next brush with Kitchener occurred in South Africa during the Boer War more than a year later. Churchill was now a war reporter for the *Daily Mail* after an initial failure to enter Parliament. He soon got on to the wrong side of the military hierarchy, including Field Marshal Lord Roberts, General Sir George White and, of course, Kitchener himself. While Churchill became almost overnight a public hero for his capture, after displaying great gallantry, and his subsequent daring escape from the Boers, he was refused permission to rejoin the army in order to see more of the fighting. He then made himself highly unpopular by writing in favour of treating the Boers generously after their rebellion had been put down.

In April 1902, now a Conservative Member of Parliament, Churchill ensured Kitchener's enduring hatred, and the deep suspicions of his own party, by attacking the authorities for refusing to allow the editor of a South African newspaper to come to England for private reasons. This editor, A.P.Cartwright, had served a year in prison after being found guilty of seditious libel in publishing a statement that Kitchener had issued instructions to the troops not to take prisoners. Churchill accused the military authorities of incompetence for abusing their powers under military law, and the British Government for violating the liberty of the subject.

Although Churchill did not come face to face with Kitchener again for more than ten years, his dislike of the General never cooled. 'I always hated Kitchener,' he told his friend Wilfrid Blunt in October 1910. 'Kitchener behaved like a blackguard in that business [Mahdi's head scandal]. He pretended to have sent the head back in a kerosene tin, but the tin may have contained anything, perhaps ham sandwiches. He kept the head, and has it still.'* A year later, after Kitchener had been appointed as British Agent, Consul-General and Minister Plenipotentiary (euphemisms for ruler) to Egypt, on 16 July 1911 by the Liberal Government, Churchill, no longer a Conservative, wrote to Blunt, 'I was glad to find from your letter ... that my belonging to a government wicked enough to send Lord Kitchener to Egypt has not altered our relations.'

To Churchill Kitchener was war stripped of all honour and glory and the trappings of action, romance and excitement, a denial of Churchill's strongly held conviction, 'In war : resolution ; in defeat : defiance ; in victory : magnanimity ; in peace : goodwill.'†

To Churchill Kitchener was the unacceptable face of war-making, an activity which dominated a great part of his life. War to Churchill was 'a vile and wicked folly' that also sent his heart beating faster and found him, when it came, 'interested, geared up & happy'. Kitchener sullied the martial spirit and the figure of the soldier.

In Churchill's mind, Kitchener, the man consumed by his own vanity, despising his own troops, cruel and relentless to a defeated foe, utterly lacking in magnanimity and goodwill, a proven threat to his ambitions, was an enemy for life. Although far distant from Churchill in India and Egypt after the Sudan War, Kitchener remained like an unsponged stain, a beastly memory in the past, a threat for the future, as Churchill climbed the political ladder with consummate ease : Colonial Under-Secretary in 1906, President of the Board of Trade in 1908, Home Secretary in 1910 ...

During these years Churchill was to establish a relationship with another great service chief – an officer of a strongly contrasting personal-

* This was quite untrue.
† 'The Moral of the Work' printed in Churchill's history of the Second World War.

ity to Kitchener – who was to become a partner to Churchill in the great trial of strength that lay ahead. These three men, the politician, the soldier and the sailor, were to figure in an unblessed trinity of mutual destruction.

2
Scottish Tryst

Winston Churchill, at thirty-two the youngest Minister of the Crown, arrived at Biarritz on the train from Paris on 19 April 1907, a cold, drizzly day with no hint of spring in the air. Biarritz is a small French resort in the Pyrénées-Atlantique Département on the Bay of Biscay and close to the Spanish frontier. The town had become fashionable under the patronage of Napoleon III and Princess Eugénie and later Queen Victoria and King Edward VII. There were at that time a number of luxurious hotels along the windy sea-front – the Continental, Grand and Hôtel des Princes among them. King Edward preferred the Hôtel du Palais, an enormous slab of a building like a highly decorated wedding cake in which he took over several floors for himself and his mistress, Mrs George Keppel, his secretary and equerries and servants.

The King-Emperor also brought with him a great number of friends who contributed further wealth to the town. Among them were his closest friend, the German-born multi-millionaire Sir Ernest Cassel, his granddaughter (a pretty little girl of four, Edwina Ashley – one day to marry Lord Louis Mountbatten), and her mother, Cassel's daughter Maud; and one of the most famous admirals since Nelson.

Admiral Sir John Arbuthnot Fisher was, in 1907, a highly controversial world figure who, at the recent Hague Peace Conference intended to humanize modern warfare, gained notoriety by exclaiming, 'You might as well talk of humanizing hell! War is the essence of violence. Moderation in war is imbecility.' The conference was not a success.

Fisher had a modest background, loathed toadies and had advanced up the navy's promotion ladder without social influence or wealth. Fisher's life cause was the Royal Navy, which he regarded almost as a branch of his beloved Church of England. As a great reformer, parables and biblical quotations and aphorisms rattled like shrapnel amidst the thunder of his naval guns, firing at failure and defects in the service or despatching spine-chilling threats at the future enemy. 'The Germans will smell Hell when they find us at Cuxhaven!' he once predicted. 'The great advantage of absence is "*litera scripta manet*".' And of dilatoriness in building submarines, '*Give peace in our time, O Lord!* for this is the old, old story! "We strain at the gnat of Perfection, and swallow the camel of Unreadiness!"'

Jacky Fisher was a twice life-size figure who in turn flattered and flattened his friends and enemies, both of them numerous. He was impatient with opposition, unforgiving with those who set out to foil him, and possessed a conspiratorial turn of mind which relished making mischief. Women with few exceptions found him irresistibly attractive. He charmed them, was kind to them, except (like Nelson) his own wife. Fisher was an ebullient man of ferocious energy who would dance the night through in his sixties and work a twelve-hour day and seven-day week.

At the time of his visit to the King at Biarritz Fisher had been First Sea Lord for two and a half years. His accomplishments had seized the imagination of the country, above all the spectacularly rapid introduction of the world's greatest battleship into the fleet. HMS *Dreadnought* bristled with innovations, from its turbine engines to its batteries of heavy guns – the first all-big-gun battleship which made all other battleships obsolete, especially as it was also the fastest in the world.

Fisher forced the navy to take the submarine seriously, and the first-ever battle-cruiser was about to be unveiled and astonish the world. Less spectacular were his reforms in training, selection of recruits, broadening of the class range of officer cadets, reform of naval ordnance supply, and other reforms in countless fields little understood outside the service.

Most important of all, Fisher was among the first to recognize the threat posed by the naval rearmament of Germany under the madly jealous eye of the German Emperor. While others hoped that the new German Navy was no more than a harmless toy to amuse the Kaiser and gratify his *amour-propre*, Fisher believed that the new High Seas Fleet was a deadly threat to British rule of the seas and to British trade in time of war.

To meet this peril, Fisher was concentrating the Fleet in home waters, denuding even the Mediterranean of its most powerful squadrons; and hastening the construction of battleships bigger and more powerful than any the Germans had built. Fisher was convinced that the Germans were hell-bent on eventual war in Europe. In December 1911 he correctly predicted that his favourite admiral, John Jellicoe, would be C-in-C, and Prince Louis of Battenberg First Sea Lord, when war came. 'The Battle of Armageddon comes along in September 1914. That date suits the Germans .... Both the Army and their Fleet then mobilized, and the Kiel Canal finished, and their new [battleship] building complete.'

For some reason neither could ever explain, Fisher and Churchill had never met before. At the King's invitation, they both travelled to Biarritz during the King's stay at the Hôtel du Palais. When Churchill arrived Fisher was already there. Fisher had received three 'extremely cordial' letters from King Edward, the last asking him to call at 3 p.m.

Edward VII had fallen under the spell of Fisher's vivacity and charm many years earlier when he was Prince of Wales. The King loved men who amused and occasionally outraged him, and he had developed the highest respect for Fisher's naval achievements. Fisher frequently stayed with the King at Balmoral and Sandringham, and developed a deep admiration for the beautiful Queen Alexandra – 'I had an affectionate half hour with the Queen.'

For Fisher, the King was a priceless ally against his enemies, many of whom were powerful and rich and high in society. Some of these enemies lost favour at Court and as a result came to hate Fisher even more intensely. Now the King felt that the time was ripe to bring together his leading admiral and the rising young politician. King Edward had a percipient eye and a practised understanding of politics and of men and their ambitions, and it is possible that he could visualize a future partnership between these two vital and brilliant men, in spite of the age gap of thirty-three years.

Fisher and Churchill remained as the King's guests for two weeks that April, and the impression Fisher, 'in the height of his reign', made on his future partner in the navy was deep and lasting.

We talked all day long and far into the nights [Churchill later recounted]. He told me wonderful stories of the Navy and of his plans – all about Dreadnoughts, all about submarines, all about the new education scheme for every branch of the Navy, all about big guns, and splendid Admirals and foolish miserable ones, and Nelson and the Bible .... At any rate, when I returned to my duties at the Colonial Office I could have passed an examination on the policy of the then Board of Admiralty.

'The teacher', as Churchill called Fisher, had completed his first lessons. There were to be many more.

Before the two men separated, Fisher proceeding with the King in the royal yacht for his annual Mediterranean cruise, King Edward noted in his diary that Churchill and Fisher 'are most amusing together. I call them "the chatterers".'

'The chatterers' met for lunch at the Ritz Hotel in London some months later when Churchill turned up unexpectedly at the Admiralty. 'I was whirled off,' Fisher recalled. 'I had 2 hours with him. He is very keen to fight on my behalf .... He is an enthusiastic friend certainly! ... He said his penchant for me was that I painted with a big brush! and was violent! I reminded him that even "The Kingdom of

Heaven suffereth violence, and the violent take it by force" ...' Fisher
was also heard to remark that Churchill was 'quite the nicest fellow
I ever met and such a quick brain that it's a delight to talk to him'.
The lunch was followed later by an invitation from Fisher to Churchill
to sail in the Admiralty yacht.

On 5 April 1908 the Prime Minister, Sir Henry Campbell-Bannerman,
resigned because of ill health and was succeeded by Herbert Asquith,
'the last of the Romans' as he was sometimes called, a patrician yet
genial figure with a brilliant brain and a highly developed understanding
of men. Among his defects was a tendency to indolence and self-indul-
gence. He was destined to see his Liberal Party and his country through
a succession of political, constitutional, international and military crises
until 1916. Among the ministerial appointments of that April were
Churchill's friend and ally Lloyd George as Chancellor of the Exchequer, and Churchill, only four years after joining the Party, as President of the Board of Trade.

Fisher told the new Prime Minister that he wanted Churchill as First
Lord, which would have led to the formation of an inevitably fiery
and fascinating partnership within twelve months of the first meeting
between the two men. 'I am only sorry', Churchill wrote to Fisher
later, 'that the drift of events did not enable us to work together.'
And he told him how much he regretted 'that I did not press for the
Admiralty in 1908. I think it would have been easily possible for me
to obtain it. I believe it would have been better for us all.' Instead,
they met in head-on conflict.

The trouble began with the publication of the new 1908 German
Navy Law which revealed that four more dreadnought battleships were
to be built, threatening even more seriously British naval superiority
which was based on a 'two-power standard', with Britain having an
advantage in numbers of heavy ships over any two foreign powers.
Fisher and the Admiralty calculated that by 1912 Germany would have
thirteen against Britain's eighteen dreadnoughts, an unacceptable
margin for security, especially because surprise is always on the side
of the aggressor, and Britain had world-wide responsibilities while
Germany's inappropriately named High Seas Fleet was concentrated
in the North Sea and the Baltic.

In answer to this German threat, Fisher demanded six new dreadnoughts instead of four, and was backed by the strong Big-Navy lobby,
the Navy League, the industrialists who could only benefit by an even
greater increase in naval construction, by the Conservatives in opposition in the House of Commons, and by the new First Lord appointed
by Asquith, Reginald McKenna. McKenna, like Churchill, was one
of Asquith's bright young men, clever, an excellent administrator, a

tenacious fighter for the navy but lacking in Churchill's positive and controversial character. In the House Churchill was hated or loved, mostly hated at this time. McKenna was simply found unappealing by almost everyone because of his rudeness and air of superiority.

Churchill in 1908–9 was publicly demonstrating for the first time his concern with the inequalities and injustices suffered by the poor. While at the Board of Trade he introduced work agencies, called labour exchanges, to help the working man to seek suitable employment. In conformity with Liberal Party principles he was among the strongest advocates of the first stages of the welfare state, and joint leader, with Lloyd George, of the social reform/arms reduction wing of the Cabinet. With his chief ally now looking after the nation's money, Churchill embarked on a campaign against increasing to what he regarded as a recklessly extravagant pitch expenditure on defence, without, of course, putting the nation at risk.

But what was the risk level? In his early days as First Sea Lord Fisher had actually pruned the navy estimates by means of increasing efficiency and elimination of waste. Now, four years later and with the German threat becoming more and more menacing, Fisher and his allies claimed that a big increase in British strength was essential; and Fisher, being Fisher, dubbed anyone who did not support his view as a 'blue funker'.

Throughout 1908 sides were taken up between those who believed that the Germans harboured no evil intentions and the battleship race was dangerous, extravagant and unnecessary, and the defence staffs, interested pressure groups, and Conservatives and the Conservative press who believed that the threat from across the North Sea was all too real. With Fisher in the vocal vanguard of the Big-Navy group as professional head of the navy, and Churchill equally convinced of the political and social need to trim armament expenditure, and with the battle becoming increasingly intense all the time, it seemed remarkable that, only a year earlier, 'the chatterers' had so exuberantly exchanged ideas and vowed eternal friendship.

Within the Cabinet the split widened. On the one side were the navalists and, on the other, the 'little Englanders' or members of 'the Syndicate of Discontent' (Fisher's definition) who threatened to resign if as many as six dreadnoughts were agreed to. But the entire Board of Admiralty declared that they would resign if only four were to be built. Fisher characteristically replied by declaring a new offensive, demanding *eight* dreadnoughts – each costing little less than two million pounds, or forty million in present-day currency. This was seized upon by the Conservative press with a nation-wide cry, 'We want eight, and we won't wait!' Was this Tory recklessness, or Tory patriotism?

The Lloyd George and Churchill versus Fisher fight went into its twelfth round in the early weeks of 1909, and Asquith, who had taken up an ambivalent stance through the contest, at last determined that something must be resolved or the Liberal Party would be fatally damaged. Should he knock heads together, or search for a compromise? 'Winston and Lloyd by their combined machinations have got the Liberal press into the same camp. They go about darkly hinting at resignation (which is bluff),' Asquith wrote to his wife. 'But there are moments when I am disposed summarily to cashier them both.'

Asquith could as well have complained of Fisher's leaks to the press about supposed German increased construction, especially to Fisher's old friend and ally, J.L.Garvin. As editor of the *Observer*, he pleaded with his readers to 'insist on "the Eight, the whole Eight, and nothing but the Eight" with more to follow, and break any man or faction that now stands in the way'.

The crisis was resolved at a Cabinet on 24 February 1909 with a typical compromise offered by the Prime Minister. Four dreadnoughts would be laid down immediately, with four more 'contingency' dreadnoughts to be laid down when the need for them was proven, with a juggling of a few million pounds here and there in order to save Lloyd George's face. Within a few weeks the Admiralty was able to 'prove' their urgent need, and the four additional dreadnoughts were authorized in July.

Churchill noted sardonically of this resolution that 'In the end a curious and characteristic solution was reached. The Admiralty had demanded six ships; the economists offered four; and we finally compromised on eight.' Fisher was vastly relieved and, for once, generous in victory, at least as far as Churchill was concerned. He told the King, 'Lloyd George and Winston Churchill, bad as they were, fought out in the open'; and he waggishly suggested to Churchill that the names of the four extra dreadnoughts should be 'Winston', 'Churchill', 'Lloyd' and 'George'.

Churchill was equally generous in defeat and wrote a long and affectionate letter to Fisher, who replied, 'Private, Personal and Secret: I confess I never expected you to turn against the Navy after all you had said in public and in private ("*Et tu, Brute!*") .... I reciprocate your grief at our separation! I retain the memory of many pleasant duets!' A few days later he was sending a further letter, 'Yours till the Angels smile on us!', and it seemed as if the breach was healed.

In the spring of 1911, Germany's despatch of a gunboat to an insignificant harbour called Agadir on the Atlantic seaboard of Morocco sounded off the alarm bells all over France. France had despatched an expeditionary force to Fez as the first step towards the annexation of Morocco. Germany, claiming to have interests which required protection at Agadir, ordered the gunboat *Panther* to proceed to the port. This was seen in France as the first step by Germany to acquire some of the spoils for herself, and by Britain as the first step towards establishing a naval base – an Atlantic Heligoland – which could threaten British trade in time of war. It was a clumsy German move, and German diplomacy compounded the error by refusing all explanation in answer to French and, later, British enquiries of German intentions.

French and British newspapers added fuel to the fires of anxiety by a somewhat high-pitched campaign of protest. 'The plain truth of the matter', ran an editorial in the *Standard*, 'is that no government ... could consent to allow a great foreign navy to station itself on the flank of our Atlantic trade and on the line of our route to the Cape.'

At a party in the Prime Minister's garden, Churchill committed his first positive act on behalf of the Royal Navy, now bereft of the leadership of Fisher, whose term of office was over. Churchill was Home Secretary, with the control of the police as one of his numerous responsibilities. Among the other guests was the Chief Commissioner of Police, Sir Edward Henry. 'We talked about the European situation,' Churchill recalled, 'and I told him that it was serious. He then remarked that by an odd arrangement the Home Office was responsible, through the Metropolitan Police, for guarding the magazines at Chattenden and Lodge Hill, in which all the reserves of naval cordite were stored.' 'A few constables' was their sole protection, Churchill learned to his amazement, and here they were in the centre of a crisis when war might lead to a crippling blow at the navy which could be struck by a handful of determined men.

Churchill hastened to his office, telephoned the Admiralty, only to learn that, with the First Lord and the First Sea Lord both absent, the admiral in charge of affairs refused point blank to send a contingent of Royal Marines to guard this treasure. It was not his business. Churchill then tried the War Office. As a result of deficiencies in the army exposed in grisly detail by the Boer War a decade earlier, new brooms had been at work. The largest broom had been wielded by Richard Burden Haldane, 'a Napoleon' as Fisher called him. He was Secretary of State for War and answered Churchill's call in this capacity. Promptly, briskly, a company of infantry was sent to the two magazines. 'By the next day,' Churchill claimed, 'the cordite reserves of the Navy were safe.'

On 21 July *The Times* carried a story that the entire German High Seas Fleet had put to sea. And where was the British Fleet at this time when war might break out at any moment? It was not concentrated in the North Sea, ready for a sudden German attack, the long-feared 'bolt from the blue'. The Atlantic Fleet, it was true, was at Cromarty on the east coast of Scotland. But of the four divisions of the Home Fleet, one was based in southern Ireland, another was at Portland on the south coast of England, with the crews just off for four days' leave, and the other two divisions had only nucleus crews on board. Fisher's successor as First Sea Lord, Admiral Sir Arthur Wilson, had gone shooting in Scotland.

Churchill complained that 'practically everybody of importance and authority is away on his holidays . . . . I cannot help feeling uncomforable about the Admiralty. They are so cocksure, *insouciant* and apathetic.' Haldane exclaimed:

What a chance for our friends across the water! Supposing the High Seas Fleet, instead of going to Norway as announced, had gone straight for Portland, preceded by a division of destroyers, and after a surprise night torpedo attack had brought the main fleet into action at dawn against our ships without steam, without coal, and without crews!

The Agadir crisis died down and finally was extinguished after prolonged negotiations between the French and Germans. For Britain, it had fulfilled a useful purpose which was to affect profoundly Churchill's career. So bad was the state and management of the navy when Fisher had been appointed First Sea Lord in October 1904 that even he had not been able to leave the Augean stables sparkling. For the reformer there remained much more work. Fisher had also perpetuated a fatal weakness at the Admiralty: it lacked a Staff – a Naval Staff that could co-ordinate and direct through the working together of the navy's best brains naval preparations for war in a new age of technology. Intellectual study of problems was no more encouraged in the navy than individualism, which was represented only by a sort of dotty eccentricity in admirals like Beresford and other cranks of the past, Sir Algernon Charles Fiesché Heneage and Reginald Charles Prothero. Any war plans the Admiralty possessed were in the personal hands (it was even said, in the brain) of the First Sea Lord and no one else. Fisher was violently opposed to a Staff to produce contingency plans. He believed in the divine right of the First Sea Lord. Admiral Wilson agreed and had been nominated by Fisher to succeed him for that reason.

When Wilson was asked by the Cabinet to produce the Admiralty's war plan to meet the crisis, he had nothing to show them. When the Director of Military Operations revealed his plans to send six divisions to France to support the left flank in the event of a German invasion, Wilson stated that he had no plans to transport them or protect them on their passage across the Channel until the enemy fleet had been dealt with and command of the sea firmly established. *Impasse!* The Admiralty believed that Britain's war effort should be restricted to the sea and that an army sent to the continent would simply be 'swallowed up in the conflict of immense land masses'. The army was for defending the homeland and for making raids on the enemy.

Asquith was horrified by these revelations, and he could hardly blame Haldane for threatening to resign unless the Admiralty put its house in order and created a General Staff with whom he could work, such as he had initiated in his own army reforms. Asquith also learned that his minister responsible for the navy, McKenna, actually agreed with Wilson and the other admirals at the helm whose training and career had been based on the First Sea Lord's prerogative and the absolute need for secrecy.

It took a three-year war in South Africa, and the loss of thousands of lives, to modernize the army and force it to accept a controlling War Staff after almost a century without a European war. The navy was more fortunate. After more than a hundred years of peace since Trafalgar, the creation of a Staff to supersede the musings of an aged admiral was brought about by the arrival of a little gunboat in a distant Moroccan bay. It had taken just seven years since a radical group of navalists had begun their campaign against the navy's shellbacks.

Asquith decided that McKenna must leave the Admiralty. 'As we are on the eve of completing our sixth year of office,' he wrote to McKenna, 'I am contemplating a certain amount of reconstruction inside and outside the Cabinet. I am going to ask you to undertake one of the most difficult and responsible places in the Government – the Home Office.'

The stiff, arrogant Reginald McKenna was furious and never forgave Haldane and Churchill, whom he suspected of plotting his downfall. For those in the heart of politics, Asquith's choice of a successor at the Admiralty was a prime issue over the following few days. Those closest to the Prime Minister believed the choice lay between Haldane and Churchill, both of whom were thought to be burning with ambition for the job.

In late September 1911 Churchill was invited by the new king, George v (acceded 6 May 1910), to stay at Balmoral. Unlike his father, George v had been a sailor and loved the navy, retaining a proprietorial interest in it all his life. The King and his Home Secretary talked together for several hours, the subjects ranging through the Agadir crisis, national and international politics, and the state of the navy.

On 27 September Churchill drove in his grand £600 six-cylinder

Napier from Balmoral to stay with the Prime Minister at a house called Archerfield owned by Asquith's brother-in-law, Frank Tennant. Archerfield was in a spectacular position on the East Lothian coast, with a private golf links stretching down to the sea. Asquith frequently week-ended there, sleeping in the train to and from London on Friday and Sunday nights, and deriving peace and relaxation in the beautiful old Adam house and its gardens, and on the links.

Churchill's arrival signified that much political business would be conducted, but the house was geared to that, and Asquith's daughter, Violet, especially welcomed the arrival of the man she admired so keenly. She knew that her father was preoccupied over the choice of a successor to McKenna, who at that time did not even know about his imminent departure from the Admiralty. Her father was not, he said, going to ask Violet's advice on the matter. 'Between Haldane and Winston you are not a judge,' he told her. 'You are a barefaced partisan. Your scales are loaded by gross favouritism and emotion.' Then, with what Violet described as a sniff and a twinkle, 'You are not thinking of a Naval War Staff being born or of the reactions of the sensitive Admirals. You are thinking how much Winston would enjoy it!' And how right Asquith was!

After Churchill had arrived the Prime Minister, his daughter and Churchill played a threesome of golf – 'all three equally indifferent and ecstatic performers'. The subject of the Admiralty did not come into their conversation.

The next arrival was Haldane, also at Asquith's invitation. 'As I entered the approach I saw Winston Churchill standing at the door,' Haldane recalled. 'I divined that he had heard of possible changes and had come down at once to see the Prime Minister'; which was not strictly fair, as Churchill had been invited as a house guest, as he had been before.

The future of the Admiralty and who should head it became a constant source of discussion between the three men. 'Obviously Churchill had been pressing Asquith hard,' Haldane remembered; and Violet knew that her father was indeed drawn to the idea of Churchill at the Admiralty. On the other hand Haldane was immensely experienced at bringing about fundamental changes so badly needed at the Admiralty, as he had shown at the War Office. Against him the fact was that he was now a viscount and therefore sat in the Lords, which was always an untidy arrangement. Then again, as Violet heard her father argue, it might be 'wounding to the *amour-propre* of the Admiralty to send it the same new broom which had already cleaned up the War Office'.

Haldane stayed until the evening and returned the following day, after giving Asquith time to think over the arguments. This time Asquith 'shut me up in a room' with Churchill, Haldane reported. We can be sure that the dialogue was courteous, civilized, well-informed and persuasive. 'The Navy and the public had to be convinced,' claimed Haldane, 'and they would be most easily convinced of the necessity of scientific preparation for naval war by someone who already had carried out similar preparations ...' He thought he could complete the job in twelve months, with Churchill running the army in the meantime, Churchill to move into the Admiralty when Haldane had completed the job. 'However, Churchill would not be moved.'

Two days later, Violet was just finishing tea when Churchill and her father came in from a round of golf. 'Looking up, I saw in Winston's face a radiance like the sun,' Violet recalled. '"Will you come out for a walk with me – at once?" he asked. "You don't want tea?" "No, I don't want tea." We were hardly out of the house when he said to me with grave but shining eyes: "I don't want tea – I don't want anything – anything in the world. Your father has just offered me the Admiralty."' Later on the walk he remarked to the young woman at his side, 'Look at the people I have had to deal with so far – judges and convicts! This is a big thing – the biggest thing that has ever come my way – the chance that I would have chosen before all others. I shall pour into it everything I've got.'

And so, with the engaging and youthful exuberance which the Prime Minister's daughter – and many others who knew him – found so attractive, Churchill sealed his career and ambition with the Royal Navy, a service which was to carry him to the heights of success and triumph and to the depths of failure.

The historian Arthur Marder has commented on Churchill at this time:

All the traits that were to win him global renown in World War II were clearly discernible before World War I: self-confidence, vivacity, inexhaustible vitality and power of work, courage, eloquence, temperament and a great brain . . . . He was aggressive and truculent in his official capacity, showing a disregard for the opinions and sensibilities of his opponents; but he was full of charm and tolerance and amiability in social intercourse.

Churchill's welcome at the Admiralty was not rapturous, nor was his appointment approved by the Conservative Opposition in the House of Commons and the Conservative press. Many people thought he was brash, arrogant, unreliable and a turncoat. His crossing of the floor in the House of Commons was not forgotten after seven years, and was linked with his robust efforts to trim the navy estimates three years ago. He was seen simplistically by many people as an unpatriotic small-navy man ; and now here he was conning the dreadnoughts at a time of acute national danger.

The traditionalist admirals loathed him or at best were deeply suspicious of him. It was known to them all that he had been appointed to turn everything inside out and to create a Naval War Staff, to which they were totally opposed. The *Spectator* considered it an appalling appointment: 'He has not the loyalty, the dignity, the steadfastness, and the good sense which makes an efficient head of a great office. He must always be living in the limelight, and there is no fault more damning in an administrator.'

Churchill was, according to the *National Review*, 'a political gambler of the worst type' and 'a self-advertising mountebank'. *The Times*, a non-admirer, did its best to be balanced. 'His countrymen will wish him well in the discharge of the great and vital duties he has undertaken.' His past inspired misgivings, certainly, 'but this must not be allowed to deprive him of fair play, or to forestall a dispassionate appreciation of his actions on their merits'.

The Palace was in two minds about the appointment. On the one hand, George v was suspicious of the ex-army officer, ex-journalist and (worst of all) ex-Conservative, now radical. But Churchill seems to have convinced George v that he was 'pro-navy' really, and 'our sailor King' warmed to that, whatever his reservations, and they were considerable. Moreover, unlike his father, George v was a strong anti-Fisher man, had 'steered well clear of the fish pond' in the current saying, and Churchill had not brought him back. Churchill had in fact thought long and hard about making Fisher First Sea Lord again, but he sensibly recognized the dangers of opening old wounds. Instead, he intended to lean on him heavily for unofficial advice. Fisher for his part was only too willing to become Churchill's 'constant and ready counsellor', but only from a distance, he decided.

For the sake of his health Fisher had gone to live in Switzerland, which was also politically judicious of him. Fisher was an admirer of McKenna and had not liked the way he had been removed by 'the dirty trick' played on him ; and while he admired Churchill's 'genius and audacity', he found it 'very awkward between McKenna and Winston Churchill – like balancing on a tight rope'. Nor did Fisher wish to be thought by the new Board to be pre-empting or embarrassing them, which might be the case if he were present in London. Finally, having been the first violin, he wasn't going to play second fiddle. 'I don't care to be understudy to anyone !'

For his part, Churchill was not in the least concerned about preempting or embarrassing his Board, or, for that matter, treating them more as if they were raw recruits of the parade ground than venerable

officers of lofty seniority. The first to be dealt with peremptorily was
the First Sea Lord himself. Churchill suspected that Wilson was going
to be the first stumbling block in the creation of a Naval War Staff,
and this was confirmed in a long memorandum 'Tug' (because he was
always working, or tugging) Wilson prepared on this subject. 'The preparation of war plans is a matter that must be dealt with by the First
Sea Lord himself,' he insisted, although he was prepared to accept
the assistance of his Director of Naval Intelligence and Director of
Naval Mobilization.

Wilson was like a granite cliff on a lee shore, battered by time and
weather, unyielding. He was sixty-nine, unmarried, his whole life dedicated to the navy. He had won the Victoria Cross not in a naval engagement, of which there were almost none throughout his long career,
but in the Sudan for beating Dervishes about the head with his broken
sword when his Gatling's ammunition was exhausted.

Wilson took his dismissal coolly. 'He was as good-tempered and as
distant as ever,' Churchill wrote. 'Only once did he show the slightest
sign of vehemence. That was when I told him that the Prime Minister
was willing to submit his name to the King for a Peerage. He disengaged
himself from this with much vigour. What would he do with such a
thing?'

So Wilson departed from the Admiralty: he was not to be idle for
long.

Churchill always let it be known that he preferred to work with subordinates who were 'in harmony' with his thinking. His critics could as
well claim that he chose only men who bent to his will and opinions.
Certainly Wilson's mind with its fixed ideas was as impregnable as a
dreadnought's 12-inch armour plate. But who was to replace him? On
16 November 1911, in office for three weeks, Churchill wrote to Asquith,
'I pronounce decidedly in favour of Sir Francis Bridgeman as First Sea
Lord.' He had 'the aptitude for working with and through a staff well-
developed'. Bridgeman was sixty-three, son of a parson but descended
from the Fitzwilliams and of solid Midland stock. He was an able, popular but undynamic officer, a first-rate number two. He had supported
Fisher's reforms but also supported the creation of a Naval War Staff.
Churchill judged him to be suitably acquiescent.

As Second Sea Lord he selected the unexceptionable Prince Louis
of Battenberg, one of the navy's few 'brains'. Of stately bearing and
handsome looks, this German-born prince was a Hessian whose father
had been a professional soldier, his mother, unfortunately, only a com-
moner. The pair had recovered from this set-back, while slipping down
in the *Almanach de Gotha* to become mere 'serene highnesses'. One
of Prince Louis's strongest advantages in Churchill's eyes was his close

connection with the Palace and 'cousin Georgie', something that still counted for a very great deal.

For Third Sea Lord and Controller, Churchill retained Admiral Sir Charles Briggs, which proved a disaster – 'the old sheep farmer' as he was called. Among his responsibilities was the supply of shell. Sir William Pakenham as Fourth Sea Lord was, by contrast, an excellent choice, an Irishman loved by all and immensely able. Fearless, yet highly fastidious, at the Battle of Tsu-Shima he acted as an observer on board a Japanese battleship, seated in a deck chair on the exposed quarter-deck, as if he were watching the racing at Cowes, but offering a target for every passing shell fragment. The Japanese officers in the armoured conning tower watched aghast and were relieved when he at last appeared to be seeking shelter. But he had merely retired temporarily to his cabin to change his uniform, which had been spattered with blood from a nearby fatally wounded sailor.

As his Naval Secretary Churchill passed over a number of more senior officers and asked the officer who had once called out from the Nile 'How are you off for drinks?' to come to the Admiralty. David Beatty's career had prospered wonderfully since he had thrown Churchill that bottle of champagne from his Nile gunboat. He had fought hard and well in several land campaigns, was awarded the DSO, was promoted swiftly to become the youngest admiral since Nelson. Socially, he had compromised himself by marrying the divorced daughter of Marshall Field, the American store millionaire; and professionally by declining a senior appointment which he did not judge to be senior enough. 'Overpromoted,' some said. 'Brash and cocky, too rich and handsome for his own good.' He was on half pay without employment, and his career looked finished. But against all advice, Churchill called Beatty to his office. He at once liked and admired what he saw. 'He viewed questions of naval strategy and tactics in a different light from the average naval officer .... He thought of war problems in their unity by land, sea and air,' Churchill wrote.

Determined to be a 'sailor's First Lord', contrary to the style of the desk-bound McKenna, Churchill began cruising in the Admiralty yacht *Enchantress* soon after assuming office, steaming from one naval base to another on tours of inspection accompanied by his professional entourage and often with friends and relations on board.

The *Enchantress* was a graceful, single-funnel steam yacht of 3,500 tons, a slightly scaled-down version of the royal yacht *Victoria and Albert*, and almost as luxuriously appointed. It was the exclusive prerogative of the First Lord and, with Admiralty House, one of the two greatest privileges of the appointment.

'These were great days,' Churchill wrote.

From dawn to midnight, one's whole mind was absorbed by the fascination
and novelty of the problems which came crowding forward. And all the time
there was a sense of power to act, to form, to organize . . . . Saturdays, Sundays
and any other spare day I spent always with the Fleets at Portsmouth or at
Portland or Devonport . . .
    The Admiralty yacht *Enchantress* was now to become largely my office,
almost my home ; and my work my sole occupation and amusement. In all,
I spent eight months afloat in the three years before the war . . .

On one of his cruises in the *Enchantress*, Churchill visited Fisher in
his retirement at Naples. A six-week-long national coal strike had
just concluded. If it had lasted much longer, the nation and the navy
would have been paralysed. But it was not for this reason that Churchill had determined to set up a Commission on Oil, although the
uncertainty of supply of this fuel was a consideration. The switch
from inefficient coal to oil as the navy's prime source of fuel
had become inevitable ; and Churchill wanted Fisher to head this
Commission.
    Fisher liked to believe that the hand of God directed him in all his
wondrous naval achievements, and now that hand appeared to be
pointing towards Islam and the young oilfields of Persia (today Iran).
On 17 June 1912, while still undecided about whether to yield to
Churchill's pleas, he wrote to his wife recounting the English chap-
lain's sermon he had heard the day before. 'He fixed his eyes stead-
fast on me and made use of the following language : "No man still
in the possession of all his powers and vitality has any right to say,
'*Now I'm going to rest, for I've had a hard life*', for he owes a duty
to his Country and to his fellow-men."'
    Two days later, Fisher returned to London and took over the chair-
manship of the Royal Commission on Fuel Oil. As a result of its findings,
the Anglo–Persian Oil Company was set up, the British Government
having the controlling interest. Storage tanks were built in Persia, and
alongside the mountains of coal at naval bases at home and abroad,
and a vast programme of tanker construction was urgently put in hand.
In his new office in St James's Square, where Fisher presided over
the Commission's meetings, an uncharacteristic silence prevailed as if
oil had even been poured on troubled waters. But the correspondence
and the meetings with Churchill continued, and great things for the
Royal Navy stemmed from this newly reconciled pair.
    One of the most important advances, and one linked with the resort
to oil fuel, was the conception of a Fast Division for the Fleet. Intelligence reports from Germany told of new battleships and battle-cruisers

of very high speed. The *Dreadnought* of 1906 had put up the speed of battleships from 18 to 21 knots. The planned maximum speed of the most recently designed German dreadnoughts was said to be 23 knots. Comparable speed of German and British battle-cruisers rose from around 24 knots to 28 knots. Soon after assuming office, Churchill was advised, and strongly encouraged by Fisher, to proceed with a class of super-dreadnoughts which would possess the speed of a battle-cruiser with an armament so superior to any other battleship or battle-cruiser afloat that it could outrange and destroy at leisure any enemy.

'The path is plain and clear,' Fisher wrote to Churchill about new designs. 'There MUST be the 15-inch gun .... There MUST be a further VERY GREAT INCREASE OF SPEED.' Other recommendations about secondary armament and sacrifice of armour were ignored by Churchill, the Director of Naval Construction and their teams. But the essence of Fisher's philosophy was manifested in a class of five battleships forming this Fast Division, which became in the eyes of the whole world the cynosure of the twentieth-century battleship. Armed with eight 15-inch guns, protected with the thickest armour plate of any British ship, and with a speed of 24–25 knots, they were priceless additions to the Fleet and gave wonderful service in two world wars.

Churchill was proprietorially proud of these five battleships, but would have given them different names, which led to so much acrimony with the Palace that all the kudos Churchill acquired from yielding to George v on senior appointments appeared to have been lost. It was customary for First Lords to submit to the sovereign suggested names for new ships, a privilege which George v enjoyed and used from the beginning of his reign. Among the names for new battleships put up by Churchill in his first months at the Admiralty was *Oliver Cromwell*, associated more with the army than the navy, although Churchill claimed that 'scarcely any man did so much for it'. Churchill also recommended *Africa*, *King Richard the First*, *Henry the Fifth*, *Liberty* and *Delhi*.

When the King turned down *Oliver Cromwell* – a man who had, after all, decapitated his sovereign and created unhappy memories in Ireland – Churchill put it up again in his next list. The correspondence between the First Lord and the King's secretary, Lord Stamfordham, became stiffer and colder as the weeks passed. Pressing again for the name *Oliver Cromwell* Churchill argued, somewhat naïvely, 'The bitterness of the rebellions and tyrannies of the past has long ceased to stir men's minds; but the achievements of the country & its greatest men endure .... I am satisfied that the name [*Oliver Cromwell*] would be extremely well received ...'

Churchill hated to be crossed and the long-drawn-out argument with the Palace (of a strictly private nature of course but bordering on disrespect) reflected his youthful bumptiousness and conceit. In the end Prince Louis, the admiral nearest to the throne, entered the argument, almost certainly at the behest of the King, and told Churchill that 'all my experience at the Admiralty & close intercourse with three sovereigns leads me to this; from all times the Sovereign's decisions as to names for HM Ships has been accepted as final by all First Lords'.

Even this did not silence the First Lord. Churchill spent further hours drafting long letters to the Palace attempting to justify names like *Pitt*, which had never been used before in the navy, and informing the King's secretary that, on the contrary, 'the custom of bringing the names of battleships to the Sovereign's notice did not exist during the reign of Queen Victoria'. He also quoted contemporary historians to whom he had turned for advice and information. George V was infuriated and gave as good as he got, terminating the correspondence by suggesting that in future Churchill should come to the Palace and talk over new names before formally submitting them. The names reluctantly accepted by Churchill in the end were *Queen Elizabeth*, *Warspite*, *Barham*, *Valiant* and *Malaya*: names which rang through thirty-five years of eventful and often glorious naval history.

This curious quarrel with his sovereign had an even more curious postscript. At the closing stages of the battle of names, Churchill's attention was coincidentally drawn 'to some very large estimates wh have been presented for the refit of the *Victoria & Albert*'. The royal yacht was indeed an extravagance, as it always had been and is today, the target for proponents of naval economy and radical anti-monarchism alike. The *Enchantress* was also an expensive item and Churchill had been obliged recently to defend – successfully, as it happens – the cost of maintaining and running 'his' yacht. Churchill, in his letter to the King's secretary, continued: 'I have also been looking into the expenditure of the last five years on this vessel. I am sure the King would be surprised to see the enormous charges wh are made for quite small things.' He told Lord Stamfordham that he was sending a delegation down to Portsmouth to look into the matter. The sum involved was £13,000, about a quarter of a million in present-day money. 'After I am more fully informed,' concluded Churchill, 'His Majesty wd probably wish me to lay the result of the investigation before him.'

Lord Stamfordham showed George V the letter the next day. How else could he reply than that he deprecated unnecessary expenditure or extravagance and that he would be glad to know the result of the investigation? No doubt this was done although there is no written record. Churchill had made his point – perhaps a crude and petty one but certainly significant of his character.

These episodes re-aroused George v's doubts and suspicions about his minister, which remained to the end of his life. Nor were they in any way modified by Churchill's promotion of the King's cousin Prince Louis to the office of First Sea Lord within a year of Churchill's arrival at the Admiralty – an event which raised yet more clamour and controversy, this time of a public and political nature.

3
Recalcitrant Admirals

Arthur Balfour, the ex-Prime Minister (1902–6), was blessed with a private secretary, J.S.Sandars, with a talent for hearing all the gossip and promptly passing it on to his master. After 'Tug' Wilson's peremptory dismissal as First Sea Lord, it was Sandars who learned that Francis Bridgeman had been astonished to be asked by Churchill to supersede Wilson and had at first expressed his unwillingness to do so. But after pressure from the First Lord and assurances that they would work well together, Bridgeman agreed to give up his senior seagoing command and dutifully tie himself to an office desk instead.

That was in December 1911. Ten months later the picture was a very different one, as Sandars learned from Bridgeman in the course of a long and 'very frank' conversation. Not only Bridgeman but the entire Board of Admiralty were up in arms about what they regarded as Churchill's arrogant and ill-mannered behaviour – so bad that it threatened to lead to their mass resignation, with all the shattering political consequences, and personal consequences for Churchill, this must have.

Churchill had had the misfortune to follow an acquiescent and amiable First Lord. Whatever the impression he gave in Parliament and public, McKenna got on well with his admirals, enquired little into their doings and was by no means so eager as Churchill for bustle and change. It had been a relatively quiet time which made the contrast with Churchill's regime unwelcome.

As one of Churchill's allies put it, in explaining the reason for the restlessness in the Admiralty: 'When, in order to secure the application of a speedy remedy, you dictate a forcible indictment of something wrong, you are condemning the subject matter; they assume you are reflecting on the individuals who have grown up with the system & have not attempted to correct it.'

It was the language and the peremptoriness of Churchill's manner that caused such outrage. As Sandars reported to Balfour, the outrage to official decorum in the Admiralty had led Bridgeman and Prince Louis to meet and talk over what to do about it. Subsequently, Bridgeman plainly told [Churchill] that he must mend his manners or his Board would have to take action ... that as Winston could not give a single order outside the Admiralty building without the consent of the Board & that he was only *primus inter pares* the terms in which he had been addressing his colleagues were most improper.

Churchill at first bridled at this questioning of his powers. Bridgeman therefore said that the Board would have to take the matter to the Prime Minister, 'and ultimately to the King'. At this Churchill appears to have suddenly broken down and, to the wonder and discomfiture of his First Sea Lord, burst into tears. 'He has behaved better since,' Bridgeman reported with some satisfaction, suspecting wrongly that Churchill was suffering from ill health.

All this took place in early October 1912. During the following month, while Churchill was acrimoniously tossing to and fro ships' names with Buckingham Palace, it was Bridgeman's ill health that came up for scrutiny. While on leave at his seat, Copgrove Hall near Leeds, Bridgeman had caught a chill which had turned to something slightly more serious. Since the scene in the Admiralty at the beginning of October, Churchill had been searching for means of ridding himself of his colleague, who had proved a good deal less acquiescent than he had expected, as the recent incident revealed. Now Churchill seized the opportunity of doing the deed decently and in a manner which, he hoped, could not be used politically against him.

On 28 November 1912 after talking to the King at Windsor about Bridgeman's health, Churchill wrote to the Admiral to commiserate, adding that he had been 'meaning to write to you for some time about your health, which causes me concern both as a colleague and a friend'. He continued:

During the year that we have worked together I have seen how heavily the strain of your great office has told upon you, and I know that only your high sense of duty and your consideration for me have enabled you successfully to overcome your strong inclination to retire .... If therefore you should feel disposed at this juncture to retire, I could not, whatever my personal regrets, oppose your wish ...

This came as a great surprise to Francis Bridgeman, who was also touched by Churchill's consideration. He said that he was much better thank you but would think the matter over and come to London as soon as his doctor permitted the journey.

Churchill at once wrote to the King as if Bridgeman's resignation were already a *fait accompli*, and hoped that he would approve a proposal that Bridgeman should be promoted Admiral of the Fleet and that the King's cousin Prince Louis should now fill the office of First Sea Lord.

Meanwhile, Bridgeman saw his doctor who gave him a clean bill of health, so he wrote to Churchill to give him the news that he would 'return for good to the Admiralty at the New Year'. This crossed with a letter from Churchill telling him that he had talked the matter over with the Prime Minister and informed the King, and that 'the conclusion at which I have arrived must necessarily be final'. This came as an unwelcome surprise to the Admiral who had not realized that everything was settled. However, he saw that there was nothing he could do but resign. 'I am happy to be able to meet your wishes,' he wrote in reply.

The matter might have rested there but with so many enemies in the land, Churchill could hardly expect it to do so. On the evidence of the deep bitterness felt by Bridgeman about his forced resignation, it can reasonably be assumed that it was he who tipped off a leading Conservative politician, or the Conservative press directly, or someone who would forward the facts to the right quarter. On 14 December, under the headline MR CHURCHILL AND SIR FRANCIS BRIDGEMAN, the *Morning Post* opened the engagement with a broadside revealing 'some particulars regarding the resignation of Admiral Sir Francis Bridgeman'. The newspaper went on to inform its readers that Churchill had urged the entire Board of Admiralty to resign on the subject of navy pay and manning on which he was in dispute with them. Churchill had then conveyed the reasons for this crisis to the Prime Minister, with the result that Churchill had been forced to give way to his admirals but had – out of revenge was the implication – forced the resignation of the First Sea Lord.

Churchill on the same day (14 December) sent the newspaper cutting to Bridgeman. 'For such a gross breach of official confidence, I am certain you cannot be directly responsible,' he wrote. But it 'raises several serious issues on which it is necessary that I should know exactly where you stand'. He then informed Bridgeman that the matter would now become 'the subject of acrimonious debate in Parliament', and that he wished to have his confirmation that there had been no dispute about pay and manning and that 'no other cause of difference or dis-agreement in policy or view existed between us which had led, or was about to lead, to your resignation'.

It was a long letter, firm and only just friendly, and with one passage that smacked of collusion against Bridgeman within the Admiralty. Three weeks earlier, it seems, Bridgeman had written privately to Prince Louis saying how rotten he felt and that he really ought to get away to somewhere warmer in the winter – 'an impossibility so long as one remains at the Admiralty'. He had also written privately to Beatty on the same theme, indicating that he had at one time taken a pen in his hand to write his letter of resignation then decided to see how he was in the morning, when he felt better.

Churchill had persuaded both these officers to give permission for their letters to be used if necessary – and in the subsequent outcry, in Parliament and the press, they were so used. Bridgeman never forgave Prince Louis or Beatty and many years later, when he was an old man, he blackballed Prince Louis's son, Lord Mountbatten, who had been proposed by Beatty, from the Royal Yacht Squadron. In Parliament, Andrew Bonar Law, the Conservative leader, spoke of Bridgeman being 'brutally ill-used'. Both Bridgeman and Churchill threatened to make public more information and letters damaging to the other, and Churchill begged the King to intervene and persuade Bridgeman not to do so. Lord Charles Beresford wheeled himself out to proclaim the wickedness and misdeeds of Churchill and Prince Louis – 'this disgraceful affair'.

At the height of the storm it was made known that Bridgeman was riding to hounds three times a week in Yorkshire, looking 'in the pink'. Churchill countered in Parliament by revealing from how many important meetings the Admiral had been absent through ill health. The storm eventually died, but Churchill's critics were confirmed in their belief that he was untrustworthy and was handling his admirals badly. The word 'disgraceful' was much used in connection with the affair, and a future First Sea Lord, Rosslyn 'Rosy' Wemyss, commented, 'the whole matter is damnable, undignified and extremely bad for the Service . . .'.

It was under these inauspicious circumstances that Prince Louis of Battenberg assumed office as First Sea Lord. George v, while deploring the events that had led to the appointment, was delighted that his cousin had achieved the peak of his ambition.

An Admiralty scandal involving Churchill, less widely known at the time, concerned Admiral Sir Richard Poore, C-in-C at the Nore (a buoy and anchorage off Sheerness and a prestigious command). Churchill, in his enthusiasm to dig out the truth about everything wherever he went on his tours of inspection, did not scruple to call for junior officers and discuss with them the merits or demerits of their superiors and what was going on. He justified this on the ground that junior officers were less likely to cover up any scandals or failings. This practice aroused much resentment and accusations of encouraging insubordination, although a number of admirals used similar methods. Jellicoe in particular, as Second Sea Lord and responsible for discipline in the navy, seethed with indignation whenever he heard of another example of Churchill's 'meddling'.

On 23–26 October 1913 the *Enchantress* was at Sheerness with Churchill on board, keen to inspect the command and check on the progress of the Naval Air Service, in which he took such a keen interest. The NAS parent ship, and the navy's first seaplane carrier, HMS *Hermes*, was there, commanded by Captain Gerald Vivian. Vivian had recently made a certain decision about the use of some nearby land which was the responsibility of the NAS. But one of his young lieutenants, while being questioned by Churchill, suggested that his commanding officer had made a mistake and put forward his own views on the subject. Churchill thought these were sensible and preferable to Vivian's – and then told Captain Vivian so.

After Churchill had left, the young lieutenant was summoned to the presence of his commanding officer and, when rebuked, unwisely told him that Churchill had instructed him to report directly to him at the Admiralty if his course of action was not followed. Vivian complained strongly to Admiral Poore, who in turn complained strongly to Prince Louis, about Churchill's disrupting intervention. Churchill, who was said to have spies everywhere, was tipped off and reacted intemperately. Any communication concerning the matter, he told Jellicoe, was to be referred immediately to him. But when just such a letter – a private one – from Poore reached Jellicoe, he returned it to the Admiral, judging 'the remarks concerning the First Lord were too strong' and writing back privately to say so.

Churchill must have given instructions to the Admiralty's post room, for he got wind of this letter, too, and (it was said) 'he went dancing mad', telegraphing the General Post Office demanding that the letter be intercepted and returned to him personally. When this was done he opened and read it, and at once informed the Board that he was going to order Admiral Poore to haul down his flag.

The entire Board said it would resign if this happened, and Jellicoe said that he would make public their reasons for doing so. Churchill, he pointed out, did not even have the powers to order an admiral to haul down his flag. Churchill blasted back a broadside: if *any* member of the Board thought fit to criticize him on any matter, this must inevitably lead to the officer's resignation. Word of all this reached the Palace, but not yet the King, in case peace could be restored speedily.

Peace was restored, thanks largely to Prince Louis's efforts. Poore, who had threatened to demand a court martial, was induced to withdraw his letter and express his regret. 'Winston would not be flattered', wrote the Additional Civil Lord, Sir Francis Hopwood, to the King's secretary, 'if he knew the arguments used by the Naval Lords to keep the Commander-in-Chief from going. They were in short that Churchill was so much off his head over the whole business that Poore need take no notice of it!' He ended his letter, 'Laus Deo! It is over for the time, but we shall have it again in some form.'

The trouble was that Churchill tended to think of admirals unfavourably as civil servants and junior officers favourably as students – precocious students to be encouraged if they showed a bit of cheek or initiative. He always preferred the young whom he regarded as malleable to his mould, creatures of promise by contrast with the has-beens with a thick gold ring on their sleeves. Although so much of Churchill's heart and sense of romance was in history, it was in the promise of youth that he saw a better future; and in the case of the navy, a better navy.

On the whole generals were let off lightly compared with admirals. For Churchill the army was always the senior service – the army in which his ancestors had flowered and in which he had begun his own career. Nothing can match the loyalty one feels for a service in which you have displayed your youthful gallantry and risked your young life. Churchill's emotional link with the army and with its generals was immutable, and coloured his relationship with the navy throughout his political life.

The Admiralty soon learned of Churchill's insistence on brevity and correct presentation of memoranda and papers. He felt strongly about correct and concise usage of the English language. But he would never have written in these terms to a general:

I find it necessary to criticise the general style and presentment of your letters. A flag officer writing to a member of the Board of Admiralty on service matters ought to observe a proper seriousness and formality. The letter should be well written or typed on good paper; the sentences should be complete and follow the regular British form. Mere jottings of passing impressions hurriedly put together without sequence . . .

And more in this vein. Churchill, two years with the navy, was writing to an admiral who had been in the navy since Churchill was two years old.

If Churchill was not rebuking his admirals, he could often be found patronizing them or instructing them in their art in an insensitive manner. Here he lays down principles and advice to an admiral twenty-two years his senior and Commander-in-Chief of the Home Fleet who, it could be presumed, had had previous experience of exercises at sea:

Although manoeuvres are only a partial resemblance to war, they afford our sole means in time of peace of testing naval dispositions & commanders; and they must therefore have a real significance as regards both conduct & results

.... The task entrusted to you cannot be called disproportionate to the forces
at yr disposal, & it is for you to find, as you wd do in war, the best method
of achieving it . . .

The only senior admiral for whom Churchill felt unqualified respect
was Fisher, and Fisher was the only admiral, retired or serving, who
could argue with him, persuade him to change his mind, attack him
with intemperate language without rebuke in return. Fisher was like
a pilot guiding an inexperienced ship's captain through shoals and cur-
rents he himself had navigated professionally for many years. Churchill
would never admit to it but his views and principles, his opinions and
prejudices, on all naval matters derived wholly, largely or in part from
Jacky Fisher. As a prophet himself, he would no doubt eventually have
embraced the causes of the submarine and aviation without Fisher's
volatile encouragement. But Fisher nudged him along with his persuasive arguments and demands in capital letters, double underlinings,
exclamation marks, quotations from the Bible, psalm book and the
classics, and apt similes. Small cruisers, he insisted, 'will all be gobbled
up by an armoured cruiser, like the armadillo gobbles up the ants –
puts out its tongue and licks them up one after another – and the bigger
the ant the more placid the digestive smile'. And on speed :

No armour for anything but the super-*Lion, and there restricted ! . . . you'll
make the Germans 'Squirm' ! You had better adopt 2 keels to 1 ! You have
it now*. It will be safe ; it will be popular ; it will head off the approaching
German naval increase. Above all remember Keble in *The Christian Year*.
'The dusky hues of glorious War !'

Time and again Fisher pressed upon Churchill the great power and
brilliance of Admiral Sir John Jellicoe, 'the coming Nelson' who would
command at the second Trafalgar when war came. Jellicoe could do
no wrong in Fisher's eyes, and for a long time Churchill accepted Fisher's
judgement on this officer. Jellicoe was not an impressive figure, being
short in stature with a big nose and 'letter-box' mouth and a style that
was not at first impressive. His health was not robust. As a young officer
he had been shot through a lung out in China. He was recovering from
Malta fever when the *Victoria*, the flagship in which he was serving,
was sunk rapidly in a collision and he suffered from severe rheumatism
as a result. He was tortured by piles and bad teeth.
Jellicoe, however, had impressive powers of reasoning, was a tidy
administrator and a fine handler of a fleet. He was widely regarded
as one of the navy's few considerable 'brains', had sat with Prince Louis
on the dreadnought committee, and although greatly admired by Fisher
was never regarded by Fisher's enemies as being in the 'fish pond'.

Churchill's respect for Jellicoe was not reciprocated. Jellicoe thought Churchill had a baleful effect on the navy. He considered him 'quite ignorant of naval affairs'. 'His fatal error', he thought, 'was his entire inability to realize his own limitations as a civilian.'

Another exception to Churchill's generally dismissive attitude towards Royal Navy admirals was Prince Louis and this was, at least in part, because of the importance of his Palace connections. But he also recognized Prince Louis's powers of organization and administration, and although Churchill frequently exasperated the Prince, there was mutual respect and never a cross word was exchanged.

It would have been difficult to establish a Naval War Staff, to learn as rapidly as Churchill did just how the navy operated in peacetime when he regarded war with Germany as imminent, to carry out much-needed reforms left behind after even Fisher's broom had swept for six years – he would not have been able to accomplish all this without arousing antagonism among a hierarchy which disliked and was suspicious of any change. But Churchill, by his brash manner, his practice of setting subordinate against superior and brushing aside criticism and argument, ensured the depth of feeling against him among almost all senior officers.

This was widely known in political circles, and Conservatives spread the word and used it to attack both him personally and the Liberal Party. The Germans were well aware of it, too. On 3 December 1913, eight months before the outbreak of war, the German naval attaché in London reported home:

The sea-officers of the British Navy are often enraged against Mr Churchill ... for the youthful civilian Churchill, on his frequent visits to the fleet and dockyards, puts on the air of a military superior. Through his curt behaviour he offends the older officers in their feeling of rank and personal pride. And thus, according to many, through his lack of tact he injures discipline by his ambition for popularity with the lower ranks.

In January 1914 Fisher prepared a memorandum on the submarine, and this was sent to Asquith to be presented at a meeting of the Committee of Imperial Defence on 14 May. 'The coming of the submarine', Fisher insisted, 'means that the whole foundation of our traditional naval strategy, which served us so well in the past, has been broken down !' As far as shipping destruction was concerned, the elaborate international rules – putting a prize crew on board an enemy merchantman, convoying the vessel into harbour, and so on – could not be observed. The very nature of the submarine prohibited doing so.

Fisher then went on to predict in unerring detail the imminent unrestricted U-boat warfare conducted by the Germans, which came within a whisker of winning them the war by starving out Britain and cutting off war supplies.

There is nothing else the submarine can do except sink her capture, and it must therefore be admitted that (provided it is done, and however inhuman and barbarous it may appear) this submarine menace is a truly terrible one for British commerce and Great Britain . . .

Asquith was so shocked by the suggestion that an enemy could descend to such depths that he suppressed the paper. Fisher sent a copy to Churchill, who was equally outraged, and found it a 'frankly unthinkable proposition . . . . I do not believe this would ever be done by a civilized power.' On 20 October of that same year (1914) the German submarine *U-17* sank a British steamer off the Norwegian coast. The sinking was in accordance with international law. But by January 1915, when the German Naval Staff had been convinced of the true potential of their U-boat force, unrestricted submarine warfare was considered and put into effect. From 18 February all merchant ships would be sunk within the waters of the British Isles 'without it always being possible to avoid danger to the crews and passengers'. As Fisher had so often declared, to humanize war is like humanizing hell.

The aeroplane and seaplane had a much stronger appeal to Churchill than the submarine. He was always prepared to go down in a submarine and showed his usual interest in the mechanical workings, but his imagination and sense of romance and wonder were quite carried away by the flying machine. When Fisher was still First Sea Lord in January 1909, it was decided to build an experimental airship for scouting purposes. The Germans were far ahead in lighter-than-air machines, and the British never got things quite right, with the result that the British airship programme was dropped during Churchill's years of office.

Encouraged by Fisher ('You told me you would push *aviation* – you are right – . . .'), Churchill fought the Treasury for funds for aviation and eventually won, after setting up a service anyway.

The Agadir crisis of 1911, which had led to Churchill's arrival at the Admiralty and all that stemmed from this appointment, also led to much bitterness and increasing paranoia in Germany, and a resolve to build up the strength of the Fleet to a point where such rebuffs and humiliations could not occur again. On his very first day in office, Churchill received a letter from the Palace telling him that one of the King's relations in Germany, recently in Berlin, had informed the King of the mood there :

At the time when the Morocco [Agadir] crisis had creached its acute stage,

Germany would have gone to war with England but her Fleet was not ready yet and would *not* be until 1915 when the Canal would be finished so that all the largest ships could pass through [between Baltic and North Sea], and by that time they would have enough Dreadnoughts launched to deal with any power . . .

Germany's determination was confirmed when a supplementary navy bill was secretly prepared authorizing the building of more battleships in order to achieve a 2:3 ratio with Britain. This provocative proposal, which soon reached Churchill's ears, did not immediately lead him to propose a counter stroke, only the promise in his first public speech as First Lord that there could certainly be a reduction in the navy estimates if Germany made no increase to the existing programme.

The picture of Churchill as a man of peace is not one that immediately comes to mind, least of all in Germany in 1911–12. But to Churchill, who had seen war at first hand, the idea of war with Germany was abhorrent. 'I deeply deplore the situation,' he wrote to his old friend Sir Ernest Cassel, 'for as you know I have never had any but friendly feelings towards that great nation and her illustrious Sovereign & I regard the antagonism wh has developed as insensate. Anything in my power to terminate it, I wd gladly do . . .' Again, at the Royal Academy banquet (4 May 1912): 'I believe that if any two great civilized and highly scientific nations go to war with one another, they will become heartily sick of it before they come to the end of it.'

Right up to August 1914 Churchill kept the door open to a reduction in warship building, proposing from time to time what he called a 'naval holiday' in which all construction should cease for a stated time. But it was like trying to halt a 30,000-ton battleship in its slide down the slipway. Moreover, it infuriated the Germans, and the Emperor, who regarded anything like it as meddling in Germany's internal affairs. As late as May 1914 Churchill, with the blessing of the Foreign Office, was trying to arrange through Cassel a meeting in Germany with Grand-Admiral Alfred von Tirpitz. Tirpitz was Germany's Fisher, inspirer, with his master, Kaiser Wilhelm, of German naval expansion. Churchill wanted to demonstrate the genuineness of his proposals for a 'naval holiday'.

'Naval holiday'? Britain could well talk about a year without any naval construction, was the orthodox German view, when her navy was more powerful than any other two navies in the world. 'It is absurd England always looking at Germany,' complained the Emperor to the British naval attaché in Berlin.

But within weeks what had been dreaded by so many and judged inevitable by others had come to pass, and Churchill had to switch his attentions from reform while searching for peace to conducting the Royal Navy in its greatest challenge since the days of Napoleon.

4
Indignant Turks

As a writer himself, Churchill learned early in his career the importance
of establishing and preserving a written record of events which ensured
for him all possible credit. With his admirals, who were not usually
concerned with the written record and with posterity, Churchill acquired
the practice of committing to paper an idea put up to him in these
terms: 'As you know, since I discussed with you the matter of ...'
and then requesting a memorandum on the subject.

Prince Louis rumbled these tricks early in his relationship with his
First Lord, shrugged his shoulders and muttered to his wife something
derogatory about 'these politicians'. In June 1913 Prince Louis received
one of these 'As you know ...' notes from Churchill. This one continued, 'this has been in my mind for some long time. I should hope
next year to obtain a mobilization of the whole of the Royal Fleet
Reserve ...'

In reality the question of a trial mobilization of the huge Fleet Reserve
had been discussed many times between Prince Louis and Jellicoe, and
other members of the Board. The Prince had been pressing for it for
ten years. A full-scale test was obviously desirable and necessary to
ensure that the complicated arrangements for moving 20,000 reservists
from their homes to their ports and ships worked smoothly.

'In the autumn of 1913,' wrote Churchill in his memoirs, 'when I
was revolving the next year's Admiralty policy in the light of the coming
Estimates, I had sent the following minute to the First Sea Lord:

October 22, 1913.

First Sea Lord
Second Sea Lord
Secretary

We have now had manoeuvres in the North Sea on the largest scale for
two years running, and we have obtained a great deal of valuable data which
requires to be studied. It does not therefore seem necessary to supplement
the ordinary tactical exercises of the year 1914–15 by Grand Manoeuvres. A
saving of nearly £200,000 could apparently be effected in coal and oil

consumption, and a certain measure of relief would be accorded to the Estimates in an exceptionally heavy year.

In these circumstances I am drawn to the conclusion that ... it would be better to substitute instead a mobilization of the Third Fleet [reserves] ...'

In one written minute Churchill acquired for the record the credit for conceiving this Reserve Fleet mobilization (already agreed to four months earlier), justifying the cancellation of the manoeuvres by the fact that data from earlier manoeuvres had not yet been studied, and confirming for all to see his desire for economies in the running of the navy at a time when this was coming up again for minute and hostile scrutiny.

'Prince Louis agreed,' Churchill added starkly in his memoirs.

Churchill announced this mobilization publicly in Parliament on 18 March 1914 and the mobilization began on 15 July. The timing could hardly have been more fortuitous. Churchill and Prince Louis visited Chatham to see if the machinery ran smoothly there. The reservists drew their kits and proceeded to their ships, which coaled and raised steam and proceeded to Spithead to rendezvous with the main permanent Fleet. Here on 17–18 July George v in the royal yacht *Victoria and Albert* inspected these combined fleets, 'the greatest assemblage of naval power ever witnessed in the history of the world', as Churchill described it.

On 19 July all the Fleets put to sea for exercises. After Churchill witnessed this impressive scene he wrote :

It took more than six hours for this armada, every ship decked with flags and crowded with bluejackets and marines, to pass, with bands playing and at 15 knots, before the Royal Yacht, while overhead the naval seaplanes and aeroplanes circled continuously .... One after another ships melted out of sight beyond the Nab. They were going on a longer voyage than any of us could know.

Domestic arrangements in the navy hierarchy for the dog days of August 1914 included a family visit to Russia by Prince Louis. The First Sea Lord's elder son was serving in the battle-cruiser *New Zealand*, but his younger son Dickie was to accompany him and join the rest of the family. Prince Louis's sister-in-law was the beautiful unbalanced Tsarina, and the Russian imperial family and the Battenbergs were to have spent those high summer weeks together at the royal summer palace, boating, fishing, swimming, talking endlessly while their children played with their pets and at numerous games.

Churchill and his wife Clementine and their children were to have occupied themselves very similarly if more humbly in Norfolk, by the sea at a village called Overstrand, near Cromer. Here Churchill had rented Pear Tree Cottage for the summer and his sister-in-law Beehive Cottage nearby. The four children, Clementine's Diana and Randolph and their cousins Johnny and Peregrine, would paddle and play in the sand.

Overstrand had been a simple fishing hamlet for many years. Lacking a harbour, the boats were drawn up on to the shelving beach beneath the low cliff. In the 1890s Cromer, Sheringham and Overstrand were developed as resorts to meet the bracing holiday needs of the middle and upper classes. The first two were for the middle classes and boasted large red-brick hotels on the front. Overstrand was more exclusive. Cyril Flower, the millionaire brewer and later Lord Battersea, developed Overstrand for grander people and commissioned the famous architect Edwin Lutyens to design him a house. Lutyens also converted several of the fishermen's cottages, including Pear Tree Cottage, with six bedrooms and a billiards room downstairs in addition to a drawing-room and dining-room.

Overstrand had become established as the summer venue for both Churchill families, and gained additional local esteem when the *Enchantress* anchored off-shore one day, Churchill coming ashore for a few days with his family. With the international scene so ominous, Churchill did not expect to be able to spend long with Clementine and the children during July and August but determined to slip down for one weekend, especially as Clementine was expecting another child and was not feeling well.

On Friday afternoon, 24 July, Churchill attended a Cabinet. The first subject on the agenda was Ireland and Home Rule, a subject which had split the nation and threatened civil war in Ireland. But in the middle of these doleful and menacing considerations, a note was delivered containing the terms of an ultimatum from Austria to Serbia, and all attention was diverted from a critical domestic scene to an even more threatening international situation.

Since the assassination in Sarajevo, Serbia, of Archduke Franz Ferdinand of Austria and his wife on 28 June, relations between Serbia and Austria had rapidly deteriorated and Germany and Russia were being sucked relentlessly into the maelstrom of acrimony and hysteria. As Churchill was to write to his wife, 'Europe is trembling on the verge of a general war.' The Austrian ultimatum, he described as 'the most insolent document of its kind ever devised'. Churchill then proceeded to the Admiralty. The First Fleet was at Portland. The Second Fleet was also at Portland after completing exercises and would shortly discharge the members of the reservist crews. The Third Fleet ships, manned almost entirely by reservists, were heading for their home ports with orders to pay off on Monday.

That night Churchill dined with Cassel and the equally wealthy German, Albert Ballin, at Brook House, Cassel's stone and marble mausoleum-like mansion in Park Lane. Ballin was in sombre mood. During dinner he recounted a prediction of the one-time German Chancellor in 1897: 'I remember old Bismarck telling me the year before he died that one day the great European War would come out of some damned foolish thing in the Balkans.'

On the following morning, Saturday 25 July, Churchill returned to the Admiralty and spoke to Prince Louis, who was to hold the fort over the weekend. Churchill assured his First Sea Lord that he would make special arrangements with the post office switchboard in Cromer to have the telephone manned day and night while he was away so that he could be kept *au courant* with developments, and would telephone the Prince every few hours. Prince Louis did not approve of the First Lord absenting himself at this critical time, and later told his younger son, 'Ministers with their weekend holidays are incorrigible.'

Churchill took the 1 p.m. train to join his family at Overstrand. That evening he telephoned the Admiralty. Prince Louis's news was slightly reassuring. Among the numerous despatches which arrived at the Admiralty was a note from the Foreign Office to the effect that Serbia, bowing its head in supplication, had accepted the terms of the Austrian note. Churchill went to bed that night feeling that 'things might blow over'.

Sunday was a perfect summer day, clear and sparkling. In the morning Churchill took the children down The Land, the 200-yard-long lane leading to the cliff top; and thence down the zig-zag path to the beach. 'We damned the little rivulets which trickled down to the sea as the tide went out,' he wrote later of this day. He called up Prince Louis again at mid-day. The Austrians appeared dissatisfied with Serbia's response and remained threatening. At dinner on Friday night Ballin had said, 'If Russia marches against Austria,' as a result of an Austrian attack on Serbia, 'we [Germany] must march; and if we march France must march, and what would England do?' Churchill had told the German magnate that it would be a mistake for Germany to presume that Britain would necessarily do nothing.

The burning question for the navy was whether or not to halt the dispersal of the reservists. Churchill would not commit himself on his decision, only emphasizing to his First Sea Lord the serious political implications if their demobilization were halted. The telephone line was poor and Prince Louis had difficulty in catching all that Churchill said, but there was no doubt that the decision must be his. Churchill also added that he would cut short his weekend and return late that night. But by then, Prince Louis knew, and Churchill knew, that it would be too late to halt the return home of the 20,000 reservist sailors, many of whom would be off at once on their own summer holidays and be scattered all over the country.

Prince Louis always believed afterwards that he had been left to carry the can in order that Churchill could not be held responsible and that it would therefore be a service rather than a political decision. 'The wrong decision now could seriously damage and even destroy the career of the man who made it,' as Prince Louis's biographer has written.

Over the next few hours the news suggested a worsening situation. At 6 p.m., the hour when Austria's ultimatum was due to expire, Prince Louis decided on his own initiative to 'stand the Fleet fast', and in his own hand wrote out the orders. Later, Churchill gave him full credit – 'his loyal hand had sent the first order which began our vast naval mobilization', and was relieved to hear late that night on visiting the Foreign Office that the announcement of this grave step 'might have the effect of sobering the Central Powers and steadying Europe'.

Over the next days, as the situation worsened still further, all the precautions and contingent arrangements worked out by the new Naval War Staff were put in hand. Coastal guns were manned day and night, bridges guarded, naval bases and barracks closed to all but authorized personnel, magazines and other vital stores protected. After Monday's Cabinet, Churchill drew up 'a very secret warning' to all Commanders-in-Chief:

> July 27, 1914.
> This is not the Warning Telegram, but European political situation makes war between Triple Entente [Britain, France, Russia] and Triple Alliance [Germany, Austro-Hungary, Italy] Powers by no means impossible. Be prepared to shadow possible hostile men-of-war and consider dispositions of HM ships under your command from this point of view. Measure is purely precautionary. No unnecessary person is to be informed. The utmost secrecy is to be observed.

The official Warning Telegram was despatched hard on the heels of this preliminary warning and was in the hands of every squadron and fleet throughout the Fleet, from Hong Kong to the West Indies, from Simonstown in South Africa to Alexandria, Malta and Gibraltar.

In consultation with the Chief of the Naval Staff, Admiral Doveton Sturdee, and Prince Louis, at 10 a.m. on Tuesday 28 July the decision was made to despatch the First Fleet to its war stations. This Fleet, soon to be renamed Grand Fleet, was the navy's first line and comprised the Battle Squadrons and supporting cruisers and destroyers of the latest and most powerful ships. It was to leave Portland, and during the hours of darkness and with all lights extinguished, the battleships and battle-cruisers, eighteen miles long in all, would steam fast through the Straits of Dover and head north for Scapa Flow, Cromarty and Rosyth in Scotland, where all ships would refuel and be put on a war basis.

By the morning of 31 July they were ready for action, and eager for it, too. Morale was good, self-confidence as high as it had been in Nelson's day. Throughout the Fleet, there was not a man who did not believe that he had the best and most battle-worthy ships in the world, and the first clash was anticipated with the conscious and frequently articulated belief in their invincibility.

On this same day Churchill wrote to his wife at Pear Tree Cottage: 'There is still hope although the clouds are blacker & blacker. Germany is realising I think how great are the forces against her & is trying tardily to restrain her idiot ally .... But everybody is preparing swiftly for war and at any moment now the stroke may fall. We are ready.'

This stroke fell four days later. At 11 p.m. on 4 August Churchill flashed the signal, 'Commence hostilities against Germany.' The civil head of the Royal Navy in peacetime was now responsible to Parliament and the nation for the efficient maintenance and running of the Royal Navy in time of war.

The duties of a First Lord were almost as undefined as the British constitution. 'Accepted practice' was an expression much used and much abused by Churchill. He had never once transgressed the law, let alone the constitution, in his 1,100 days in office; but he had departed from the practices of his predecessors in almost every department. His early excesses which had caused such outrage had been somewhat mitigated. There was less friction with his admirals in 1914 than in 1912, but that was largely because these admirals had come to terms with his style and behaviour and complained less because they were on the whole a stoic body of men and could see that nothing could be gained by getting upset. Moreover, his most stubborn opponents had by now been overthrown. Relative calm reigned. As the German Naval Attaché wrote home in one of his last despatches, 'On the whole the Navy is satisfied with Mr Churchill ...'

There was no hint, in Churchill's style of leadership as First Lord in peacetime, to lead Prince Louis and the Naval Staff to believe that he would be less exacting and less commanding in time of war. But the keenness with which he followed every move, the depth of detail into which he at once plunged, and the authoritarian and completely dominating manner in which he took over control of the main thrust of events, came as a great shock to that professional body of men within the Admiralty who had trained for years in their roles. Like some maritime Marlborough, Churchill *was* the Admiralty, *was* the navy – supremo, admiralissimo, dictator.

Churchill, in conducting the naval war, listened to the Chief of Naval Staff, Admiral Doveton Sturdee, listened to Prince Louis, sought answers to his questions, delegated relatively minor matters – there were after all only eighteen working hours in the day. But there was never any shadow of doubt that he was the hub of this giant steel wheel. It was not in the office of the Chief of Naval Staff, nor the First Sea Lord. It was mid-way between the Admiralty War Room with its charts of the world's oceans upon its walls, and Churchill's private office overlooking the Horse Guards Parade. Because Churchill reigned supreme, increasingly when absent he left a vacuum, a sense of impotency almost, initiative shrivelled among those whose real business it was to supervise the conduct of the war at sea. Because he *was* the dynamo, when it was switched off the lights went out.

The public, who had expected an immediate and glorious victory in the North Sea, were disappointed. The Germans remained in harbour in home waters. It was in distant seas, where they had a scattering of ships, some of them powerful, that the first naval events occurred, and they were disappointing to the British. In the Mediterranean, the modern German battle-cruiser *Goeben*, supported by a light cruiser, escaped from a more powerful British force and was welcomed with open arms by the sympathetic, but still neutral, Turkish people. Unfortunately, Churchill had just ordered the seizure in British shipyards of two dreadnoughts being completed (and paid for) for the Turkish Navy.

On the same day that Churchill learned of the safe arrival of the German ships in Turkish waters, Prime Minister Asquith noted:

We had a Cabinet this morning as usual. The only interesting thing is the arrival of the *Goeben* in the Dardanelles & her sale to Turkey! The Turks are very angry – not unnaturally – at Winston's seizure .... As we shall insist that the *Goeben* shall be manned by a Turkish instead of a German crew, it doesn't much matter: as the Turkish sailors cannot navigate her – except on to the rocks or mines ...

Thus, with stratospheric arrogance and complacency, Asquith disposed of *that* incident in a war now seven days old. Lloyd George thought quite otherwise. He was convinced later that Churchill forced Turkey into the war in 1914, and told him so, to his outrage.

There were several set-backs for the navy during the month of August besides the failure to intercept the *Goeben*, including the loss in a mine-field (after sinking the German minelayer) of the light cruiser *Amphion*. From now on, almost until the war's first Christmas, the Admiralty had very little but bad news to report, and Churchill became more and more depressed. On 24 October Captain Herbert Richmond, the Assistant Director of Operations, who had Churchill to dinner that evening, noted that he was 'oppressed with the impossibility of *doing* anything .... I have not seen him so despondent before.' Far from fighting a fleet action with the Germans, Jellicoe had been obliged to retreat from his insecure base at Scapa Flow for fear of submarine attack. Even on the west coast of Scotland it seemed that the Fleet was not safe from the much feared underwater weapons. The new super-dreadnought *Audacious* was sunk by a mine off Loch Swilly three days after Churchill had dined with Richmond. So finely balanced numeri-cally were the two battle fleets now that if the German Navy had sought a major action at this time it could very well have inflicted a decisive defeat – and that would have meant the end of the war.

On 22 September 1914, soon after dawn, three old *Bacchante*-class cruisers, the *Aboukir, Hogue* and *Cressy*, manned in all by over 2,200 men, were steaming in a straight line on patrol, unescorted (the weather had been too bad for destroyer escort) at 10 knots. A single, small, obsolescent German U-boat stalked them and put a torpedo into the *Aboukir*, which sank in twenty minutes. The other two big ships came alongside her to lower rescue boats and were in turn themselves sunk. Twelve hundred officers and men perished, and being reservists were mostly married men with families, an infinitely worse loss than the worthless ships which should never have been there.

Churchill, in his account of the catastrophe, made much of a minute he wrote four days earlier – 'the *Bacchantes* ought not to continue on this beat' – and recounted the chapter of accidents which led to action being taken too late. He failed to mention that Commodore Roger Keyes, senior naval officer at Harwich, had warned of the risks being taken on this patrol in a letter he wrote on 21 August. 'For Heaven's sake,' he pleaded, 'take those "Bacchantes" away! ... the Germans must know they are about, and if they send out a suitable force, God help them!' It is unlikely that Churchill, with his eye on everything, failed to see this or have his attention drawn to it, especially as it came from a real fire-eating commander whom he admired.

Up at Scapa Flow during those anxious autumn weeks of 1914, fears grew of U-boats entering the anchorage and causing mayhem. Jellicoe was becoming jittery and there were early signs that his health was being affected by the weight of his responsibilities. As he wrote to a friend: 'I am laid up for a bit. It is of course due to the worry of trying to get things done which ought to be done without my having to step in . . .'

It was the lack of a secure anchorage for his great Fleet that was his first concern. 'I *long* for a submarine defence at Scapa; it would give such a feeling of confidence,' he wrote to Churchill a week after the loss of the three cruisers. 'I can't sleep half so well inside as when outside, mainly because I feel we are risking such a mass of valuable ships where, if a submarine did get in, she practically has the British Dreadnought Fleet at her mercy . . .'

Churchill had already attracted strong professional and public criticism for what came to be known as his Antwerp escapade. From the earliest days of the war the navy had to concern itself with the German advance through Belgium. Not only were the Channel ports at stake, but if they fell the supply lines to the British Army fighting in France would be cut. The Naval Air Division was soon operating from French soil near Dunkirk and by the middle of September a large quantity of guns and ammunition had been supplied to the Belgian defenders and the Royal Marines Brigade of 3,000 men despatched as support.

The most important Belgian port was the fortified city of Antwerp which was still holding out, the King and the Government in residence, at the end of September. Once Antwerp had fallen, the way was open for the Germans to advance upon Dunkirk, Calais and Boulogne. With the fall of Brussels, the Germans turned their attention on Antwerp, bombarding the forts with howitzers. Belgian morale slumped and by 2 October it was clear that they would not hold out for long without help and the Belgian Government announced that it would evacuate the next day. Churchill was informed of the depth of the crisis and was recalled from a visit to the naval aerodrome at Dunkirk. He decided to go to the rescue of the Belgians personally, to put spine into the Antwerp defenders, reinforce and reorganize the city's defences, and prevail upon the King and his Government not to quit.

Churchill left London in his personal train at 3 a.m. on 3 October, promising a report as soon as possible. The spirit of Marlborough was already flowing through his veins. He observed with an expert eye German howitzers demolishing the powerful Belgian forts. The principles of land warfare were something that he had fully comprehended and fully mastered many years ago, and the prospect of saving a great city and changing the course of the war filled him with anticipatory excitement. 'I cannot but think that he will stiffen them up to the sticking point,' Asquith commented. And he was right. The Belgian Government agreed not to evacuate if the British agreed to give strong support. Churchill called for the Naval Brigades from their base in England

and toured the city's defences in a Rolls-Royce with a rifleman in the front seat.

The rifleman, many years later, recalled this picture of Churchill the soldier far from the First Lord of the Admiralty's office :

He put forward his ideas forcefully, waving his stick and thumping the ground with it. After obviously pungent remarks, he would walk away a few steps and stare towards the enemy's direction. On other occasions he would stride away without another word, get into the car and wait impatiently to go off to the next area.

With the scent of battle in his nostrils – he was under fire more than once – Churchill decided that he would like to stay and see it through 'provided that I am given necessary military rank and authority, and full powers of a commander of a detached force in the field'. He wished to resign from the Cabinet, and his post as First Lord, and become a soldier again. 'I feel it my duty to offer my services, because I am sure this arrangement will afford the best prospects of victorious result ...' He even proposed a successor at the Admiralty.

Asquith read out this startling document to the Cabinet, members of which were anxiously enquiring about the likely date of his return as he was too often given to these dashes across the Channel, which were not welcomed by the Government or the Admiralty. Asquith later reported the Cabinet reaction. 'I regret to say that it was received with a Homeric laugh. W. is an ex-Lieutenant of Hussars, and would if his proposal had been accepted, have been in command of 2 distinguished Major Generals, not to mention Brigadiers, Colonels &c ...' In fact Asquith had already telegraphed his refusal to Churchill's proposal.

By 8 October Churchill knew that it was all over. 'Poor Winston is very depressed,' Asquith wrote to his confidante Venetia Stanley, 'as he feels that his mission has been in vain.'

Arthur Gwynne, editor of the *Morning Post* and a violent Churchill-hater, published these patronizing injunctions : 'What we desire chiefly to enforce upon Mr Churchill is that this severe lesson ought to teach him that he is not, as a matter of fact, a Napoleon ; but a Minister of the Crown with no time either to organise or to lead armies in the field.' Being photographed under fire (as indeed he was), the *Morning Post* charged, 'is an entirely unnecessary addition to the risks and horrors of war'.

Sir John French did not agree. Churchill enjoyed a great fellow feeling with the Commander-in-Chief of the British forces in France. Churchill had frequently visited him at his headquarters to discuss the problems and progress of the war on land as well as on sea. 'You did splendid work at Antwerp,' French wrote to Churchill when he was at his lowest. 'When are you coming to me again ? For God's sake don't pay attention to what those rotten papers say.'

Churchill could not entirely avoid doing so, but felt able to reply: 'I clear my heart of all hostile reflections and sterile controversies. It is vain to look backwards.'

But the navy's fortunes did not prosper. The German armed merchantman *Kaiser Wilhelm der Grosse* (her name alone a provocation) was responsible for a number of losses in the Atlantic before being tracked down and destroyed by a British cruiser. The German cruiser *Karlsruhe* in the Caribbean and off Pernambuco evaded a powerful force sent in search of her and notched up a steady toll of victims, seventeen in all, by 1 November.

The career of the *Emden* in Indian and South-East Asian waters became something of a *cause célèbre*, and for a while she paralysed trade over a wide area. She, too, was still untraced, still continuing her depredations, at the beginning of November, her captain assuming even in British eyes something of the guise of a heroic privateer of old.

The most serious commerce-raiding problem, however, was in the vast reaches of the Pacific, where it could truly be said for a time that Britannia no longer ruled the waves. Besides the *Goeben* and *Breslau* in the Mediterranean, the German Navy had on station at the outset of the war a powerful squadron in China, consisting of armoured and light cruisers under the command of a skilful and determined officer, Vice-Admiral Count Maximilian von Spee.

After detaching the *Emden* from his squadron, Spee disappeared from sight, posing a threat to all Australasian shipping and later, as he took his force from west to east, to the equally important Pacific South American trade routes. A veritable armada of searching men o'war – French, Australian, New Zealand and Japanese as well as British – spread out to locate the German force, listening all the while for the faintest message on the w/T.

The force most likely to intercept Spee was a squadron of mainly elderly cruisers under the command of a gallant but unwell and sketchily organized officer called Christopher Cradock. Admiral Cradock finally caught up with the overwhelmingly superior German squadron off the Chilean coast on 1 November 1914. His flagship and his second armoured cruiser were instantly sunk with no survivors. Churchill then self-righteously declared, 'I cannot accept for the Admiralty any share in the responsibility [for this tragedy].' Moreover, he presented to Asquith and the Cabinet a wholly distorted account of the events, and the exchanges of signals leading up to the Battle of Coronel. Cradock, Churchill told his fellow ministers, was at fault in disobeying 'his instructions, which were express to the effect that he must concentrate his whole squadron . . .' But Cradock had been denied the one ship that could have given him a chance against the Germans. And the truth was that, however ill-judged was the action of the courageous admiral, he had been confused by contrary orders stemming from Churchill personally and from the Admiralty's craven, inexperienced and not sufficiently brainy Naval War Staff.

Prince Louis of Battenberg at least escaped all blame for the disaster in the Pacific because three days before Coronel he resigned his office as First Sea Lord, his own battle finally lost after weeks of bloodless struggle. Before the war Lloyd George had warned that the public would not stand for a German-born admiral being professional head of the navy in war. Asquith, too, thought that there might be trouble but that if everything went well he might expunge the 'crime' of being a blood relation of the German hierarchy: after all, the Kaiser was King George's cousin. But that was not to be. Prince Louis was told to go.

Of Churchill at this time Asquith wrote to Venetia Stanley on 28 October: 'Poor boy, he has just been pouring out his woes.' The sinking of the *Audacious* was a great worry, but 'Winston's real trouble however is about Prince Louis & the succession to his post. He *must* go, & Winston has had a most delicate & painful interview with him – the more so as his nephew Prince Maurice was killed in action yesterday.'

Who was Churchill to choose to replace his First Sea Lord, now that the pressure had, by Prince Louis's sacrifice, been lifted from his own shoulders? Haldane had written to Churchill a few days earlier, 'The nation thoroughly believes in you. I should like to see Fisher and Wilson brought in.' Their advent, he claimed, 'would make the country feel that our old spirit of the Navy was alive and come back'.

The more Churchill thought about Fisher as his partner the more he liked the idea. Conflicts they had had, but these had been inevitable in the turbulent times through which the navy had recently lived; they had always come out beaming at one another in the end, to settle down to another ferociously long talk, sparks flying, beating the best out of each other. Fisher the stimulant was what Churchill needed in these pallid days of worry and inaction.

'Lord Fisher used to come occasionally to the Admiralty, and I watched him narrowly to judge his physical strength and mental alertness,' Churchill wrote later. 'There seemed no doubt about either . . . he left me with the impression of a terrific engine of mental and physical power burning and throbbing in that ancient frame.'

Churchill sounded him out forthwith and found, unsurprisingly,

that he was fiercely eager to lay his grasp on power, and was strongly inspired
with the sense of a message to deliver and a mission to perform .... I was
well aware that there would be strong, natural and legitimate, opposition in
many quarters to Fisher's appointment, but having formed my own conviction
I was determined not to remain at the Admiralty unless I could do justice
to it. So in the end, for good or for ill, I had my way.

Churchill and Fisher had a mutual compulsion for one another,
drawn to some shared drug which raised them to a new 'high' of
hyper-stimulation. Contentment for them both lay in rapid debate,
sparks flying, which was a wonder to those present who were themselves stunned into silence. When they wanted one another, nothing
was allowed to stand in their way – not even the words of caution
to her husband uttered by sensible Clementine. As for Fisher, the
lust for renewed power, like one of his battle-cruisers under forced
draught, swept him ever more swiftly back to the Admiralty, listening to no one. Lord Northcliffe wrote to the journalist Hugh
Massingham: 'I expended one hundred and twenty minutes of as
much energy as I possess in giving him [Fisher] my views of Churchill's character – its many good qualities, its many bad – gained in
a great many years of acquaintance with Churchill. I might have
been talking to a stone . . .'

Shortly before Churchill visited Asquith to pour out his woes, Lord
Stamfordham had been at 10 Downing Street. Asquith had mooted
to him the likely turn of events at the Admiralty, and the return to
power of Jacky Fisher. The King's secretary was clearly appalled at
the prospect for, as Asquith wrote to Venetia Stanley, 'Stamfordham
declares the King's unconquerable aversion to Fisher . . . and suggests
nonsense people .... I said nothing would induce me to part with W,
whom I eulogised to the skies, and that in consequence the person
chosen must be congenial to him. So for the moment there is a complete
impasse . . .'

There now developed another row between sovereign and First
Lord, this time with Asquith as a highly prejudiced referee. At first
the King used the argument that Churchill had been trying to leave
the Admiralty himself for some time because he wanted to see action
as a soldier. Then why not go now? Kitchener would ensure that he
was given an appropriate rank, and Sir John French would welcome
him to the battlefields. It was Asquith who threw over this idea, declaring that Churchill was irreplaceable at the Admiralty. The King
argued that the service did not trust Fisher, he would open up old
wounds, etc.

'I cannot help feeling that his presence at the Admiralty will not inspire the Navy with that confidence which ought to exist,' the King wrote to Asquith, 'especially when we are engaged in so momentous a war. I hope that my fears may prove groundless.'

Churchill, with Asquith adding up the points in his favour, knew that he had only to stick it out. In fact a few more hours sufficed. The King gave in, but not without putting it on record that he approved the appointment 'with some reluctance and misgivings'.

George v was not the only doubter. Besides those who had never been in the fish pond, several admirals, including Rosslyn Wemyss, experienced forebodings for the future. 'They will be as thick as thieves at first until they differ on some subject,' wrote this percipient and highly experienced sailor, 'probably as to who is to be No 1, when they will begin to intrigue against one another.'

Another admiral with doubts, and who would never work in harmony with Fisher, was the Chief of Staff and Fisher-hater, Doveton Sturdee. Churchill knew that he would have to go, and in his place he wanted to bring back 'Tug' Wilson – a curious choice for an admiral who had been sacked for opposing the introduction of a Staff in the first place. Wilson refused anyway, but agreed to work in a supernumerary and advisory capacity – no special title, no pay : typical of the man.

But the newspapers, with few exceptions, were delighted at the news, as were the public at large. Churchill was right. The Admiralty's reputation was redeemed overnight, and with it his own reputation even before anything had been accomplished. It was at this moment, fortuitously, that news of Coronel was published. The disaster could be laid at the feet of the old regime. There would be no more defeats now ; vengeance would be on the way.

The wheels of vengeance for Coronel were thrust into motion within just one hour of the news being confirmed that Cradock and his two cruisers had gone down off the Chilean coast. Fisher was in his element, in command again at this hour of need for his beloved navy and his country. At the Admiralty it was at once evident that, for the first time since October 1911, professional control was no longer exclusively in the hands of the First Lord. Fisher changed all that overnight. There was no branch of the elaborate and powerful Admiralty machinery with which he was not familiar. He knew everyone in command, their strengths and weaknesses, and could identify without a glance his enemies and friends.

After clearing out all weak elements, Fisher got down to the business of running the war at sea with Churchill. At this stage it was Fisher who made most of the operational decisions, the new Chief of Staff,

Henry Oliver, being no more than a rubber stamp. The new dispositions were entirely Fisher's and characteristically positive they were, too. He proposed to send to the South Atlantic without delay two battle-cruisers, each capable of outgunning and outpacing Spee's entire squadron. They did so, in short order, and on 8 December 1914 a British squadron caught and sank all but one of von Spee's five cruisers off the Falkland Islands – the fifth was caught later.

The navy and the Admiralty were reinstated in the hearts of the people. 'A brilliant feat of arms', 'Coronel avenged' and simply 'A great naval victory' were the expressions used by the press. Letters from his friends and contemporaries in the service, from politicians, from the general public, poured in to the Admiralty for Fisher. But the message he treasured most was from Churchill;

December 10

This was your show and your luck .... Your *flair* was quite true. Let us have some more victories together, and confound all our foes abroad – and (don't forget) at home.

Churchill had not been so politically secure since the outbreak of the war, the partnership with Fisher had never been so close, and they were soon to share in another victory at sea, this time in home waters.

Two days after the defeat at Coronel, German cruisers struck again, this time in the North Sea. On 3 November four battle-cruisers under the command of Admiral Franz von Hipper had crossed the North Sea to cover a mining operation and bombarded Yarmouth on the coast of Norfolk. Only a few shells were fired, damage was negligible, and no one was hurt. But the implications were serious. For the public, it was a rude slap in the face.

Fisher at once matched his preparations for a counter attack here with those he was taking against Spee on the other side of the world. By happy chance a set of German cipher and signal books had come into the hands of the British recently through the good offices of the Russian Admiralty. (They had been found on the corpse of a German sailor: Churchill referred to them as 'these sea-stained priceless documents'.) With the guidance of these codes and the extremely sophisticated listening-in and direction-finding devices installed along the English coast, the Admiralty could by this time not only locate and listen in to German men o'war and to German shore transmitters; the Admiralty through its hush-hush 'Room 40' learnt in advance of certain German operations.

Thus, on 23 January 1915, it was learned that Hipper's battle-cruisers were about to embark on an operation against the English coast again.

There was plenty of time to prepare a trap. All the auguries were favourable. A crack battle squadron of dreadnoughts and Beatty's battle-cruisers were poised to destroy the German force as it advanced across the North Sea. The Germans fell into the British trap and lost a powerful battle-cruiser-cum-armoured-cruiser, the *Blücher*.

The action was hailed as a great British victory and photographs of the sinking *Blücher* on her side were relished by millions. Referring to Hipper (who had earned the sobriquet 'Baby-Killer') one newspaper noted with satisfaction, 'It will be some time before they go baby-killing again.' And *The Times* rejoiced

to announce that the German battle-cruiser squadron was caught by the Royal Navy in the North Sea yesterday while steaming at full speed towards the east coast of England on another of its murderous raids. The powerful cruiser *Blücher* was sunk, and two other German battle-cruisers were seriously damaged. Such is the crushing reply of British sailors to the raiders who bombard undefended towns and slaughter helpless women and children.

For Churchill the Battle of the Dogger Bank was another much-needed gift. How fortunes had swung in the Admiralty's favour since he had recalled Fisher ! But never for one moment did he relate Fisher's return to the relative non-interference in operational matters he was now permitted as a result of Fisher's firm control and total authority over the day-to-day running of the Royal Navy and all matters of communication between the Admiralty and commanders at sea. Churchill, while following events in the Dogger Bank with intense keenness, limited himself to informing the King about what was happening rather than shooting off loosely worded instructions like those sent to Admiral Cradock.

The Dogger Bank battle marks the completion of a brief but critically important phase in Churchill's relations with the Royal Navy. Since Fisher's return he had handed over numerous controls of the great and complex Admiralty to Fisher, who was handling this ship with all the old brilliancy and fervour he had demonstrated when, as a younger man, he had virtually run the navy unaided from 1904 until 1910.

But it would be quite wrong to deduce from this that Churchill had in any way reduced his own steam pressure. His mind did not rest during any waking moment in the long day and half the night when he worked, and he was soon back to his old tricks, trying to run everything. The range of his thinking was infinitely wider than Fisher's, embracing as it did not just the needs and activities of sea power but the entire broad spectrum of the war and how and where it must be won.

Back in 1911 Churchill had prepared a long memorandum for a meeting of the Committee of Imperial Defence, 'to instil into this important body an alertness such as he felt himself'. It assumed an alliance between France, Russia and Britain and a joint attack on this alliance by the central powers, Germany and Austria. On the Western Front, Churchill predicted, a massive German advance would break through the line of the Meuse on the twentieth day, after which the French armies would fall back on Paris. But, claimed Churchill the military prophet, the rate of the advance would be slowed by German losses, by the need to guard their extended lines of communication and supply, by the vast diversion (half a million men) required for the investment of Paris, by the growing pressure from the east as the vast Russian armies gained momentum and by the arrival of the British Army. By the fortieth day Germany would be at full strain and the 'opportunities for the decisive trial of strength may occur'.

Three years later, as the German armies poured through Belgium, Churchill circulated copies of this document to the Cabinet, not as a boast of his prophetic powers but to put some steel into their spines. As Balfour wrote at the time, 'It is a triumph of prophecy!' Beyond the fortieth day this prediction did not reach. It did not predict the land war's lapse into stalemate, ineffective and bloody attrition in the tortuous maze of trenches and barbed wire, blasted dwellings and forests. But even before the fortieth day had come and the German Army had ground to a halt, Churchill was seeking an alternative to an impasse in the west.

Churchill's strategic eye was attracted to the east. Here was the partner in the alliance whose armies and geographic advantage of vast spaces could exhaust the enemy. Influenced historically by Napoleon's exhaustion and final retreat, Churchill saw on the Russian front the means for the eventual crushing of Germany and Austria – if contact could be made and lines of communication and supply set up.

For almost as long as Churchill had known him, Fisher had preached the Baltic Project as the master stroke, the decisive campaign, to win a war against Germany. In common with received opinion in the navy, Fisher disapproved of sending the small, professional British Army to France on the outbreak of a war where it must soon be surrounded and destroyed. He wanted it reserved for amphibious warfare. 'Fisher's view was that a country like Britain with a relatively large and highly trained Navy, but only a small professional Army, could use that Army to the best effect by throwing it, at a critical moment, on the flank or in the rear of the main body of the enemy.'

The Baltic Project provided this opportunity. The British Fleet would force its way into the Baltic, and with an armada of hundreds of shallow-draught landing vessels, put a Russian army ashore on Pomerania. Churchill was much taken with this concept, had digested it over the years and, when war came, even before the stalemate in the west, began to make projections. He first sounded out the Russians on a joint amphibious attack on 19 August 1914 in a memorandum addressed to Grand-Duke Nicholas, the C-in-C of the Russian Army.

The Russians welcomed this approach: 'We therefore gratefully accept in principle the First Lord's offer.' As a first step, Churchill calculated that it would be desirable if not necessary to seize an island close to the German coastline. Various schemes were analysed, including the capturing of neutral Danish, Norwegian or Dutch islands. Churchill's favourite island as a target was Borkhum.

Fisher, not yet back in the First Sea Lord's office, enquired anxiously from Churchill about his own favourite Baltic Project. Churchill confirmed enthusiastically that it was by no means dead. 'But you must close up this side first,' he wrote to him. 'You must take an island and block them in .... The Baltic is the only theatre in which naval action can appreciably shorten the war.'

These schemes came to nothing, frustrated by lack of enthusiasm or downright disapproval from inside the Admiralty, and the looming of new priorities. But the fundamental need to establish links with Russia and to support her in her isolation remained steady in Churchill's mind.

With the declaration of war on Turkey on 5 November, attention turned sharply to the ever-troubled, mutually antagonistic states of south-east Europe and Asia Minor. Serbia looked set for being crushed by the Central Powers and no one trusted Bulgaria, least of all her neighbour Greece who was in turn at daggers drawn with the Turkish Empire. Turkey also threatened Egypt and the Suez Canal and the Russian frontier in Armenia. Italy continued to sit on the fence, ever alert to the tides of military failure and success. German influence and military infiltration in Turkey was by now total. The *Goeben* and *Breslau* were ranging across the Black Sea, bombarding Russian targets with impunity.

The key to the Russian Caucasus and the crushing of Turkey lay in the Gallipoli peninsula and the Dardanelles, that surrealist example of geographic extension which just splits Asia from Europe and forms the narrow, hazardous sea link between southern Russia and the rest of the world. Since mankind had become mobile and bent on conquest this fast-flowing (4-knot) natural canal had figured in eastern Mediterranean military considerations, from Xerxes in 480 BC and Alexander the Great in 334 BC to a meeting of the British Committee of Imperial Defence in 1906 when Turkey and Britain came close to war.

The seizure of the Gallipoli peninsula and the passage through the Dardanelles of the British Fleet would be sufficient to force the Sultan to his knees – or so were the findings of a report by this committee at the time. But how this was to be accomplished was not explained. The recent British record in this part of the world was not encouraging. In 1807 a British fleet had got through to the Sea of Marmara, but took a savage drubbing returning down the Dardanelles. When, during the Armenian massacres eighty-eight years later, a repeat of this operation was considered, this time with powerful ironclads, the commander on the spot advised against. Suicide, he said.

Once again in November 1914, with Britain in desperate need of an alternative to the Western Front where the small British Army – the 'old Contemptibles' – was being savaged, the Dardanelles came up on the agenda. Churchill, strongly supported by Fisher, presented the idea of a joint military–naval attack on the Gallipoli peninsula, which initially would allay the worst fear in this theatre now that Turkey was an enemy – a Turkish attack on Egypt.

The tall, grave, revered figure of Field Marshal Kitchener at once took the centre of the stage as Churchill, the leading actor, completed his opening lines in the Dardanelles drama now unfolding. Kitchener at once made it abundantly clear that no troops would be available for such an operation. And that was that.

Churchill and Kitchener had enjoyed the barest minimum of social or professional contact since the Boer War. When Kitchener was C-in-C Indian Army in 1905 and wished to extend the power of the military administration against the Viceroy, Lord Curzon, Churchill expressed himself opposed to acquiescing 'in the handing over of the Indian Empire to an ambitious and indocile soldier'. He wrote to his mother: 'Of course I am all for Curzon as against Kitchener, and for Constitutional Authority against military power. I cannot believe a Liberal Government will allow the Commander-in-Chief in India to engross himself in so much power.'

In 1912 the two men met in Malta when Kitchener was Agent-General in Egypt and reached a formal agreement over naval strength and dispositions in the Mediterranean. When Kitchener became Secretary of State for War in 1914 the two men came into close contact again for the first time for a dozen years. The gulf between their processes of thought and standards of conduct was as wide as it had been in Egypt and South Africa. For Kitchener, Churchill the clever, cocky braggart on the make, three-quarters scribbler for the gutter press, one-quarter bogus soldier, had grown into a self-seeking, untrustworthy politician;

and to Kitchener politicians, like journalists, were a breed which he both despised and utterly failed to understand.

Churchill took a more relaxed and pragmatic view of the most famous soldier of his day. He did not see Kitchener as an alien species. He disliked him as much as ever, but feelings of antipathy were, he believed, of no consequence when it came to working in harness with him. Kitchener was head of the army ; Churchill was head of the navy. A sudden dreadful danger had struck Britain and the empire and they were fighting for their lives against a gross tyranny.

The press and public response to the news that Lord Kitchener of Khartoum ('K of K') was back and would lead the army to victory was as enthusiastic as it was to be for Fisher's return twelve weeks later. Like Fisher, Kitchener was a man with a record behind him and a public *persona* representing the conquering soldier just as Fisher was seen as the ultimate sailor.

Kitchener was the first serving soldier to be employed in a Cabinet since 1660. His experience of war was confined to distant theatres and he had no interest in or knowledge of European land war on a large scale. According to his biographer he 'despised the regular Army because it was much too small for the part which it was certain to have to play'. In this his view was in accordance with accepted Admiralty thinking up to the advent of Churchill. He also 'despised the Territorial Army of fourteen divisions ... on account of its amateur spirit which he regarded as incurable'.

The hierarchy of the War Office did not want him ; they thought he would be manipulated by the politicians. He also held the French Army in total contempt and expected that the Germans would march through them as they had in 1870. At the same time, and somewhat contradictorily, he judged that it would be a long war and that Britain must at once start creating a people's army of millions for a great continental campaign. With this in mind he had ordered the printing of tens of thousands of posters bearing his fierce and formidable visage exhorting, with pointed finger, the man in the street to volunteer – 'Your country needs you'.

Kitchener's staff and paperwork were appalling and rapidly became a byword at the War Office : 'Kitchener of Chaos', he was nicknamed, and with very good reason. His first important decision, in the teeth of the opposition of Field Marshal Lord Roberts, the nation's second most famous and revered soldier, and the commander in the field Sir John French, was that the British Expeditionary Force should be concentrated at Amiens, some seventy miles behind the point desired by the French military authorities. He did not wish them to begin their war with a retreat, he said. He turned upside down the pre-war arrangements for alignment with the French Army, which he believed would soon fold up.

Churchill was at first as impressed as he expected he would be at Kitchener's firm and decisive leadership and they worked together satisfactorily over arrangements for the transportation of the army to France. It was Kitchener who encouraged Churchill to rush to Antwerp during those desperate days before the city's investment and was undisguisedly admiring of the manner in which he rallied the Belgians and organized the Royal Marines and scratch Naval Divisions. When Asquith read out to the Cabinet Churchill's offer to give up the Admiralty and remain to continue the fight, Kitchener did not laugh the idea to scorn; he said he would make Churchill a lieutenant-general on the spot.

To Churchill's amazement Kitchener's enthusiasm and admiration for him in these early days appeared to know no bounds. 'My dear Churchill .... Please do not address me as Lord as I am only yours Kitchener.' When Churchill approached Kitchener about finding some war work for his cousin the Duke of Marlborough and Kitchener responded, Churchill wrote to him : 'I am touched by the promptness with wh you have looked after Marlborough. It is a gt pleasure to work with you, & the two Departments pull well together . . .'

Within a very short time, a matter of about four weeks, cracks began to show in Kitchener's relations with Sir John French. Kitchener felt obliged to make a visit to his C-in-C in France. It was not a success. Churchill, as an old friend of French, tried to mediate by letter. French replied about Kitchener's behaviour in the same terms as Churchill's admirals might have complained of his relentless interference with them : 'I do beg of you, my dear Friend, to add one more to all the many & great kindnesses you have done me & *stop this interference* with field operations. Kitchener *knows nothing* about European warfare . . .'

When matters went from bad to worse, Kitchener asked Churchill to act as liaison between himself and his commander. Bedevilled by a thousand problems in his own department, Churchill agreed and made his first visit in this capacity on 15 September. He felt a fulfilled being touring the front, watching the shelling, lying in a haystack observing French artillery fire. 'When darkness fell,' he wrote, 'I saw the horizon lighted up with the quick flashing of the cannonade. Such scenes were afterwards to become commonplace : but the first aspect was thrilling.'

Churchill's visits to General French became more frequent and were soon being made on his own account. To his detractors, this activity was seen as 'Winston playing soldiers again'. Kitchener took a more serious view. From being a mediator, was Churchill not now becoming a collaborator with his difficult Field Commander? Churchill's wife, ear to the ground as always and a shrewd observer and judge, counselled caution before he embarked on his fourth visit to French's HQ. 'Of course I know you will consult K,' she wrote. 'Otherwise the journey will savour of a week-end escapade & not of a mission. You would be surprised & incensed if K slipped off to visit Jellicoe on his own. I wish my darling that you didn't crave to go . . .'

Churchill took his wife's advice, asked for and received Kitchener's assent. 'How right you were about telling K,' he wrote to Clementine humbly.

But no amount of advice, no words of warning, seemed able to curb Churchill's involvement in every theatre of war, by land, sea and air. By mid-November, at a time when Sturdee was heading south towards his fateful meeting with Admiral Spee and the Admiralty was dealing with the grouses of Admiral Jellicoe over the threat from mines and U-boats and inadequacies in the strength of his Fleet, Churchill was deeply embroiled in plans for a joint military and naval attack along the Belgian coast towards Ostend.

In addition to the installation of naval air squadrons in northern France, Churchill had stationed, ostensibly for the defence of the navy's airfields, a mixed bag of armoured cars, including forty-five Rolls-Royces and a hundred others, 'vy well designed & stand all bullets'. These were under the command of the gallant Josiah Wedgwood, a particularly staunch defender of Churchill who later was wounded and won the DSO at the Dardanelles.

This coastal attack was really the joint brainchild of French and Churchill, and it soon came up against niggling enquiries and directions from Kitchener in Whitehall which were uncannily similar to Churchill's interventions from Whitehall into his admirals' operations. The truth was that Kitchener could not bear all this independent planning. He would much rather have been back in Egypt, but (as he saw it) if he was supposed to be running the land war, that was what he was going to do. Again Churchill tried pouring oil on to the troubled army waters and with Kitchener's blessing visited French's headquarters on 6 December.

The First Lord of the Admiralty's efforts to bring peace to the army's hierarchy at this critical juncture was seen by Opposition politicians and hostile newspapers as at the best bizarre and at the worst a dereliction of Churchill's proper duties. Very few people knew that they were, for the present, effective. Returning from France, Churchill saw Kitchener, patched up peace between the soldiers, and was able to write to French (8 December, as Sturdee was sinking Spee):

Kitchener agrees entirely with yr view. We held an immediate conference with the PM & Sir E. Grey .... Nothing cd exceed the urbanity of 'our mutual friend' on my return .... I cannot tell you how much I enjoyed our talks, & my visit to the front was a pure delight. I shall try to come & see the working out of the plan, if all goes well.

So, for a few days at least, Churchill was in his room at the Admiralty, ready to give some attention to strictly naval matters. Fisher, for one, was glad to see him. 'Welcome back!' he wrote to him early on the same morning. 'I don't hold with these "outings" of yours! I know how you enjoy them! Nor am I afraid of responsibility when you're away. But I think it's too venturesome! Also it gives your enemies cause to blaspheme! ...'

Nine days later, 17 December, Churchill proposed to cross the Channel yet again to 'see the working out of the plan'. The temptation to become involved on the spot was irresistible. But he took the precaution this time of informing Asquith first. Asquith, after consulting Venetia Stanley, his ever-wise confidante, replied that 'I do not think that you ought to go again to French without first consulting Kitchener & finding that he approves'.

So Churchill did as he was told – '... have you any objection to my staying with French as he wd like ...?' Instead of answering direct, Kitchener went to see Asquith at 10 Downing Street to present his objections and persuade him to prohibit Churchill from staying with French again.

My dear Winston,

There can, of course, be no objection to your going to Dunkirk to look into naval matters, but after talking with Kitchener, who came to see me this morning, I am clearly of opinion that you should not go to French's headquarters or attempt to see French.

These meetings have in K's opinion already produced profound friction between French & himself ...

Yrs always
HHA

'Profound friction' indeed! Who had begged Churchill to act as a peacemaker? That same afternoon (18 December) Churchill stormed out of the Admiralty and made his way to Downing Street. He was furious at Kitchener's back-door methods of by-passing him and going to the top without speaking to him first.

After Churchill left, the Prime Minister wrote to Venetia (sometimes he wrote three times a day): 'He has just been to see me, very sore & angry with K, upon whom he poured a kettle-full of opprobrious epithets. Of course he acquiesced in the decision ...'

As the Prime Minister's daughter had already observed, of Kitchener and Churchill at Malta during their meeting in 1912, 'their relationship has always been a prickly one'. From this time, the prickliness had hardened into a hostility between the two men that was as total and relentless as the war itself, camouflaged as it might be to the outside world, and even to members of the Cabinet, by the courtesies of correct public behaviour. Private communication was something different.

'The question I asked was one wh you cd easily have answered yourself,' Churchill snapped in a letter he wrote the same day. '... It was not necessary to trouble the Prime Minister; and some of the statements you appear to have made to him are not well founded, & shd certainly in the first instance have been made to me.'

Asquith directly, and Venetia Stanley indirectly but promptly, were at once wide-eyed amused witnesses and conciliators in this fracas between the two war leaders at this critical hour.

Kitchener replied with an even heavier shell:

My dear Churchill,

I cannot of course object to your going over to discuss naval co-operation with Sir J.French; but at the same time I think I ought to tell you frankly that your private arrangements with French as regards land forces is rendering my position and responsibility as S of S impossible. I consider that if my relations with French are strained it will do away with any advantage there may be in my holding my present position and I foresee that if the present system continues it must result in creating grave difficulties between French & myself. I do not interfere with Jellicoe nor do I have a personal correspondence with him.

He concluded with the extraordinary suggestion that Churchill should take over the War Office and let Fisher become First Lord – 'then all would work smoothly I hope'. Although this was not sent, Kitchener was not going to deprive himself of the satisfaction of telling Churchill that he had written it and been persuaded by Asquith not to send it, with all the implied dark hints about its contents.

Back came Churchill on this hectic day (19 December) of hurled Whitehall insults with messengers running hither and thither. Claiming reasonably that he had on every possible occasion and by every possible means promoted confidence and goodwill between Kitchener and French, Churchill said bluntly that 'there was no need to make charges or statements of the character to wh I have referred. They are vy unfair to a colleague', he concluded, 'who has worked with you with the utmost loyalty.'

To clear the air, and calm down 'my stormy petrels', as Asquith described Churchill and Kitchener, he decided to bring Sir John French over secretly from France for conversations. These covered a whole range of subjects, but during them French let drop that, much as he admired and felt affection for Churchill, he did find his judgement 'highly erratic'. But then he also told Churchill later that 'Kitchener *ought* to be shot !'

5
The Bombardment

Acrimony was rife, optimism a rare commodity, disenchantment widespread early in 1915. The small British Army in France – what was left of it – was exhausted and in the judgement of its commander incapable of offensive action. Casualties during the first months of the war had been far beyond anyone's reckoning. At sea Jellicoe complained of inadequate strength, inadequate bases, the deadly and continuous threat of the mine and the U-boat; he also complained about his health, pyrrhoea and piles in particular. Beatty complained, too, about the withdrawal of three of his battle-cruisers for the Admiral Spee hunt, U-boats and the activities of the Admiralty – 'If only we had a Kitchener in the Admiralty!' Nothing seemed able to winkle the High Seas Fleet out of its bases for the big showdown. Beatty was furious about his squadron's failure to sink all four German ships at the Dogger Bank battle.

The King and the Prime Minister were unhappy about the state of affairs. George v, while pleased at the outcome of the last two engagements at sea, saw his beloved navy in the hands of two men whom he distrusted. Asquith surveyed the state of the war bleakly, sat bored through interminable meetings, read Chekov, dined out constantly, played bridge and derived life-giving support from the letters that he sent to, and those that arrived almost every day from, Venetia Stanley with whom he enjoyed this 'wonderful and unique relationship'.

The German armies beat their way farther into Russia and the Turks opened an offensive in the Caucasus. It was this attack, and the *cri de coeur* from the Russian C-in-C, which forced the Cabinet and the War Council to take some sort of positive action and at last break the frustrating and gloomy impasse which had gripped the nation's war-making powers for so long.

The Russian appeal for action to relieve the pressure being applied to them was received on 2 January. The response was immediate. The Foreign Office despatched a telegram promising some sort of action against Turkey. As in the previous November, Gallipoli and the Dardanelles became the military planners' first target. And again Fisher, by a long way the oldest member of the War Council, was first off. He drew up, within twenty-four hours, and with the guidance of Maurice Hankey, Secretary of the Committee of Imperial Defence, a new strategic plan, written characteristically with many capital letters, underlinings and exclamation marks. 'I CONSIDER THE ATTACK ON TURKEY HOLDS THE FIELD! but ONLY if it's IMMEDIATE! However, it won't be! ... We shall decide on a futile bombardment of the Dardanelles which wears out the irreplaceable guns of the "Indefatigable" which probably will require replacement .... And so the war goes on! You want ONE man!'

Not a very helpful beginning. Then, more positively, it went on to recommend the formation of an Expeditionary Force of seasoned troops from France, replacing them with Territorials from Britain, a Greek attack on Gallipoli and a Bulgarian attack on Constantinople. There were two main snags to this plan: Bulgaria and Greece, arch-enemies anyway, were both neutral; and neither Kitchener nor the French command would countenance for one minute the withdrawal of seasoned troops from France.

There was, however, a last paragraph which caught Churchill's eye: force the Dardanelles with old battleships. 'But as the Great Napoleon said "Celerity"!' Fisher concluded, ' – without it – "FAILURE"!'

Ignoring the complementary proposals for combined attacks by land, Churchill seized the last item in Fisher's proposal in isolation, regarding it as an inspired idea which, if successful, could reverse the damage done by the escape of the *Goeben* and the seizure of the Turkish battleships back in August, and force Turkey to surrender. Suddenly he saw British battleships, white ensigns flying, cleared for action, and flinging shells at the Turkish batteries, steaming up the Narrows to the Sea of Marmara, and thence to the Bosporus and the Moslem seat of power itself – Constantinople.

Acting on Fisher's plea for speed, Churchill despatched a telegram that afternoon to the C-in-C Allied Forces Eastern Mediterranean.

3 January 1915   Admiralty
1.28 p.m.
Secret
Do you consider the forcing of the Dardanelles by ships alone a practicable operation.
It is assumed older Battleships fitted with mine-bumpers would be used preceded by Colliers or other merchant craft as bumpers and sweepers.
Importance of results would justify severe loss.
Let me know your views.
W.S.C.

The C-in-C was Admiral Sir Sackville Hamilton Carden, a fifty-six-

year-old Irishman who had earlier been placed in command of Malta
dockyard in order to serve out his time in relative obscurity. No one
seemed able to explain how or why he had been given this appointment,
obscure though it was. Fisher had no time for him ; Churchill was 'not
aware of anything that he has done which is in any way remarkable'.
In the light of his future responsibilities, the only remarkable thing
is why Churchill was prepared to retain the unenterprising and negligible
Carden at this critical juncture.

Carden replied to Churchill's enquiry on 5 January. He did not think
it possible to 'rush' the Dardanelles, 'but they might be forced by
extended operations with a large number of ships'. Churchill came back
the next day asking the Admiral to 'forward detailed particulars' and
assuring Carden that 'high authorities here concur in your opinion'.

It is difficult to identify these 'high authorities'. The Fisher–Hankey
plan expressly called for attacks by land, on three fronts, *in conjunction
with* a purely naval attempt to force the Dardanelles. Certainly Fisher
was not among them ; at the Dardanelles Commission enquiry later
Churchill specifically excluded Fisher's name. Admiral Sir Henry
Jackson of the War Staff Group did not condemn the navy-only plan,
neither did he show any enthusiasm for it, pointing out the 'unenviable
position' of the fleet under these circumstances. And in any case his
written appreciation was not received by Churchill until after Churchill
had written to Carden of the high authorities' concurrence. Admiral
Henry Oliver, Churchill's Naval Secretary, did not support the navy-
only proposal on paper but Churchill later claimed that he had done
so verbally.

Hankey 'thinks very strongly that the naval operations should be
supported by the landing of a fairly strong military force, and I think
we ought to be able to do this without denuding French', Asquith confided to his diary. As joint author of the plan in which the forcing
of the Dardanelles by ships was only a subsidiary operation, Hankey
was certain that authoritative naval opinion was against a naval-only
operation. 'From Lord Fisher downwards,' he wrote to Balfour, 'every
naval officer in the Admiralty who is in the secret believes that the
Navy cannot take the Dardanelles position without troops. The First
Lord still prefers to believe that they can do it with ships, but I have
warned the Prime Minister that we cannot trust to this.'

Hankey was certainly right about naval opinion in the Admiralty,
where a feasibility study in 1906 was recalled. This insisted that a navy-
only attack on the Dardanelles 'would be fraught with great risk'. But
it is also true that for a time, such was the heat of Churchill's enthusiasm
and the fervour with which he assailed all about him with his arguments,
that Jackson, Oliver and even Fisher himself succumbed and gave their

uneasy approval. It is not possible to overestimate the power of persuasion that Churchill wielded at this time. No one could match his rhetoric, and tough, wise old admirals like Wilson who had not been endowed with much power of dialectic debate fell down like ninepins before the momentum of Churchill's animation.

Admiral Sir William James has written that 'Mr Churchill's powers of argument were so extraordinary that again and again tired Admiralty officials were hypnotized into accepting opinions which differed vastly from those they really held'. The brilliant Director of Naval Intelligence, Captain W.R.Hall, recalled a meeting with Churchill very late at night at which Churchill was 'determined to bring me round to his point of view. It was long after midnight, and I was dreadfully tired, but nothing seemed to tire the First Lord.'

Later, Captain Hall knew that he was succumbing against his better judgement.

I began to mutter to myself: 'My name is Hall, my name is Hall . . .'

Suddenly he broke off to look frowningly at me. 'What's that you're muttering to yourself?' he demanded.

'I'm saying', I told him, 'that my name is Hall because if I listen to you much longer I shall be convinced that it's Brown.'

'Then you don't agree with what I've been saying?' He was laughing heartily.

'First Lord,' said I, 'I don't agree with one word of it, but I can't argue with you, I've not had the training.'

Lloyd George once wrote that when Churchill had 'a scheme agitating his powerful mind . . . he is indefatigable in pressing it upon the acceptance of everyone who matters in the decision'. If Churchill could sway the War Council with the blast of his argument, what sort of chance had admirals who neither had his brains nor 'had the training'?

Possibly the only Admiralty official who was not bamboozled by Churchill's powers of persuasion was Captain Herbert Richmond. 'Winston proposes mad things . . .', he wrote in his diary on 9 February, 'very, very ignorant, believes he can capture the Dardanelles without troops.' But then Richmond was not one of Churchill's prime targets even though he possessed the finest intellect and all-round strategical grasp in the Admiralty in 1915. For example:

We seem to have no idea of using our Fleet & Army in combination. The sole thing the soldiers are able to imagine is plugging a host of troops into North France .... Whereas, with our power of carrying troops by sea we can give him [the Germans] a very nasty tweak at the tail. Thirty thousand men at the Dardanelles next week would make more impression on the Continental campaign than five times the number on the banks of the Yser.

In these early days of January 1915, then, Fisher was negatively acquiescent in the navy-only plan and preparations, and to his later regret even made one positive contribution. HMS *Queen Elizabeth*, the first of the mighty 15-inch-gunned fast oil-burning super-dreadnoughts of the 1912 programme, had now been completed and was due to carry out her all-important gunnery trials off Gibraltar. Rather than firing off her 15-inch shells into the sea, why not lay her guns on the Turkish forts? Churchill responded enthusiastically to Fisher's proposal. Surely even the most strongly defended fort could not stand up to salvoes of these almost one-ton projectiles?

Carden responded to Churchill's order for more detailed proposals on 11 January. In effect they recommended a piecemeal bombardment of the lines of forts at the entrance to the Dardanelles and up the narrow channel, followed by a minesweeping exercise, after which 'battle force proceeds to Marmara preceded by mine-sweepers'. He wanted three battle-cruisers, twelve battleships, three light cruisers, a flotilla leader, sixteen destroyers and numerous auxiliary craft. On the duration of the operation: 'Might do it all in a month about.'

All this was laid before the War Council on 13 January by Churchill, who had convinced himself that, though a gamble, it was worth trying and that it had the expert and professional support of Fisher and the Naval War Staff. There is no doubt that he would have preferred a combined operation with a powerful land force but he was reconciled to the fact that Kitchener, General Sir John French and the French High Command would not spare any troops from the Western Front.

Hankey later told of the effect of Churchill's eloquence as he laid the navy-only proposal before Asquith and the War Council members:

At this point events took a dramatic turn, for Churchill suddenly revealed his well-kept secret of a naval attack on the Dardanelles! The idea caught on at once. The whole atmosphere changed. Fatigue was forgotten. The War Council turned eagerly from the dreary vista of a 'slogging match' on the Western Front to brighter prospects.

Carried forward on this wave of enthusiasm the War Council agreed that 'The Admiralty should prepare for a naval expedition in February to bombard and take the Gallipoli Peninsula, with Constantinople as its objective.' How a Franco–British Fleet (for the French Navy would contribute) was to take the heavily fortified peninsula, occupied by well-armed German-trained Turkish troops and a sprawling city of 875,000 people, were not discussed. 'Once the forts were reduced the minefields would be cleared, and the Fleet would proceed up to Constantinople and destroy the *Goeben*.' Thus would the humiliation of last August be avenged.

Fisher and Wilson remained silent throughout this War Council. 'Neither made any remark and I certainly thought that they agreed,' Churchill noted. But no; the Admirals' minds were at work, doubts already flooding in. 'Anyone who attacks a fort is a fool.' Was that not Nelson's conclusion after being a 'fool' himself and paying the price with an arm – and almost his life? Did this truism no longer apply when 15-inch guns could fire their great high-explosive shells from 20,000 yards, far beyond the range of the Dardanelles forts' ancient guns? Churchill answered equivocally, 'No absolute rule can be laid down about fighting between ships and forts. It depends on the ship; it depends on the fort.'

After uttering no word of doubt or complaint at this meeting, Fisher let his real feelings be known in a letter to Jellicoe the following day. '*In everything we are confronted by some political expediency! and my patience is pretty near exhausted! ... I really don't think I can stand it!*' Jellicoe had been writing frequent letters, all of them full of complaints. After citing figures showing how alarmingly narrow was his margin of strength over the High Seas Fleet and how inadequate were his defences: '*I wonder I can ever sleep at all.*'

But Jellicoe could still do no wrong in Fisher's eyes, and within a week of the War Council meeting approving of Churchill's navy-only plan, Jellicoe's relative (and dangerous) weakness was used as the first weapon in the sustained attack he was about to open on his partner.

On 19 January, under the heading PLEASE BURN, Fisher revealed exasperation with Churchill mixed with his sympathy for Jellicoe:

It's amusing how Winston makes out that in all types [of warships] you are ever so much stronger than when you assumed command of the Fleet. I simply keep on reiterating, '*He has only 29 battleships available at present.*' He can't get round that fact! So goes off on another attack on your arrangements ....
And now the Cabinet have decided on taking the Dardanelles solely with the Navy, using 15 battleships and 32 other vessels, and keeping out there three battle cruisers and a flotilla of destroyers – *all urgently required at the decisive theatre at home*! There is only one way out, and that is to resign ...

Fisher was an habitual 'resigner'. He had already handed in his resignation on 4 January over some trivial matter of aerial defence. He 'resigned' again in a letter to Asquith on 28 January, to Churchill on the same day, and at a meeting of the War Council. 'He is always threatening to resign,' Asquith complained to Venetia Stanley, '& writes an almost daily letter to Winston, expressing his desire to return to the cultivation of his "roses at Richmond".'

The Dogger Bank engagement intensified Fisher's opposition to the navy-only Dardanelles plan because it highlighted the narrow naval balance of power in the North Sea – Fisher's 'decisive theatre'. The battle had been between five big British ships against four German big ships.

Carden's Dardanelles requirements called for three battle-cruisers. Four days after Dogger Bank, Fisher wrote to Churchill: 'The Battle cruiser action shewed very conclusively the absolute necessity for a *big* preponderance of this type of ship and I hope will at any rate result in no diversion of ANY "Queen Elizabeths" or ANY Battle Cruisers FROM THE DECISIVE THEATRE. It [Dogger Bank] might easily have been a disaster. Had we lost the Lion victory would have been turned into defeat.'

Fisher wrote in similar vein to Jellicoe, and on 21 January wrote uncompromisingly to the Admiral. 'I just abominate the Dardanelles operation unless a great change is made and it is settled to be made a military operation, with 200,000 men in conjunction with the Fleet.'

In making much of Jellicoe's inadequate strength and emphasizing the need to concentrate the navy in 'the decisive theatre at home', Fisher had a second reason which he never raised in his arguments at this time, knowing that it would carry less weight because, in the eyes of many of his enemies, it was his hobby-horse. This was the Baltic Project, so recently supported by Churchill and now lost in the cordite smoke of the Dardanelles' battleships. In every shipyard in the land vessels big and small, all of shallow draught, were being hastened to completion for this pet operation of Fisher's. And Fisher knew deep in his heart that all were likely to be swallowed up in the eastern Mediterranean instead of the Baltic.

This was the reason why his opposition to the Dardanelles project, at least in War Council meetings, was mainly silent; this silence, alas, being taken by many as, if not assent, at least muted agreement. It was not until the Commission of Enquiry interrogated Fisher, long after he and Churchill had been cast into the wilderness, that the truth about the first reason for Fisher's opposition became known. Asked if his main objection 'was that it might interfere with your Baltic Project?' he answered, 'Quite right. I was going to lose ships in the Dardanelles that I wanted to lose only in the Baltic, besides losing officers and men.'

Fisher might be flaying about wildly in his frustration and the feeling that only fiasco could be the outcome of the navy-only plan. He might often be sulkily and dangerously threatening to resign. He can be

The 21st Lancers charge at the Battle of Omdurman.

Lieutenant Winston Spencer Churchill, 4th Hussars, 1895.

Budget Day, 1910. Lloyd George and Churchill (centre figures) hasten down Whitehall to the House of Commons.

Churchill as First Lord of the
Admiralty.

With the First Sea Lord, Admiral
Prince Louis of Battenberg, father of
Lord Mountbatten and soon to be
cast into the wilderness because of
his German connections.

Admiral Cradock's flagship *Good Hope* (below) sunk at Coronel by Admiral von Spee's armoured cruisers *Scharnhorst* (above) and *Gneisenau*, marking the low point in Churchill's fortunes in 1914.

Admiral of the Fleet Lord Fisher (above left) and Field Marshal Earl Kitchener, who were responsible for Churchill's downfall in May 1915. Churchill never lost his love and admiration for 'Jacky' Fisher and never ceased to hate and despise the soldier. Under the influence of Fisher, Churchill at first admired Admiral Sir John Jellicoe (below) and ensured that he was appointed C-in-C of the Grand Fleet at the outbreak of war in 1914. Later, his confidence waned.

Admiral of the Fleet Alfred von Tirpitz (left) and Kaiser Wilhelm II, who together led the massive build up and modernization of the German Navy and the creation of the High Seas Fleet of 1914. Below: Herbert Asquith, the Prime Minister who was forced to replace Churchill as First Lord of the Admiralty during the shell scandal and Dardanelles crisis of May 1915.

Until the Battle of the Falkland Islands in December, very little went right for the Royal Navy, and for Churchill, in 1914. The significance of the escape from a massively superior British force of the German battle-cruiser *Goeben* to Turkey was not fully appreciated at the time. Then following the seizure of two new Turkish battleships completing in British shipyards, this escape led directly to Turkey allying herself with the Central Powers, to the Dardanelles fiasco and the downfall of Churchill. Below: The loss of three armoured cruisers and over 1,400 officers and men, sunk by a single small and elderly German U-boat, was a savage early blow and revealed the effectiveness of the torpedo.

HMS *Queen Elizabeth*, the newest and most powerful super-dreadnought in the world, early in her career became a symbol of the Royal Navy's commitment to the Dardanelles campaign, and a bone of contention between Fisher and Churchill. Below: Admiral Fisher's infamous '30 pieces of silver' letter which was not very secret or private for long. Addressed to Reginald McKenna, it was dated 22 May. Churchill was out of office a few days later.

REMARKABLE PHOTOGRAPHS OF THE DARDANELLES BOMBARDMENT.

PHOTOGRAPHS BY C.N., ILLUSTRATIONS BUREAU, AND OTHERS.

IN THE DARDANELLES : A GREAT BRITISH WAR-SHIP.   FIRING A BROADSIDE : H.M.S. "QUEEN ELIZABETH" IN THE DARDANELLES.

EVIDENCE OF THE PERILOUS CHARACTER OF THE ALLIES' TASK IN THE DARDANELLES : A FRENCH BATTLE-SHIP ENCIRCLED BY TURKISH PROJECTILES.

SHOWING (RIGHT) A GREAT COLUMN OF WATER THROWN UP BY A SHELL FROM ONE OF THE TURKISH FORTS : H.M.S. "AGAMEMNON."

DURING THE BOMBARDMENT : A BRITISH BATTLE-CRUISER.   NEARLY STRUCK : A SHELL BURSTING NEAR THE "AGAMEMNON."

'I thought he would never get over the Dardanelles; I thought he would die of grief,' Clementine Churchill of her husband after he left the Admiralty.

accused of acting subversively in his communications with Jellicoe and negatively in refusing to utter a word against the plan in the War Council, or absenting himself altogether, to the chagrin of Churchill and Asquith. He was, in short, being as unreliable and untrustworthy as George v had feared he would be. Nevertheless his instinct was right, as it had been so often in the past. If the February naval attack had been made in conjunction with 200,000 well-led troops as he surmised, or even 20,000, there was a very good chance of success, and all the massive benefit – and saving of life – that would have accrued from a decisive victory.

But Fisher knew, and Churchill knew, that the Western Fronters, and predominantly Kitchener, were not going to make any troops available. 'And it will be the wonder of the ages', Fisher wrote to Churchill on 29 January, 'that no troops were sent to cooperate with the Fleet with half a million soldiers in England.'

On this same day Fisher wrote to Jellicoe, 'I had fierce rows yesterday with Winston & the Prime Minister .... I was SIX hours yesterday with them at War Council and sat till 8 p.m.! They are a *"flabby"* lot!' Asquith's interpretation of the meeting was more temperate: 'Fisher is still a little uneasy about the Dardanelles.'

In spite of Kitchener's implacable opposition to the loss of any troops from Britain or France for Churchill's Dardanelles expedition, Fisher still prayed that it was not too late to make him change his mind. He wrote despairingly to Churchill, 'I hope you are successful with Kitchener in getting a Division sent ... *tomorrow*!'

Then, as if by magic, a bright shaft of light appeared bringing into view an entirely new aspect to the operation. In spite of Kitchener's total intractability up to now, while approving of the navy-only plan in principle, the Field Marshal suddenly let it be known to the War Council that a regular professional Division, the 29th, based at home but intended eventually for France, could be diverted to the Mediterranean and the Dardanelles to support the two battalions of Royal Marines already assigned to that theatre, and any troops that could be spared from Egypt.

So it was no longer to be navy-only but a combined operation as it should have been all along. In a few words, delivered with stately deliberation, Kitchener had transformed the operation. Asquith was greatly relieved, Churchill was delighted and his soldier's mind was already full of plans of how best to utilize this sudden access of strength. He ordered transports for their passage and arrangements of all kinds.

As if Churchill's difficulties with Fisher were not enough, there then took place the most acrimonious exchange yet with Kitchener. The subject in dispute was the Naval Division and Churchill's armoured cars. And the timing could not have been worse. Churchill had offered to French over Kitchener's head a brigade of the Naval Division and two squadrons of his armoured cars – 'those famous Armoured Cars which are being hawked about from pillar to post', as Asquith referred to them. 'My conversation with French was of course quite unofficial,' Churchill wrote later in mitigation. But knowing as he must have known by now from past experience, it was an ill-considered step. He may not have realized how arrogant and overbearing this kind of behaviour appeared to others. But he certainly knew how ultra-sensitive the equally arrogant, not to say megalomaniac, Kitchener was about interference in his department.

Once again Kitchener marched to Downing Street. He was 'in a state of some perturbation', Asquith reported to Churchill in a letter of complaint:

He has just received two official letters from French, in which he announces that you have offered him a Brigade of the Naval Division, and 2 squadrons of armoured cars. Kitchener is strongly of opinion that French has no need of either. But, apart from that, he feels (& I think rightly) that he ought to have been told of, & consulted about, the offer before it was made.

And that night Asquith wrote in his diary of 'the folly of the offer'. Told of this new row brewing up, Asquith's wife wrote more strongly in her diary: 'Of course Winston is intolerable – he is devoured by vanity .... It's most trying as K and he had got a modus vivendi.' And Asquith described the business to Venetia Stanley as a 'bad *bêtise*'.

Ignoring Asquith's advice to 'go & see him & put things right', Churchill instead wrote a cross reply to Asquith:

The whole thing is a mare's nest .... I wish you had heard what I had to say before assuming that I was in the wrong. This is not the first time that Kitchener has troubled you about matters which a few moments' talk with me would have adjusted. I do not remember that I have ever claimed your aid against any colleague otherwise than in Cabinet.

Churchill waited until the next day before writing, coolly rather than crossly, to Kitchener: 'You must know what care I have taken in these last few months to avoid anything wh cd cause difficulties ...' It was a long letter, packed with self-justification. There was to be a Cabinet on the afternoon of the following day, 19 February. In the morning, Churchill wrote again to Kitchener about his ubiquitous armoured cars, which according to Asquith were not wanted in France, except for their Maxim guns. 'You have known for months past of the armoured cars,' ran his letter, a sharper one this time, '&

the naval battalions, & what was the intention with which they were called into being . . .'

It was an afternoon of high hopes and expectations at the Cabinet. The decision to send out the 29th Division urgently was to be confirmed. Details and dates were to be discussed. Kitchener spoke first, and his words broke over the assembled members like the first salvoes of the Dardanelles bombardment which had opened that morning at 8 a.m. 'In view of the recent Russian set-back in East Prussia,' ran the minutes, 'he was averse to sending away the 29th Division at present.' For the time being any troops required to follow up the naval bombardment must come from the Corps of New Zealanders and Australians – the 'Anzacs' – encamped in Egypt, fresh, enthusiastic but only half trained.

As Churchill's biographer has written, 'Churchill was totally unprepared for such a volte-face. It was only three days since Kitchener had agreed to release the 29th Division without detriment to the European situation.' What had brought about this reversal of decision? Could it be coincidence that in those three days the situation had changed so dramatically for the worse on the Eastern Front? Or was the real reason the sudden plummeting to new depths of relations between Kitchener and Churchill?

The minutes do not record Churchill's fury, only:

MR CHURCHILL said it would be a great disappointment to the Admiralty if the 29th Division was not sent out. The attack on the Dardanelles was a very heavy naval undertaking. It was difficult to over-rate the military advantages which success would bring . . . . We should never forgive ourselves if this promising operation failed owing to insufficient military support at the critical moment.

Asquith appealed to Kitchener to change his mind, emphasizing the dangers of weakening the force by depriving it 'of the one Regular Division so necessary to its effective composition'. Churchill was not quite right in claiming that 'the whole Council, with the exception of Lord Kitchener, were of one mind. I urged the Prime Minister to make his authority effective,' Churchill later wrote, 'and to insist upon the despatch of the 29th Division . . . . I felt at that moment in an intense way a foreboding of disaster. I knew it was a turning-point in the struggle as surely as I know now that the consequences are graven upon the monuments of history.' But Asquith wrote in his diary that night, 'Kitchener, I think on the whole quite rightly, insisted on keeping his 29th Division at home.' So what *did* Asquith think? It really does seem as if he did not know what to make of the whole business and was stunned into silent acquiescence (not for the first time) by the omniscience of the stern Field Marshal. Thor had spoken, and that was that.

Kitchener did not rule out the prospect that the Division might be allowed to leave at some time in the future. On the day after the meeting as a further slap in Churchill's face he cancelled, without authority and without informing Churchill, all the arrangements for the despatch of the troops, and the numerous transports were dispersed.

In renewed fury Churchill wrote to him:

The War Council on the 18th instructed me to prepare transport inter alia for the 29th Division, and I gave directions accordingly. I now learn that on the 20th you sent ... a message that the 29th Division was not to go, and acting on this the transports were countermanded without my being informed .... I have now renewed the order for the preparation of the transports; but I apprehend that they cannot be ready for a fortnight ...

On the same day Churchill took the precaution of circulating a note recording his opinion that the alternative military force to the 29th Division 'is not large enough for the work it may have to do; and that the absence of any British regular troops will, if fighting occurs, expose the naval battalions and the Australians to undue risk ... the weakness of the military force may compel us to forego a large part of the advantages which would otherwise follow.'

At length, Kitchener changed his mind again and released the 29th Division on 10 March. Due in part to the cancellation of the transports, the last of the vessels carrying these professional regulars did not get away until 23 March, three weeks later than it would have done if Kitchener had not cancelled the order. Characteristically understating the consequences, Asquith wrote in his diary, 'There is no doubt that this delay ... gave the Turks time to improve their defences.'

It was not possible then, and remains impossible today, to discern and analyse all the motives for this grave and infinitely damaging decision to cancel the departure of this Division. But a strong if not a dominant influence was the abiding hatred and jealousy Kitchener felt for Churchill; young, aristocratic, happily married to a beautiful woman and with three children, journalist and successful political careerist, and in every aspect of his being and character the diametric opposite to Kitchener. Fifteen years after their African confrontations – fifteen years when Kitchener saw himself as loyally carrying out his imperial duties in India and Egypt whilst Churchill was ruthlessly hewing out political advancement – fate had brought them together again. But now the one-time insubordinate lieutenant was head of the navy, and as powerful as he was.

Kitchener had done his best, he would say, to bring about good relations by supporting Churchill during those critical days at Antwerp, defended him against those who mocked and denigrated his efforts, and even encouraged him to quit his post at the Admiralty and become a soldier again. And what did he receive in return? Constant visits to Kitchener's commander in France, undermining his authority, sowing seeds of discord, encouraging plans contrary to Kitchener's own policy and creating acrimony with the French Army commanders. Churchill had interfered with military plans and arrangements at every level and in every theatre: at home over the threat of invasion, which Churchill constantly pooh-poohed, in France and Belgium with his rag-tag and bob-tail Naval Division and his useless armoured cars – mostly driven by his friends. And now in the eastern Mediterranean, Churchill, having accepted that the navy could do the job alone, was trying to pre-empt him again and demand, as if by right, Kitchener's last professional reserves.

This in simple summary was Kitchener's view and assessment of the situation as the navy-only plans went ahead. But increasing anxiety in Whitehall – felt especially by Hankey – and some of his own War Office Staff as to the navy's ability to pull off this coup alone had led Kitchener to send out General Sir William Birdwood to draw up a report. It was Birdwood's opinion that the navy could not do the job alone that led to Kitchener's first reluctant agreement to send out the 29th Division. 'If the Fleet would not get through the Straits unaided, the Army ought to see the business through.' He recognized that British prestige was at stake.

But even as Kitchener made the decision to support Churchill's navy-only plan he was assailed by doubts. As A.J.P.Taylor has written: 'Again, there was no rational calculation, no cool determination ...' *If* the navy pulled it off on its own it would enjoy enormous popular acclaim and prestige. So would Churchill. If it failed, the danger to Egypt would greatly increase and would demand further troop reinforcements from Britain anyway. Kitchener's excuse for holding back the 29th Division because German successes on the eastern front might lead to greater pressure in the West can be quickly discounted. Churchill wrote that Kitchener

gave as his reason the dangerous weakness of Russia and his fear lest large masses of German troops should be brought back from the Russian Front to attack our troops in France. I cannot believe that his argument had really weighed with him. He must have known that, apart from all other improbabilities, it was physically impossible for the Germans to transport great armies from Russia to the French Front under two or three months at the very least, and that the 29th Division – one single division – could not affect the issue appreciably if they did so.

Churchill concluded significantly: 'He used the argument to fortify a decision which he had arrived at after a most painful heart-searching on other and general grounds.'

The conclusion of the Dardanelles Commission was uncompromising: 'We think that Mr Churchill was quite justified in attaching the utmost importance to the delays which occurred in despatching the 29th Division ... from this country.'

Had Asquith had the courage and strength of will to overrule the Secretary of State for War, as was his perfect right; had Balfour, Churchill's successor at the Admiralty, or McKenna his predecessor, been First Lord in these critical weeks of 1915, there can be little doubt that the 29th Division would have sailed in the transports Churchill had made ready on 22 February. Personal prejudice played its disagreeable part in what Arthur Marder has called 'the three weeks of shilly-shallying'. Perhaps after two of those weeks had passed Kitchener's doubts began to disperse, like the transports for his troops' rapid embarkation. Perhaps he began to recognize a different balance of accruing kudos from a successful joint attack. Be that as it may, when he announced to a greatly relieved War Council that the 18,000 professionals of the 29th Division could go with his blessing after all, and when he appointed his old crony from the days of the Boer War, General Sir Ian Hamilton, as commander of all land forces for the Gallipoli campaign, his orders were to capture Constantinople. 'If you do,' Kitchener told him, 'you will have won not only a campaign, but the war.' And the contribution of the navy and of Churchill personally would be seen as very small beer by contrast with his own and the army's.

Two feuds broke the Dardanelles Expedition and Churchill himself: Churchill's naval feud with Fisher and his army and personal feud with Kitchener. A number of men who knew Fisher and Churchill had predicted the clash of wills which could only lead to catastrophe. Only one man, and he was not the supine, complacent Asquith, anticipated the even more dangerous jealousies, competition and resentment, with their roots deep in earlier wars, that would develop between Churchill and Kitchener. And that man was Kitchener himself, who had first begged Churchill to go to Antwerp and then did his utmost, when the opportunity so fortuitously occurred, to recruit him as a subordinate in the army rather than continue to suffer him as an equal in the Cabinet.

At nine minutes to ten o'clock on the fine, clear morning of 19 February 1915 the Anglo–French naval force under Admiral Carden opened the bombardment on the Dardanelles outer forts. Twelve ships were involved, four French battleships of undistinguished vintage, six British pre-dreadnought battleships, the battle-cruiser *Inflexible* and – the star of the show – HMS *Queen Elizabeth*. (Her 15-inch guns were to fire in the first major Allied bombardment of the First World War and again in one of the last bombardments of the Second World War.)

The Dardanelles bombardment was the first in which spotting aircraft took part, employing one-way radio. The observer of one of the aircraft wrote later:

It was a glorious day of brilliant sunshine, and from my seat in the nose of our seaplane, I had an ideal view of the bombardment. It was like watching a theatre scene from the front row of the dress circle. Beneath us lay the Dardanelles: on the European side one could see over the Gallipoli peninsula and as far as the Sea of Marmara; while on the Asiatic side the Plains of Troy were visible in the distance.

Immediately beneath us were the ships of the Fleet, underway and steaming up and down and banging off at the forts. It was a rare spectacle . . .

In the afternoon the big ships closed the entrance to the straits and reopened fire. Carden was pleased with the results and reported to Churchill that things went well. The seaplane observer did not agree and made himself thoroughly unpopular by saying so. His pilot flew him low over the outer Turkish forts – 'in no case had any damage been done to the guns'.

There are numerous reasons why a gun duel between a fort and a ship is strongly balanced in favour of the fort. To damage a gun it is necessary to obtain a direct hit and a gun makes a very small target, often invisible until it fires, no matter that it is a fixed target. For the shore gun the target is the entire ship, hundreds of feet long and of relatively massive silhouette; and the gun-layer ashore has a fixed, steady platform and the fall of shot is readily spotted – no spume misting lenses, no funnel smoke blotting out the target. 'Ships are unequally matched against forts . . . . A ship can no more stand up against a fort costing the same money', wrote Admiral Mahan in 1911, 'than the fort could run a race with a ship.'

The disadvantages for the ship gunner were compounded by his high-velocity, low-trajectory guns. The battleships' guns elevated to a maximum of 15 degrees, in a few cases 20 degrees, which was all right for long-range ship-to-ship action but necessitated great accuracy and most sensitive range adjustment to score a hit against a fort's gun; especially a gun cleverly camouflaged and cleverly concealed. The Fourth Sea Lord's private secretary recalls an occasion just before the bombardment was due to open:

When the Naval attack began, I was sharing a room with Captain (afterwards Admiral) Leonard Donaldson RN. When I suggested that the ships would get through, he shook his head. 'I am afraid', he said, 'the trajectory of Naval guns is too low for attacks against forts.' And then he explained that for attacks on land defences a high trajectory was essential. That was the cause of the German success in attacking the Belgian forts. What a disaster it was that Donaldson or some other gunnery officer was not at hand to inform Churchill of the difference.

Churchill the soldier now recalled how he had witnessed the German howitzers reduce the Belgian forts to rubble. If these howitzers could destroy land forts with such apparent ease, then 12-inch and 15-inch naval guns should surely have no difficulty in dealing with the Turkish forts guarding the Dardanelles. That was Churchill's military reasoning and unfortunately Admiral Oliver, who was with him in Belgium at the time, was inclined to agree after no doubt being bowled over by Churchill's enthusiasm and rhetoric. Oliver did not seek advice elsewhere, either.

Extreme accuracy of shooting was demanded by the low trajectory of the naval guns but it was unfortunately not demonstrated. In spite of numerous reforms and improvements in recent years, British naval gunnery was still relatively poor. At the Battle of Dogger Bank the guns were fired with the battle-cruisers at full speed for the *first time*. One of them, the newly commissioned *Tiger*, had *never once* fired its guns against a moving target. Apart from the *Blücher*, which was latterly a sitting target, the British guns made just six hits out of 1,150 shells fired, or ½ per cent, against the German figure of 2.1 per cent. The author clearly recalls a conversation with Captain H.C.B.Pipon, the gunnery authority, on the fiftieth anniversary of the Battle of Jutland. He was highly critical of the battle-cruisers' gunnery at that battle.

Like everyone else, our gunnery officers had the outlook of amateurs. They were good fighters at heart and longed to fire their guns at the enemy – *and* that the enemy should fire at them and so provide the spice of danger without which the programme would be dull – but, like many of the best fighters, they were not thinkers; they were used to shooting at floating targets and could not adapt themselves to shooting at targets on shore. Indirect firing seemed beyond most of them.

If the spotting officer could not see the fall of shot he behaved like a blind man. On several occasions in subsequent 'shoots' when air spotting was available, observers attempted to correct the poor shooting but the gunnery officers were incapable of bending their imagination to this information coming in from a new-fangled one-way wireless from a new-fangled flying machine. None of them had ever practised this sort of shooting and this sort of co-operative effort in peacetime.

Finally, the Turkish guns were much more cleverly sited and better manned than the British gave them credit for. The German instructors had done a good job. Characteristic British arrogance played its part in this belief. But poor intelligence, which failed to comprehend the danger from, or even the existence of, numerous mobile howitzers, further handicapped the attackers.

Nevertheless, in spite of all these difficulties and unfavourable weather conditions (which caused the breakdown of Carden's health and his resignation), the main Turkish forts were in turn knocked out progressively. By 18 March the battleships were able to penetrate six miles up the straits and had silenced most of the big guns, which were in any case now desperately short of ammunition.

At this point another factor and one of a deadly nature stepped in. Conditions in the straits were ideal for mining and the Turkish minefields had been a menace from the beginning. Time and again the British minesweepers were driven back by a hail of Turkish fire. Their fate was no better on this day and they were forced to retire before they could clear a minefield which began to take its toll with the blowing up of the French battleship *Bouvet*. This ship sank in a few minutes with the loss of almost all her 640 officers and men. Three British ships were then struck, two of them foundering. The third was the prized battle-cruiser *Inflexible* which was badly damaged. Two more French battleships were put out of action by Turkish gunfire. The whole operation was then called off and the new C-in-C, Admiral John De Robeck, refused to persevere further without the support of the army.

Churchill was horrified when he heard. 'I regarded it as only the first of several days' fighting,' he said of the 18 March débâcle, 'though the loss in ships sunk or disabled was unpleasant. It never occurred to me for a moment we should not go on.' Asquith was of the same view but not until after his usual vacillation. On 12 March he noted that the Admiral 'is quite right to proceed cautiously. Winston is rather for pushing him on.' But by 23rd, 'the Admiral seems to be in rather a funk'. On the following day he noted in his diary that the naval experts too 'seem to be suffering from a fit of nerves'.

The underwater mine, then, was the real villain of the navy-only Dardanelles attack. Fisher was one of the few who had ever taken the mine seriously and then seemed to forget all about mines when he became First Sea Lord. To the authorities it had the twin demerits of being unethical and defensive. The gunnery officer still reigned supreme in 1915, and for long after. The navy was deeply imbued with the spirit of the offensive and against the defensive. So, at the outbreak of the war there were few British mines and they were of poor quality. The German Navy, concerned as it had to be with whittling away Royal Navy superiority and making secure its bases, the Kiel Canal and a short coastline, gave more thought and money to mines. They were deadly in their effect – for example, the 23,000-ton *Audacious* went to the bottom after striking only one mine.

The Germans applied all their mining skills to the defence of the Dardanelles. The British minesweepers were recently converted North Sea trawlers, manned largely by North Sea fishermen with no disciplined training. In carrying out their dangerous trade, these trawlers had not only to contend with numerous concealed Turkish howitzers but also a 4-knot current.

Recalling this set-back a future admiral and deputy director of Naval Intelligence wrote :

The Navy had no system of clearing a big minefield in narrow waters under fire. No one had even thought how it could be done. It was clearly impracticable unless the minefield batteries were mastered. The urgent and dominating necessity of clearing the minefield was fully appreciated by Admiral De Robeck and indeed by everyone, but some who clearly knew nothing about the practical aspects of the task thought it could be done by piffling about with trawlers . . .

Hearing of the minesweepers' failures, Churchill regarded the crews as scrimshankers. Casualties and losses must be expected, he kept reiterating. The Turkish guns must be attacked at decisive range and, if necessary, landing parties should be put ashore to destroy the forts' guns.

Reading these instructions, an officer on the spot expressed a widely held opinion when he wrote, 'It is one of those peculiarly objectionable messages, in which the man on the spot is not only urged to attack but told how to do it . . . . In its easy and superficial reference to very difficult or impracticable tasks, it bears the unmistakable impress of the First Lord's hand.' But Fisher and Oliver would no doubt have seen it.

The fearless Commodore Roger Keyes summed up the dilemma in a letter to his wife, Eva :

The position is – we can silence – temporarily – I think the guns at the Narrows at Chanak whenever we wish – but in order to take advantage of this we must have a clear channel through the mine field for the ships to close to decisive range to hammer the forts and then land men to destroy the guns. Progress in the mine field has been slow latterly. And in the mean time we cannot afford to waste ammunition in bombardments which necessarily can't be decisive until the channel is clear . . .

The refusal of Admiral De Robeck to continue to repeat the attack after the expensive failure of 18 March to break through infuriated Churchill. He sat down and drafted out a long telegram detailing the action the Admiral should now take.

You ought to persevere methodically but resolutely with the plan contained in your instructions . . . . You should dominate the forts at the Narrows and sweep the minefield and then batter the forts at close range . . . taking your time, using your aeroplanes, and all your improved methods of guarding against mines. The destruction of the forts at the Narrows may open the way for a further advance. The entry into the Marmara of a fleet strong enough to beat the Turkish Fleet would produce decisive results on the whole situation . . .

The telegram was never sent. Fisher, whose support for the navy-only enterprise had become increasingly tepid and intermittent, opposed its despatch. He was supported by Wilson and Jackson. For the first time the strongest members of the Admiralty War Group not only held together but directly and firmly opposed the First Lord.

Churchill was reduced to appealing to the Prime Minister for his support – twice in one day. Asquith believed Churchill was right but refused to overrule three such powerful naval figures. If De Robeck attacked again and suffered a further rebuff with more heavy casualties, when the facts were known it would doubtless lead to the end not only of Churchill's political career but also of his own.

Churchill was more positive. 'If by resigning I could have procured the decision [to renew the navy-only attack], I would have done so without a moment's hesitation . . .', he wrote later. Now he drafted out another even longer telegram of reasoned appeal to De Robeck and, emphasizing that this was not an executive order, only a 'Personal & Secret' comment, showed it to Fisher for his approval.

Fisher remained adamant. 'Although the telegram goes from you personally, the fact of my remaining at the Admiralty sanctions my connection with it, so if it goes I do not see how I can remain.' The indefatigable Churchill was not yet finished and Fisher was obliged to write again, this time one of his 'we are the lost ten tribes of Israel!' letters, ending with the postscript, 'Send no more telegrams! Let it alone!'

Churchill did no such thing. He battered away until the old Admiral's forts crumbled and he capitulated. But the message, when it was received, did not affect in the smallest degree De Robeck's determination to waste no more ships and men until the army arrived and they could proceed with a combined operation. '"No" had won,' wrote Churchill bitterly, 'with general assent and measureless ruin.'

6
'My regiment is awaiting me'

From these last days of March cordiality and co-operation between Fisher and Churchill declined rapidly. Churchill despatched men o'war of all kinds, including the first of Fisher's completed Baltic Project vessels, just as Fisher had feared. All these ships departed from home waters – Fisher's 'scene of decisive action' – to reinforce De Robeck for his decisive action. Every man o'war, every officer was wrenched from Fisher's unwilling fingers. His anxiety about the balance of naval power in the North Sea was heightened by intelligence coming in that Germany was likely to succeed in bringing Holland into the war on her side, which would almost certainly lead to the High Seas Fleet's emergence from its bases and a direct challenge being offered to Jellicoe.

'We can't send another rope yarn even to De Robeck!' Fisher wrote to Churchill on 2 April. 'WE HAVE GONE TO THE VERY LIMIT!!! And so they must not hustle and should be distinctly and most emphatically told that no further reinforcements of the Fleet can be looked for! *A failure or check in the Dardanelles would be nothing. A failure in the North Sea would be ruin . . .*' And to Jellicoe he cried, '*This Dardanelles entirely exhausts my time.*'

Above all, Fisher was anxious about the super-dreadnought *Queen Elizabeth*, whose handsome, stately and omnipotent silhouette dominated the naval scene off the Dardanelles and became for the army as it began to arrive the symbol of naval power and tangible confirmation of the navy's commitment to the operations.

For Fisher the presence of this precious ship, which he had intended to be attached to the force only for testing her guns, was now the manifestation of Churchill's intention to drain the strength of the Grand Fleet for the benefit of the Mediterranean – a reverse process to Churchill's peacetime policy when the High Seas Fleet was not yet a daily and deadly threat.

'It seems desirable to send a telegram to Admiral De Robeck that on no account whatever is the *Queen Elizabeth* to be risked as was the *Inflexible*,' Fisher wrote to Churchill nine days later, 'and she should be kept solely for long-range firing from the northern side of the

Gallipoli peninsula and not risked inside the Straits . . .'

Churchill would not agree to this restriction – '. . . it would not be right at this moment to make a rigid prohibition of her entering the Straits . . .' And in reply to another anxious and critical message from the First Sea Lord, Churchill replied (11 April 1915): 'Seriously, my friend, are you not a little unfair in trying to spite this operation by side winds and small points when you have accepted it in principle? It is hard on me that you should keep on like this – every day something fresh: and it is not worthy of you or the great business we have in hand together.' And later, Churchill wrote in his memoirs how 'every officer, every man, every ship, every round of ammunition required for the Dardanelles, became a cause of friction and had to be fought for by me, not only with the First Sea Lord but to a certain extent with his naval colleagues . . .'

The weeks between De Robeck's flat refusal to continue the navy-only attacks and the first landings of Allied troops on the Gallipoli peninsula showed Churchill at his bulldog best. Blow after blow fell upon him and his pet enterprise. He suffered them stoically, refused to lose heart, never for one moment relaxed his aggressive stance, and continued to feed De Robeck with encouragement and advice. Today we can see him as a figure ten times larger than the other effete, arrogant, scheming, self-concerned, trivial-minded Cabinet members – all of them pygmies except for Lloyd George by comparison with this scion of the Marlboroughs. He might be encroaching far beyond the traditional boundaries of his responsibilities, but at least he was spreading life and fire when he did so.

The minefields of the Narrows may have destroyed Churchill's dream of the Fleet standing off Constantinople with its population cowed, the *Goeben* a smoking ruin, but his overall faith in the expedition had not declined by one degree. His brother Jack had joined the Staff of General Sir Ian Hamilton, and from the eastern Mediterranean now wrote to Churchill that, 'We call this expedition the last "Crusade" and shall expect a papal cross for it!!' But Jack Churchill also confirmed to his brother the reality of the frustrated navy-only operation.

We are up against a very tough proposition . . . . The sailors are now inclined to acknowledge that they cannot get through without the co-operation of troops. Long range fire on forts is no good unless infantry occupy the forts afterwards and maintain themselves there. Stronger minesweepers are necessary against the current . . . . Half the targets are concealed and the ships have the greatest difficulty in locating and firing at mobile guns.

As a further blow to the enterprise, and also an explanation of why it had been such hard going for the navy, Churchill learned that Romania had opened her frontiers to German trains carrying war material and military experts to Constantinople. At first the crates of mines, guns and ammunition had been marked with the Red Cross, but all pretence at concealment soon ceased, and British protests had no effect. It now seemed as if the Balkan states were backing a victory for Turkey before the Allied army had even arrived.

Churchill's two main antagonists within, both of them wily and unscrupulous in their methods, continued their independent attrition. Now that Kitchener had accepted under Asquith's pressure the necessity of sending the 29th Division to Gallipoli, he visualized the whole operation in army terms and declined to take Churchill into his confidence, isolating him from information about the army's movements and plans. Kitchener seems to have persuaded Asquith, as a *quid pro quo* for involving the army in the operation at all, not to convene a meeting of the War Council to discuss plans. This was Kitchener's show. On 25 March he told Churchill in very general terms that 'We are pushing on preparations for land operations.' He also expressed his hope that the navy would continue to bombard the Turks so that they used up their ammunition. And that was about all. Asquith has left no evidence that he was a party to Kitchener's intention to distance Churchill from arrangements about the military landing, but he must have divined that this was what was happening.

Aboard the *Queen Elizabeth* off the impregnable Dardanelles De Robeck was being similarly isolated from the army's intentions, or so it seemed. On 4 April De Robeck sent Churchill a telegram explaining in general terms how he hoped to co-operate with Hamilton. But he could not get down to details. 'General Hamilton has not informed me yet whether the covering force will land at night and attempt a surprise or by day and obtain maximum assistance from gun fire of Fleet.'

An outside eye would find it hard to discern the depths of the hostility between Kitchener and Churchill. For their immediate colleagues there was no such difficulty. Kitchener's slovenly working methods and his conscious urge to 'take it out on' Churchill conspired to frustrate co-operation between the two men who, above all others, were really running the war. The supply of ammunition for the Fleet, for example, might be considered an important matter, especially with the colossal expenditure of shells and cordite charges at the Dardanelles. The 'shell scandal' about the shortage of ammunition for the army in France was already a political issue and was soon to rock the nation. Ammunition was clearly a subject demanding the closest co-operation between the two services, but Churchill was repeatedly frustrated in achieving this co-operation. Official letters on the subject from the Admiralty to the War Office were written on 16 February, 1 March, 18 March and 2 April 1915. 'Up to the present,' Churchill wrote to Kitchener in vexation on 8 April, 'no answer has been given to us. I am afraid I must ask you for this information without wh it is impossible to arrange about the ammunition of the Fleet, the supply of mines, bombs, explosive sweeps etc.' He continued: 'It adds enormously to the labour of official work when reasonable & necessary inquiries by one department are not taken any notice of by the others', and added the threat that he would have to take up the matter in Cabinet, but discreetly deleted all this last part before despatching his letter.

Churchill could not, however, always contain the anger that welled up against the more ridiculous and damaging postures of this mad old field marshal. And yet he could see with absolute clarity the need to repair fences as soon as they were broken down at what he called 'this vy anxious time'. After high words between the two men at one Cabinet, Churchill felt impelled to write a note of apology to Kitchener. 'I am distressed to have got into a dispute with you this morning. It was far from my intention to do so, & I am vy sorry I allowed myself to become angry . . .'

Some weeks earlier Churchill's cousin Freddie Guest had sounded a warning note about Churchill's relations with Kitchener. 'I see signs of strained relationship between you and tremble for an explosion.' It did not look now as if it could be long delayed.

Fisher's attacks were open and extrovert by contrast with Kitchener's, and he did not hesitate to let anyone know of his antagonism towards the whole Dardanelles project. Jellicoe especially was aware of this as Fisher continued to fuel the C-in-C's anxieties about his inadequate strength in ships. He also continued to speak his mind to Churchill on every subject, and vitriolic attacks were not in his case followed by sweet apologies. 'Never in all my whole life have I ever before so sacrificed my convictions as I have done to please you! – THAT'S A FACT!' And, 'You are simply eaten up with the Dardanelles and can't think of anything else!' he told Churchill on 5 April. 'D—n the Dardanelles! They'll be our grave!'

Only the last words carried the message of truth. Churchill was never single-minded, in or out of office. Always his percipient mind was ranging far and wide. And in a moment of extreme frustration with De Robeck, he raised again the subject of Borkum with Fisher. For a few hours on 25 March it was like old times with the two men in high but now quite unacrimonious debate, discussing how the navy could seize that island and how an army would then soon be marching through

Germany *en route* to Berlin. But within days the scene had faded and was absorbed in some Admiralty file under the press of new crises and the weight of momentum of plans and proceedings in the eastern Mediterranean.

The days and weeks passed. Hamilton's transports arrived at the island of Lemnos, 'borrowed' from Greece as a base for the landings. Like Kitchener's working methods, and his desk, these transports were found to be in such chaotic disorder that the whole armada had to proceed to Egypt to be reloaded. Hamilton departed from Egypt again on 8 April and steamed north while more and more German military supplies poured into Turkey and the defences of the Gallipoli peninsula were further strengthened. De Robeck still had no idea how or when the attack was to take place. The reason for this was at last clear : Hamilton did not know either and was still discussing the merits of certain landing places with General Birdwood, who was to lead the Australian and New Zealand forces.

At last, on 11 April 1915, combined discussions began on board the *Queen Elizabeth*, and very cordial they were, too. De Robeck and Hamilton got on well, and a new and much-needed sense of optimism prevailed. This was not the mood back home where grave doubts and suspicions were being raised by Churchill's enemies in Parliament and Fleet Street even before the much-heralded operation began. 'Remember Antwerp !' some people were crying. The editor of the *Morning Post* wrote to Asquith suggesting again that Churchill was not fit to hold office – or be 'in charge of the Fleet during this war'.

On 19 April, six days before the first landings, Hankey dined with Churchill and found him 'extremely optimistic'. Hankey did not share this optimism. He was, as Asquith told Venetia Stanley, 'very anxious about the Dardanelles'. These anxieties were passed on to, and shared with, Balfour. 'As you know, I cannot help being very anxious about the fate of any military attempt upon the Peninsula,' he wrote.

Nobody was so keen as myself upon forcing the Straits as long as there seemed a reasonable prospect of doing so by means of the fleet alone . . . . But a military attack upon a position so inherently difficult, and so carefully prepared, is a different proposition ; and, if it fails, we shall not only have to suffer considerably in men, and still more in prestige, but we may upset our whole diplomacy in the Near East . . .

Fisher's boldly expressed opposition was echoed in milder and more considered – but firm – tones by the Second, Third and Fourth Sea Lords among others ; and on 8 April Richmond recommended to Fisher (as if he needed the encouragement !) that the Dardanelles Expedition should be abandoned.

General Hamilton's plans for the landing were completed by 20 April, and De Robeck issued orders in detail for putting the troops ashore and supporting the attack with a renewed bombardment. He hoped to begin his part on 24 April, he told Churchill, who was sternly realistic about the difficulties and dangers that lay ahead. 'Winston had given the whole subject most anxious consideration,' according to his friend Sir George Riddell, who wrote in his *War Diary*: 'If the operation is successful, its effects will be most important. They are worth the risk . . . . If the operation is unsuccessful, Winston recognises that the effect on his career may be serious. "They may get rid of me," he said. "If they do I cannot help it. I shall have done my best. My regiment is awaiting me."'

The tragedy of Gallipoli and the Dardanelles has been told many times, never more poignantly than by Churchill himself.

The landings themselves, on the bloody dawn of 25 April, set the high note of catastrophe and gallantry, with the raw, eager young Australians and New Zealanders facing the white heat of modern war for the first time and falling in hundreds on beach after beach. An old collier with holes cut in her sides, the *River Clyde*, came nearest to being a landing-craft, and she grounded at a long, lethal distance from the shore at V Beach. As Basil Liddell Hart has written:

Here the invaders ran, like gladiators, into a gently sloping arena designed by nature and arranged by the Turks – themselves ensconced in surrounding seats – for a butchery . . . . The tows, checked by the current, were caught up by the *River Clyde*, and as it grounded hell yawned. In the incoming boats oars dropped like the wings of scorched moths, while the boats drifted helplessly with their load of dead and wounded. Many men jumped overboard only to be drowned in water stained with their own blood . . .

All hope of surprising the enemy had long since gone. With the passing of so many weeks, German instruction, German Western Front experience and German equipment led to the narrow peninsula of Gallipoli becoming a distant reflection of the war in France. The same trenches and barbed wire, the same machine-guns and artillery, set the same pattern of deadlock. The only difference for the defenders was that they enjoyed geographical advantages and forthe attackers that they suffered the disadvantages of restricted space and seaborne 2,800-mile-long supply lines. As Jack Churchill wrote home to his elder brother, 'It has become siege warfare again as in France . . .'

In unison with Jack Churchill's cry, 'We must have lots more men', came inevitably the demand for more ships. And as the army ground to a halt the renewal of a naval bombardment and penetration of the Narrows was considered, both on the spot by De Robeck and at the Admiralty. Thus, by the early days of May 1915 the sequence of events in the Dardanelles was: (1) 19 February, navy-only bombardment opens; (2) 18 March, navy-only attacks cease and combined army–navy attack deemed essential: (3) 25 April, combined army–navy attack takes place; (4) 9 May, army attacks held and renewed navy-only bombardment considered.

Deeply depressed at the early failure of the army to take the Gallipoli heights and capture the gun positions which had checked the Fleet, Churchill was now obliged to go to Paris to join the negotiations for the entry of Italy into the war. Fisher was therefore in sole charge of Admiralty affairs for a few days. Instead of relishing this brief freedom from restraint, Fisher soon felt the strain. The degree of strain was revealed when Clementine Churchill invited Fisher for lunch. On his departure he confided in his hostess that her husband was really in Paris to see his mistress. This facetious and coarse remark gave great offence.

When Churchill returned he showed every intention of ordering De Robeck to take his battleships into the attack again. Fisher's first thought was for the *Queen Elizabeth*, his second thought for the reinforcements Churchill would inevitably be demanding, as loudly as Hamilton was demanding (and getting) heavy reinforcements for the army. More than ever the giant battleship with its twin funnels and four turrets of 15-inch guns had become the heart of the whole operation, by land and by sea. Beneath its heavily armoured decks, the army and navy chiefs met in this floating headquarters to discuss their problems and make their decisions. In a talk with Fisher on 11 May Churchill did indeed make clear that he sought navy-only action again, on a limited basis; but Fisher knew that if it was successful it would rapidly be developed into a full-scale attack with the Sea of Marmara again as the Fleet's destination.

To counter this threat Fisher, with the sympathetic help of Hankey, drew up a memorandum clarifying his views that 'any attempt by the Fleet to rush the Narrows, is doomed to failure, and, moreover, is fraught with possibilities of disaster utterly incommensurate to any advantage that could be obtained therefrom'. He concluded with a further implied threat of resignation.

Churchill replied at once that there was no intention of rushing the Dardanelles and then lapsed into an appeal, a *cri de coeur* even : 'Surely here is a combination and a situation which requires from us every conceivable exertion and contrivance which we can think of. I beg you to lend your whole aid and goodwill, and ultimately then success is certain.'

Relations between admiral and minister now sped towards a supreme crisis. Fisher asked Hankey to have a word with Asquith to explain his opposition to further independent naval action and to emphasize that he would resign if his wishes were not met. Hankey noted in his diary that Asquith thought 'it was a very foolish message', but that 'to keep him quiet' he would not authorize such action without Fisher's concurrence.

Fisher quite reasonably supposed that Asquith had granted him the means of veto over Churchill, something he had never before been given. Fisher therefore felt inflated with new power which led him to reject entirely Churchill's last letter, and he sent to Asquith, on Hankey's advice, a copy of the memorandum he had prepared for Churchill.

Unaware that Fisher's new firmness and implacability stemmed from Asquith's supposed support, Churchill decided that he and Fisher must come to terms urgently or, this time, the Admiral might really resign and so inevitably put the Government and Churchill's political future at risk. He knew that the first bone of contention was the continued presence of the *Queen Elizabeth* at the Dardanelles, especially since Fisher had heard that U-boats were on their way from the Adriatic, and that the battleship *Goliath* had been sunk by a torpedo boat the previous day. Therefore, as a peace offering, he told Fisher that he was ordering the *Queen Elizabeth* to come home without delay, and that no action by De Robeck would be taken for the present.

Fisher, temporarily mollified, agreed not to resign, and agreed to a meeting with Kitchener at the Admiralty on the evening of 13 May.

Churchill recounted :

We sat round the octagonal table, Lord Kitchener on my left, Lord Fisher on my right, together with various other officers of high rank. As soon as Lord Kitchener realised that the Admiralty were going to withdraw the *Queen Elizabeth*, he became extremely angry. His habitual composure in trying ordeals left him. He protested vehemently against what he considered the desertion of the Army at its most critical moment. On the other side Lord Fisher flew into an even greater fury.

Fisher declared that unless the battleship came home that very night he would walk out of the Admiralty. Churchill did his utmost as peace-maker between the two men who had brought him such sore trial over the past months, working against him sometimes behind his back, some-times openly, but always with the intention of frustrating his wishes – or so it seemed. He recounted to Kitchener all the naval reinforce-ments which would be despatched to make up for the loss of the *Queen Elizabeth*, including two powerful new monitors, 'the last word in bom-barding vessels', which Fisher had built at record speed for his now deeply interred Baltic Project. This news may have eased the anxieties of Kitchener on Churchill's left; they did not make good listening on his right. Eventually the meeting broke up, still heavy with suspicion and acrimony.

On the following day, 13 May, Churchill became increasingly aware of his enemies closing in. The dispute with Fisher was now widely known, thanks in part to Fisher himself, and was pointedly raised in Parliament by the Conservative member William Joynson-Hicks. Was it not true, he asked, that Lord Fisher, 'regarding the March attack on the Dardanelles expressed the view that it would be wiser to wait for the co-operation of a military force; and if so, who over-ruled such advice?'

Churchill answered defensively: 'I am sure this House will not approve of this kind of question, which is calculated to be detrimental to public interests of serious importance.'

Kitchener, and later De Robeck, could be pacified only by reassur-ances from Churchill of still greater reinforcement, and Churchill knew that every ship despatched (never mind Fisher's 'We can't send another rope yarn') would have the opposite response from Fisher and the Board of Admiralty. In less than a month from the date of the invasion, the Dardanelles had become an ever-widening vortex drawing in to its limit-less depths more ships and men and armaments of all kinds. Fisher may have recovered his *Queen Elizabeth*, but, as Churchill reassured those in the battle line, more suitable bombardment ships would soon be heading for the eastern Mediterranean. 'I am determined to support you and the army in every way to the end,' he telegraphed De Robeck.

The War Council meeting of 14 May, a 'sulphurous' occasion ac-cording to Churchill, was remarkable not for being dominated by Kitchener, but for what he had to say. After the meeting at the Admir-alty Kitchener had sent Asquith a note couched in a curiously facetious tone, attempting on behalf of the army to draw a parallel with the navy's decision. Because the army was to be denied the big guns of the *Queen Elizabeth*, then, he wrote, 'We may have to consider ... whether the troops had better not be taken back to Alexandria, as there may be a Moslem rising in Egypt, and we have denuded the garrison to help the operations.' It was not, in the circumstances, a joke in the best taste ; more an ill-considered effusion from this crazed egocentric.

Now at the War Council, 'in a strain of solemn and formidable complaint', Kitchener raised again the question of the missing battleship. He said he had been persuaded to despatch the 29th Division on the assurance that the navy with army assistance would force the Dardanelles. Now the navy had given up the attempt and sent home its mightiest ship just when the army was fighting for its life with its back to the sea.

Fisher broke in, truculently one imagines and certainly not usefully, to say that he had been against the operation from the start. Nobody said anything to this. At length Churchill was allowed to speak in his own defence, stating that if only he had known that by this time, mid-May, an army of 80,000 to 100,000 men would be available, the navy-only operation would never have been authorized. As for the *Queen Elizabeth*, she was not considered as a participant when the War Council had approved in principle the navy-only attack, and had been thrown in as a bonus by Fisher, the one member who claimed that he was always against the undertaking and now wanted the ship back with the Fleet.

Churchill then went on the offensive on a wider front, dismissing the recent loose talk about the likelihood of a German invasion, claiming that the Grand Fleet was relatively more powerful than the German High Seas Fleet now than it had been at the outbreak of war. As for the Western Front (now speaking as a soldier though he did not say so), he advised : remain on the defensive ; no more expensive attacks, until sufficient reserves of men and shells had been built up before a big push.

Churchill's remarkable power to persuade, even when on the defensive, was never shown better. 'His stout attitude did something to hearten his colleagues,' Hankey wrote later. It did better than that: even Kitchener was drawn from the bowels of pessimism.

It had been a long meeting, but Churchill was not yet finished. As soon as he reached the Admiralty he wrote a long letter to Asquith, couched in the strongest terms, attacking both Fisher and Kitchener. Of Fisher he wrote :

The First Sea Lord has agreed in writing to every executive telegram on which the operations have been conducted ; and had they been immediately successful the credit would have been his .... I wish now to make it clear to you that a man who says 'I disclaim responsibility for failure', cannot be the final arbiter of the measures which may be found to be vital to success.

As for Kitchener:

It is also uncomfortable not to know what [he] will or won't do in the matter of reinforcements. We are absolutely in his hands, and I never saw him in a queerer mood – or more unreasonable. K will punish the Admiralty by docking Hamilton of his divisions because we have withdrawn the *Queen Elizabeth*; and Fisher will have the *Queen Elizabeth* home if he is to stay.

It was a day of immense activity and conspiracy, testing to the utmost the powers of endurance of all those concerned in this crisis. For quite different reasons Asquith and Fisher were worst equipped to suffer the strains imposed upon them. Three days earlier Asquith had suffered a personal blow which left him lost, distraught and in great mental pain. Venetia Stanley had written to say that she was to marry and that their letters must cease. Deepening the wound, she told him that her husband was to be Edwin Montagu, Asquith's friend and recently his Parliamentary Private Secretary.

Asquith wrote back swiftly and simply:

Wed 12 May 1915

Most Loved –
As you know well, *this* breaks my heart. I couldn't bear to come and see you. I can only pray God to bless you – and help me.

On the same day he wrote to Venetia's sister Sylvia, 'I don't believe there are two living people who, each in their separate ways, are more devoted to me than she and Montagu: and it is the irony of fortune that they two shd combine to deal a death-blow to me ...' The distress reflected in his personal letters continued unabated during these bitter days of multiple crises, headed by Churchill, Kitchener and Fisher. In one way it is remarkable how he preserved his sanity; but it has also been argued that though this blow might have impaired his judgement, the mounting tide of events and personal-professional conflicts within the War Council anaesthetized him against the pain in his heart. In the still of the night it was different. After the day of the War Council struggle, Asquith at midnight wrote again to Venetia: 'This is too terrible. No Hell can be so bad. Cannot you send me one word? it is so unnatural. Only one word.'

It was age that was burdening Fisher. The last six months of labour and strife had made their mark, and it was not just the age difference of twenty-four years between him and his partner. Their working timetables failed to synchronize by many hours. Churchill's flood-tide followed a late convivial dinner, when the memoranda and imaginative ideas flowed until the early hours, by which time Fisher would soon be up after retiring at nine o'clock the evening before. He would be at prayer in Westminster Abbey at 5 a.m. or thereabouts and at his desk before the cleaners arrived. He had done five hours' work before Churchill arrived and was whacked by 6 p.m. when Churchill's dynamos were still at high revs. As a consequence the hours together when both were at their best were few, and Fisher caught the full brunt of his partner's output when quite often Churchill's imaginative processes outstripped his practical judgement. 'It was said of Churchill', wrote one naval officer who had tried to implement one of Churchill's less practical ideas for air–submarine work at the Dardanelles, 'that he produced a hundred new ideas a week, and that four of them were fairly sound.'

When Fisher was intriguing with Hankey at the height of the May crisis, Fisher asked him to call at the Admiralty in the afternoon. Fisher had been at work for close on ten hours. 'I found him asleep, tired out, so slipped out again ...' There is every reason to suppose that Fisher was at least as tired and certainly more depressed late on the afternoon of 14 May after sitting through the long and acrimonious War Council meeting. Worn out, he told his Naval Assistant Captain T. E. Crease that he would shortly be resigning. Then, as he was about to go home at 6.30 p.m., Churchill appeared in order to discuss in detail the nature of the reinforcements to be sent out to De Robeck. These included fifteen new monitors, four 7,000-ton cruisers and a number of heavy guns including a 15-inch howitzer.

Churchill was at his most gently persuasive, Fisher in an unusually submissive and weakened state. No voices were raised, and Captain Crease overheard Churchill saying as he left, 'Well, good night, Fisher. We have settled everything, and you must go home and have a good night's rest. Things will look brighter in the morning and we'll put the thing through together.'

Crease found Fisher 'much relieved'.

Lord Fisher at once called for me, and said that he wanted to sign his papers and get home, and he then told me that he had had a very satisfactory discussion with the First Lord, and that they had peaceably settled what ships and reinforcements should go to the Dardanelles, and that things were amicable again, and he added, quite cheerfully, 'but I suppose he'll soon be at me again'.

Churchill worked late at the Admiralty that evening, not returning home until after 11 p.m. By that time he had drafted four minutes purporting to confirm their agreement on the reinforcements for De Robeck for Fisher's attention in the morning. He handed them to his secretary James Masterton-Smith to pass to Captain Crease. When

Crease read them he said to Masterton-Smith, 'In my opinion Lord Fisher will resign immediately he receives these.' They would be, Crease considered, 'the last straw'. Masterton-Smith therefore took the proposals back to his master, who reassured him that Fisher would not object to them.

On 15 May Fisher made his customary early start, giving immediate attention to the four minutes from Churchill laid out for him by Crease. Things certainly did not 'look brighter in the morning', as Churchill had predicted. Fisher's reaction was all that Crease had feared it would be. Churchill had slipped in additionally two of the navy's best and newest submarines in addition to an increase in the number of monitors and heavy guns.

This further increase 'convinced Lord Fisher that there was no finality about any agreement reached with Mr Churchill on the subject of Dardanelles reinforcements,' wrote Crease, 'and caused his immediate resignation when it reached him'.

If 14 May had been Kitchener's day, 15 May was surely Fisher's – from five in the morning until late into the night, with Churchill a confused and then increasingly anxious figure thrown into another day of hustle and general post about Whitehall. Churchill was walking to the Admiralty across Horse Guards Parade when he was met by Masterton-Smith who greeted him with the words, 'Fisher has resigned, and I think he means it this time.' Churchill then opened the letter from Fisher. It was indeed the Admiral's resignation. '. . . I find it increasingly difficult to adjust myself to the increasing daily requirements of the Dardanelles to meet your views – as you truly said yesterday I am in the position of continually vetoing your proposals – This is not fair to you besides being extremely distasteful to me. I am off to Scotland at once so as to avoid all questionings.'

No specific reference was made to Churchill's revised minutes. Fisher had been so cordial at their parting the night before that Churchill was puzzled. Churchill had, it seems, managed to convince himself that his minutes merely confirmed what had been agreed the night before.

It was a Saturday, but the war had reformed the week-ending habits of most ministers and all the leading figures in the crisis were about Whitehall – all except Fisher himself who had disappeared without trace. Churchill walked to 10 Downing Street and told Asquith what had happened and showed him Fisher's letter. Asquith thought the old Admiral was bluffing again. But he scribbled a note: 'In the King's name, I order you at once to return to your post.' But what address should he give? There was not much time as Asquith was about to leave for the wedding between his one-time Parliamentary Private Secretary, Geoffrey Howard MP, and the daughter of a field marshal, Christina

Methuen, at Henry VII's Chapel, Westminster. So he sent his secretary, Maurice Bonham Carter (who would shortly marry Asquith's daughter Violet), to find Fisher and give him the peremptory note.

Fisher had in fact slipped unnoticed into Westminster Abbey, for the second time that morning, and prayed. Then he hastened to the Charing Cross Hotel where he had booked a room, intending to hole up there until the night sleeper left for Glasgow, and into the comforting arms of Nina, Duchess of Hamilton, at Dungaval.

But he was not after all to take this train journey, not yet anyway. Bonham Carter tracked him down and delivered the note from Asquith like a bailiff with a summons. Fisher most reluctantly emerged from his retreat and went down Whitehall to 10 Downing Street. It was now the afternoon and the Prime Minister was at the wedding. Fisher decided to await Asquith's return. He was rewarded by the unexpected sight of Lloyd George. They sat down like two patients in a dentist's waiting-room.

Fisher poured out his heart to him. This time Lloyd George believed he would resign. 'His curiously Oriental features were more than ever those of a graven image in an Eastern temple, with a sinister frown.' Lloyd George pleaded with him not to resign and then became firm, pointing out that he had spoken no words at War Councils against the expedition – 'not one word of protest'. Fisher answered that nothing would induce him to stay, he had 'made up his mind to take no further part in the Dardanelles "foolishness"'.

Asquith now returned, still in frock-coat and grey top hat, from the wedding reception. Neither Churchill nor he had emulated the King in abstaining from drink for the duration of the war. Fisher repeated his complaints and reiterated his intention to resign forthwith and leave for Scotland. Deaf to all pleas from Asquith, except to remain in London for the weekend, he left, again telling no one where he was going.

Asquith now called Churchill back to Downing Street and they discussed the crisis at some length. They both knew that if Fisher did not relent the Government might fall. On the previous day *The Times* had headlined the fact that a British attack in France had been checked for lack of shells. The news from the Dardanelles was grim, too, and if Fisher resigned as an opponent of Churchill's latest adventure (as it would be seen by Churchill's enemies), this would further discredit the First Lord. Churchill was also held responsible by many of his wilder opponents for the sinking of the *Lusitania* and the multiplying losses from U-boats.

The two men agreed that a last appeal in writing must be made to the Admiral, and Churchill used all his experience, skill and guile in the composition of a long letter intended to bring Fisher back.

My dear Fisher,

The only thing to think of now is what is best for the country and for the brave men who are fighting. Anything which does injury to those interests will be vy harshly judged by history on whose stage we now are.

I do not understand what is the specific cause wh has led you to resign. If I did I might cure it. When we parted last night I thought we were in agreement . . .

In order to bring you back to the Admiralty I took my political life in my hands with the King & the Prime Minister – as you know well. You then promised to stand by me and see me through. If you now go at this bad moment and thereby let loose upon me the spite and malice of those who are your enemies even more than they are mine it will be a melancholy ending to our six months of successful war and administration . . .

Though I shall stand to my post until relieved, it will be a vy great grief to me to part from you : and our rupture will be profoundly injurious to every public interest.

Yours ever
W

This new plea fell on deaf ears. Fisher did not receive Churchill's letter until late on Saturday evening. He replied the next day, Sunday, reiterating that he had been opposed to the Dardanelles from the start, and that it was the revision of the agreed figures for reinforcements Churchill had made overnight that had finally decided him to resign.

YOU ARE BENT ON FORCING THE DARDANELLES AND NOTHING WILL TURN YOU FROM IT – NOTHING. I know you so well ! . . . *You will remain*. I SHALL GO. It is better so. Your splendid stand on my behalf with the King and the Prime Minister I can NEVER forget, and you took your political life in your hands and I really have worked very hard for you in return – *my utmost* . . .

As the word spread beyond the confines of Whitehall and the Cabinet, the appeals to Fisher to stay gathered volume. McKenna was as dismayed as Lloyd George and Hankey. The King, who had done his best to keep Fisher out of the Admiralty, now let it be known that he thought his resignation 'at such a moment is bound to have a deplorable, if not a disastrous effect upon the public . . .' Fisher's dear friend Queen Alexandra wrote, '*Stick* to your post like *Nelson* ! The Nation and we all have full confidence in you and *I* and they will not suffer you to go. You are the Nation's hope and we trust you !'

The Liberal press deplored Fisher's threatened departure. The Conservative press used it as a spearhead to a sustained new attack on Churchill – 'Lord Fisher or Mr Churchill ? Expert or amateur ?'

That weekend Churchill planned his own policy for survival and counter attack. First he investigated how he stood within the Admiralty. After Fisher himself, 'Tug' Wilson represented the solid virtues of a great admiral in the eyes of the public. Would he resign with his chief, Churchill asked? Wilson said he would not. Would he be prepared to act as First Sea Lord? The old Admiral, who had been peremptorily dismissed by Churchill before the war, dutifully said that he would. The other Sea Lords confirmed that they would remain. Churchill began to feel that he might survive after all, and that by Monday he would be able to inform the House of Commons that the crisis within the Admiralty was already over – a weekend squib.

On Sunday Churchill drove out of London to see Asquith and told him that Fisher's resignation appeared final, and that his own resignation was immediately forthcoming if Asquith wished to make a change. Asquith said he did not wish that, 'but can you get a Board?' Churchill told him that he could and that Wilson was willing to take Fisher's place. That evening of Sunday 16 May Asquith, through his personal misery, still felt that he might be able to hold things together. Churchill, with the Prime Minister behind him, was increasingly confident as he drove himself back to London that he would not be forced out.

Neither of these statesmen, for all their joint wisdom, canniness and experience, took full account of the nation's reaction to Fisher's resignation and to the nation's judgement on the man who had brought it about. No matter where the truth lay, up and down the land Churchill was seen as the too-clever-by-half politician who put personal ambition before everything and was prepared to cast adrift a loyal and selfless admiral – 'worth ten tuppeny politicians' – for his own ends. It was an unpleasant and deadly image which was given detail and warm encouragement by the newspapers, which were unanimous in their appeal: 'LORD FISHER MUST NOT GO' cried the *Globe*. *The Times*, the *Daily Telegraph*, the *Daily Express* and the *Army and Navy Gazette* all advocated promoting Fisher to First Lord in place of Churchill.

Bigger changes than this were behind political moves in and around the Palace of Westminster many hours before these press attacks appeared. By the early morning of Monday 17 May Churchill had completed writing his speech defending his action and claiming that all was well again at the Admiralty, with a strong and admired officer as professional head of the navy. At the same time, Andrew Bonar Law, the Conservative leader in the House of Commons, called on Lloyd George at the Treasury to ask if it was true that Fisher had resigned. On receiving confirmation, Bonar Law regretted that he did not think he would be able to stem the discontent within his party any longer, but that the Conservative Party recognized the vital importance of avoiding any split within the nation. He also made his party's position clear on the question of Churchill continuing at the Admiralty. If he remained, they would force a parliamentary challenge.

Bonar Law did not have to spell out his message any more clearly than this. Lloyd George hastened to Downing Street. Asquith was equally quick to take the hint. Churchill would have to go, said Lloyd George, and Asquith must broaden the Government – that is to say, form a Coalition Government with the Opposition. Flattened by personal grief, there was no fire left in the Prime Minister and he capitulated immediately. The reason for the speed of this surrender was not understood by Lloyd George, nor later by Churchill. No one knew except Venetia Stanley, to whom he addressed a letter the moment Lloyd George had left Number 10:

one of the most hellish bits of these most hellish days was that you alone of all the world – to whom I have always gone in every moment of trial & trouble, & from whom I have always come back solaced and healed and inspired – were the only person who could do nothing & from whom I could ask nothing. To my dying day, that will be the most bitter memory of my life . . .

It was indeed a day of bitter memories and feverish activity. Churchill went to the House, the list of members of his new Board of Admiralty in his pocket with his speech, his heart high as always before a big occasion. He broke off to have a quick word with Lloyd George, who told him that Fisher's resignation, together with disclosures about the shell shortage, had created a crisis which could be resolved only by the formation of a new Government. He did not divulge the fact that he and Asquith recognized that this new Government could not include Churchill any longer at the Admiralty. Churchill expressed himself in favour of that development but hoped innocently that 'it might be deferred until my Board is reconstituted and in the saddle at the Admiralty'.

Churchill next called on Asquith and showed him his new proposed Board of Admiralty, headed by Wilson. 'No, this will not do,' Asquith responded. 'I have decided to form a national Government by a coalition.' A 'very much larger reconstruction will be required'.

Churchill's suspicions were growing as the Prime Minister spoke. Then Asquith asked: 'What are we going to do with you?'

Churchill knew now, with terrible certainty, that it was the end. Asquith continued: 'Would you like to take office in the new Government, or would you prefer a command in France?'

Churchill had no time to reply before Lloyd George came in; and, like an admiral offering a dreadnought captain an obsolete torpedo boat, suggested to Asquith, 'Why don't you send him to the Colonial Office?'

Churchill barely had time to refuse this offer before another figure stepped into the room. The interruption was excusable this time. A secretary said to Churchill, 'Masterton-Smith is on the telephone, sir. Very important news ... has just come in. You must come back to the Admiralty at once.'

It took Churchill five minutes to reach the Admiralty. There he learned the news for which he had been awaiting since 4 August 1914. As if scenting the crisis and confusion in London, the whole German Fleet was out; and a single intercepted message, as brief as it was dramatic, revealed its plans: 'Intend to attack by day.'

It was a relief to have something to do, and something a great deal more important and more appetizing than the activities at the House of Commons. For the rest of the day, instead of justifying the past work of the navy and the Admiralty, Churchill busied himself with the important work of contriving the Fleet's dispositions to meet every future battle contingency, concluding with a message to Jellicoe: 'It is not impossible that to-morrow may be The Day. All good fortune attend you.'

But it was not quite the end of Churchill's day. Late in the evening the press of politics was felt again when a red box arrived from Asquith with a message confirming that he was forming a Coalition Government and requesting Churchill and all other ministers to hand in their resignation. Churchill did so, indicating that he would be prepared to accept, 'assuming it was thought fitting' and if he was *offered* it, a military department, but none other – that is, the War Office to replace Kitchener, or the Admiralty again.

'Having despatched this, I went to bed. In the morning I had prepared for a Parliamentary ordeal of the most searching character,' Churchill wrote of this day, 'in the afternoon for a political crisis fatal to myself; in the evening for the supreme battle on the sea. For one day it was enough.'

Enough. Enough for Winston Churchill, in spite of a personal political disaster, but still buoyed up by the expectation of a new Battle of Trafalgar on the morrow. Enough for Fisher, bitter, enraged, but still plotting in his room at the Charing Cross Hotel. Enough for broken-hearted Asquith going through the motions of forming a new government like an automaton.

Those who felt a sense of imminent fulfilment that night of 17 May, experiencing the sharp tang of adrenaline and that unique strain of excitement which only a warrior experiences before battle, were the commanders and the men of the battleships and battle-cruisers, the whippy light cruisers of men like Commodores Reginald Tyrwhitt and William Goodenough, and the young bloods of the black destroyers pounding through the darkness towards their destiny. Theirs was the reality of war, far distant from the squalid manoeuvrings of the Westminster mandarins.

In Whitehall and London's political homes, men slept uneasily, their minds restlessly concerned with the political upheavals and manipulations of the next day, and how, above all, that day would affect them and their future status and power. They were unaware of those hurrying men o'war and their crews who slept not at all.

A great victory in the North Sea would have saved Churchill. But as the signals arrived at the Admiralty in the early hours of 18 May indicating that the Germans were on their way home again and that there would be no new Battle of Trafalgar, Churchill made the decision to fight his own battle. For him there would be no tame retreat on this Whitehall battlefield. Until Asquith formally accepted his resignation, he remained First Lord, with a chance of holding on. Fisher's behaviour – 'Lord Fisher madder than ever,' Hankey commented – gave Churchill some additional strength. Max Aitken, proprietor of the *Daily Express* and later Lord Beaverbrook, recalled a conversation at Admiralty House on the evening of 18 May which showed Churchill's determination to remain as First Lord. 'He was clinging to the desire of retaining the Admiralty as if the salvation of England depended on it.'

For a few hours Churchill misguidedly entertained the idea that the Conservatives might save him and, disregarding Fisher's much quoted adage 'Never explain!!!', made contact with Bonar Law. Two of the greatest disasters of his wartime period of office for which he was held to blame by the Conservatives were the sinking of the *Aboukir*, *Hogue* and *Cressy*, and the Coronel defeat. Recovering from the Admiralty files the papers covering these two events, he sent them with a letter to Bonar Law because, as he wrote, there was a 'good prospect of our becoming colleagues'. 'You must not suppose', he concluded his letter, 'that in sending you these I want to claim all the credit or avoid the blame, only hitherto the principle has been that the blame only came to me.'

Next, Churchill drafted a long public statement defending his Dardanelles policy and actions. On 19 May he took it round to show the Foreign Secretary, Lord Grey, and Lloyd George, who begged him not to publish it because it would reveal all too starkly how bad things were if they required such vehement justification. According to Lloyd George's mistress and secretary, Frances Stevenson, Churchill lost his temper at this rebuff and accused Lloyd George of not caring if he was 'trampled under foot by my enemies. You don't care for my personal reputation.' To which Lloyd George agreed. 'I don't care for my own at the present moment. The only thing I care about now is that we win in this war.' But this is highly suspect evidence, published in Frances Stevenson's diary, which shows heavy prejudice against Churchill and, naturally, in favour of her paramour.

According to a more reliable source, however, Churchill did in desperation turn once again to his old partner before Fisher finally left for Scotland. Hankey reported that Churchill offered Fisher a seat in the Cabinet if he would withdraw his resignation and return as First Sea Lord. 'I rejected the 30 pieces of silver to betray my country,' Fisher told McKenna sanctimoniously.

On that same evening, 19 May, Arthur Wilson wrote to Asquith to inform him that, 'in view of the reports in the papers this morning as to the probable reconstruction of the Government', he was not prepared 'to undertake the duties [of First Sea Lord] under any new First Lord'. For Churchill, who learned of this letter through some undisclosed source, this was the first sign of light in the darkness into which he had been plunged, and he wrote to Asquith the following morning. Not only would Wilson stay; he would stay with no one else but Churchill. 'This is the greatest compliment I have ever been paid,' ran the next desperate appeal. 'The three Naval Lords are also ready to serve under me. They take a vy serious view of Lord Fisher's desertion of his post in time of war ...' Asquith had not yet learned of Churchill's attempt on the previous day to reinstate the admiral Churchill was now calling a deserter.

Asquith received another letter that morning, 20 May, about Churchill's future, this one from Clementine, the fierce, loyal letter of a loving, admiring wife who feels passionately about the injustices inflicted upon her husband. 'There is no man in the country who possesses equal knowledge capacity & vigour .... Why do you part with Winston? ... Is not the reason expediency .... If you throw Winston overboard you will be committing an act of weakness ...' Asquith did not trouble to answer, succinctly referring to the letter as having been written by 'a maniac'.

Churchill was floundering now, and he knew that no one of influence would come to his support. On the contrary, Asquith received many more letters besides Clementine's, but hers was the only one supporting Churchill; the rest demanded his dismissal.

Still Churchill struggled – a meeting with Bonar Law, whom Churchill knew to be no friend but who was immensely influential, followed by a long letter. Next a long letter to Asquith – 'It is no clinging to office or to this particular office, or my own interest or advancement wh moves me . . .' This letter was devoted mainly to the Dardanelles and to the risk of German U-boat attack on the ships there, something which only days earlier, on hearing rumours through the Russians of German U-boats' imminent arrival off the Dardanelles, he had described as 'incredible'. 'If the Admiralty were in uninstructed or unfriendly hands,' he feared, the whole Dardanelles operation might be abandoned, '& then on my head for all time wd be the blood of the 30,000 brave men who have fallen, killed or wounded or sunk in deep water. My responsibility is terrible. But I know I cd sustain it . . .'

In a postscript he asked if he might see Asquith. But like Churchill's last message to Admiral Cradock, he was 'already talking to the void'. All he had in response was a letter which at last convinced him that the fight was over. 'You must take it as settled that you are not to remain at the Admiralty.' A few hours later, like a stab wound after the *coup de grâce*, there arrived a letter from Bonar Law which made clear there would be no support from that quarter either.

On 21 May, just one week after the advent of the crisis, Churchill was finally out of office. He had said he would be prepared to take any post, however lowly, but only the Chancellorship of the Duchy of Lancaster came his way, a sinecure for 'distinguished politicians who had reached the first stages of unmistakable decrepitude', as Lloyd George venomously put it.

There was worse to come. Almost all the newspapers expressed relief and there was scarcely a good word about his record, let alone appreciation for what he had done in three and a half years. Almost alone, J.L.Garvin, the editor of the *Observer*, offered a morsel of cheer. 'He is young. He has lion-hearted courage. No number of enemies can fight down his ability and force. His hour of triumph will come.'

The navy, too, expressed its heartfelt relief from almost every quarter and every rank. Beatty, whose cause and career had been so strongly supported by Churchill, wrote that 'the Navy breathes freer now it is rid of the succubus Winston'. Vice-Admiral the Hon. Sir Stanley Colville, a past naval ADC to the King's father, wrote to George v, 'He was, we all consider, a danger to the Empire.' Jellicoe wrote that he had for long 'thoroughly distrusted Mr Churchill because he consistently arrogated to himself technical knowledge which, with all his brilliant qualities, I knew he did not possess'. Writing in general terms of the navy's reaction to Churchill's resignation, *The Times* naval correspondent believed that 'the news that Mr Churchill is leaving the Admiralty has been received with a feeling of relief in the Service, both afloat and ashore'.

Not content to see him go there still remained poisoners to administer vitriol to the dead, among them Frances Stevenson who even let it be known that the ever-loyal Masterton-Smith had said that Churchill was 'most dangerous' at the Admiralty. Hankey knew otherwise and recorded that Masterton-Smith missed him 'owing to his great driving force & capacity for work'. As an antidote to some of the more lethal poison, Garvin expressed his outrage that Churchill 'should have been malignantly and ungenerously attacked and made the scapegoat for all [mistakes and losses] is an injustice which must rouse the blood of any man with a spark of the sense of justice . . .'

Of his two closest military colleagues, Fisher from his Scottish eyrie wrote to his wife that he was '*not going to say one single word* or answer any speeches or letters on the subject of Churchill, his dismissal and his own resignation'. He wrote similarly to Jellicoe and others whom he then in the following weeks plagued with his usual excited condemnations of almost everyone in paranoid outbursts – '1 believe Bonar Law and McKenna are with me, but none else !' To George v, whose antagonism he seems to have forgotten, he addressed several letters of self-justification. And to Bonar Law he complained that 'W.C. is a bigger danger than the Germans by a long way in what is just now imminent in the Dardanelles'.

Lord Kitchener, exuding dignity and consciousness of the forgiving spirit he was demonstrating, called at the Admiralty to deliver the last rites. 'I had the honour of receiving a visit of ceremony from Lord Kitchener,' wrote Churchill with a touch of irony. '. . . He asked what I was going to do. I said I had no idea ; nothing was settled. He spoke very kindly of our work together . . . . As he got up to go he turned and said, in the impressive and almost majestic manner which was natural to him. "Well, there is one thing they cannot take from you. The Fleet was ready." After that he was gone.'

Churchill believed at the time that if Asquith had been prepared to make a stand he could have fought off demands for a coalition and voluntarily accepted the need for one later, incidentally keeping Churchill at the Admiralty. He still had no knowledge of the emotional pressure under which the Prime Minister was suffering. Later he wrote :

I am confident that had the Prime Minister, instead of submitting to the demand of the Chancellor of the Exchequer [Lloyd George] to form a Coalition Government, laid the broad outlines of his case, both naval and military, before both Houses of Parliament in Secret Session, he and the policy he was committed to would have been supported by large majorities . . . . I am sure I could have vindicated the Admiralty policy . . . . The Prime Minister's personal share in this event was a tremendous fact. I am certain that had he fought, he would have won ; and had he won, he could then with dignity and with real authority have invited the Opposition to come not to his rescue but to his aid . . .

Although to some extent rehabilitated, at least in his own mind, by the findings of the Dardanelles Commission of 1916–17, Churchill never ceased to believe that he was made the scapegoat for the military failure of the Dardanelles Expedition, which he had begun so lightly as a result of a paragraph in a memorandum read out of context.

As Chancellor of the Duchy of Lancaster he was permitted to sit on the War Council but he had no executive powers whatever, and the deprival, after so many years in office and so much promise of greatness, was almost beyond bearing; although he wrote of his first reaction: 'The more serious physical wounds are often surprisingly endurable at the moment they are received. There is an interval of uncertain length before sensation is renewed. The shock numbs but does not paralyse; the wound bleeds but does not smart. So it is also with the great reverses and losses of life.'

Churchill's old friend Wilfrid Blunt found him 'deeply embittered' and considered that if it had not been for Clementine's support 'he might have gone mad'. Churchill was distracting his mind with painting a portrait when Blunt arrived, and broke off to speak to him. Blunt recalled his saying, '"There is more blood than paint on these hands", showing his paint-smeared fingers with a queer little tragic gesture. "All those thousands of men killed. We thought it would be a little job, and so it might have been if it had been begun in the right way . . ."'

For Clementine the pain was instant and quite unendurable. Cynthia Asquith, lunching at the Admiralty before the Churchills moved out, found her alone for a moment. 'She looks very sad, poor thing.' Edwin Montagu reported to his fiancée, Venetia Stanley, that he found her 'so miserable and crying all the time'. Later, he wrote to Clementine:

My dear Mrs Winston,
My heart bled to see you so unhappy and I came back from your house to write a line in the hope of atoning for my lack of capacity to express myself verbally.

It is a hard time and it is true that Winston has suffered a blow to prestige, reputation and happiness which counts above all . . .

But it is also indisputably true that Winston is far too great to be more than pulled up for a period. His courage is enormous, his genius understood even by his enemies and I am as confident that he will rise again as I am that the sun will rise tomorrow . . .

Be as miserable as you must about the present; have no misgivings as to the future . . .

Yrs ever to command
Edwin S. Montagu

Many years later Clementine told Churchill's biographer: 'The Dardanelles haunted him for the rest of his life. He always believed in it. When he left the Admiralty he thought he was finished . . . . I thought he would never get over the Dardanelles; I thought he would die of grief.' Churchill's private secretary, Eddie Marsh, said that the blow to Churchill was 'a horrible wound and mutilation . . . it's like Beethoven deaf'.

Churchill's quiet dignity and the brave face he presented to the outside world gained him great credit, even among his enemies. However unjustly he felt he had been treated, however deep his conviction that if he had remained he could have done great things to help bring the war to a conclusion, and however bitterly he felt he had been let down by his friends and treacherously dealt with by his enemies and supposed friends like Asquith and Lloyd George, he made no public word of complaint.

Churchill was proud of his youthfulness. But in the final judgement, his youth combined with his zeal and intolerance and impatience, his consuming admiration for his own instinct for war, his unusual blend of romanticism and ruthlessness, told against him fatally. At forty years of age he had not yet tamed his dictatorial manner of commanding a department – it had been worse still at the Home Office but there was not, by an infinite margin, so much at stake there. Whatever he did for the Royal Navy in those months of peace when he worked so hard and against such odds to prepare it for war, the overall results of his performance in time of war were more baleful than beneficial.

Certainly the ineptitude of the Naval War Staff was a contribution on a massive scale to the failures and disasters at sea, and the performance of a number of admirals at sea left a great deal to be desired, too. But while Churchill justly takes the credit for creating a Staff against the sternest opposition, it was he, more than any of his less power-assuming predecessors, who must be charged with selecting or retaining these incompetent men.

The soldier and the statesmen still had much to learn in 1915. As Richmond summed him up with his usual sharpness, after Churchill had left the Admiralty: 'Undisciplined in mind, Churchill was not a success; he had studied war, but not sea war.' But in what Churchill liked to call 'the great sweep of history', the trials he underwent and the lessons he learned in those apprentice ten months of war in 1914–15 were to pay incalculable dividends to the greatest Briton of the century in the fifty-seven months of war from 1939 to 1945.

The shrewd, perceptive wife of the Prime Minister confided to her diary a sparkling thumbnail sketch of Churchill in this brief wartime period when he was head of the Admiralty:

What is it that gives Winston his preeminence? [asked Margot Asquith.] It certainly is not his mind. I said long ago and with truth Winston has a noisy mind.

Certainly not his judgement – he is constantly very wrong indeed (he was strikingly wrong when he opposed McKenna's naval programme in 1909 and roughly speaking he is always wrong in his judgement about people). It is of course his courage and colour – his amazing mixture of industry and enterprise. He can and does always – all ways put himself in the pool. He never shirks, hedges, or protects himself – though he thinks of himself perpetually. He takes huge risks. He is at his·very best just now; when others are shrivelled with grief – apprehensive, silent, irascible and self-conscious morally; Winston is intrepid, valorous, passionately keen and sympathetic, longing to be in the trenches – dreaming of war, big, buoyant, happy, even. It is very extraordinary, he is a born soldier.

Churchill resigned his sinecure appointment in November 1915. 'My regiment is awaiting me,' he had said; and so it was. After training with the Grenadier Guards, the 'born soldier' took over command of the 6th Battalion, Royal Scots Fusiliers.

As to the fate of the other leading figures of the May 1915 crisis, sad to relate it is the professional sailor Fisher who comes out of it worst, although in mitigation it can be said 'while the state of his mind was disturbed'. Having made his gesture of resignation so resolutely, he behaved without dignity, honour or good sense. On learning from Crease that the German Fleet was out, he refused to return to the Admiralty, claiming that his subordinates could manage quite well without him. Those who learned of this dereliction turned sharply against him in consequence. Now, far from ordering him to return to his post, Asquith said that he ought to be shot for desertion. George v took a similar line, satisfied only that he had been proved right about the Admiral. The Board of Admiralty was equally shocked and made it clear that, if he came back, they would leave in a body.

Unaware of the outrage he had caused, Fisher gained sudden confidence and comfort from the fall of the Government and the simultaneous appeals by the newspapers that HE MUST NOT GO. In a fit of confused megalomania and misjudgement he issued an ultimatum to Asquith giving him the terms upon which he would be prepared to return. These would make him a complete admiralissimo, dictator of the navy in all departments. The First Lord (not Churchill or Balfour) would stick to policy and parliamentary procedure and nothing else. When he heard, Asquith told the King that Fisher 'indicated signs of mental aberration'. That was about the best that could be said about this once mighty and magnificent naval officer who had done so much for the service during his lifetime.

Fisher made his belated journey to the Duchess of Hamilton in Scotland and little was heard of him for a while. But such was the power of his personality and the past admiration he had enjoyed that there were efforts to resuscitate him as First Sea Lord, which he did everything to encourage, and he did serve on a Board of Inventions without notable effect. He died, with the Duchess whispering a prayer in his ear, on 10 July 1920. His unhappy wife Kitty had died two years earlier.

Asquith survived as Prime Minister until 7 December 1916, when he was superseded by Lloyd George as Prime Minister in an attempt to bring more drive into the war effort. Balfour took Churchill's place at the Admiralty and limited himself to the more traditional role of a First Lord. His ineffectual regime was brought to an end shortly before that of Asquith. Jackson took over as First Sea Lord, until Jellicoe left the Fleet at the end of 1916. Kitchener, the great survivor, retained the public's (but not the Government's) esteem to his end and created Britain's first great continental army of recent times. He was never a friend of the navy and, ironically, met his end on board HMS *Hampshire* when it was sunk *en route* to Russia on 5 June 1916.

There is little that makes attractive reading following Churchill's departure from the Admiralty. The shell scandal, which jointly with Fisher's resignation had brought down Asquith's Government, continued for many weeks and led to many more thousands of unnecessary deaths. It was eventually resolved under the control of Lloyd George as Minister of Munitions. The Dardanelles campaign was equally expensive in casualties – 252,000 in all – and absorbed ever more troops and material of all kinds, including naval vessels from Fisher's 'decisive theatre', before it finally petered out with the evacuation of the Gallipoli peninsula at the end of the year.

Futile and extravagant trench warfare continued into infinity, or so it seemed to the participants on both sides of the barbed wire. U-boat warfare was intensified until the German dream of starving Britain into submission came near to fulfilment. Nothing much changed until the Americans came into the war two years later, and then only slowly. The war ceased with the moral and military disintegration of Germany, brought about by the drain of manpower and lack of food. If any one branch of arms was responsible for destroying the Teutonic imperial dreams of the Kaiser and his Prussian military, it was the Royal Navy, which with its unbreakable blockade in the end squeezed the life and spirit out of the Central Powers. No major battle was sought by the

High Seas Fleet, and when by chance it met the Grand Fleet head on, it was concerned only with escape, as had the German admirals at the Falklands, the Dogger Bank and in the Mediterranean. The fact that it sank some British ships before disappearing into the mist and dusk at Jutland was of no strategical consequence whatever. The fifty-one-month-long Great War was the Royal Navy's greatest victory in its history.

7
'Disentangled from the ruins . . .'

For a man who was a soldier to his fingertips, as distant from fear as the Western Front trenches from Whitehall, it is no surprise that Churchill acquitted himself with élan and success as a battalion commander when he left politics in December 1915. His example and dedication, his intelligence and courage, were admired by officers and men, and his superiors. He shared all their dangers, was several times close to death, supported the wounded, wrote letters of sympathy to the next of kin of those who died. 'He would often go into no-man's-land,' one of his lieutenants recalled. 'It was a nerve-racking experience to go with him . . . . He never fell when a shell went off; he never ducked when a bullet went past with its loud crack.'

If Churchill had stuck to soldiering after Omdurman he would by 1916 have been promoted to very high command with strong influence on the way the war should be fought. As it was, this period in France and Belgium served only to underline in his mind the futility and waste of trench warfare and led him to regret ever more bitterly the unreliability of Kitchener and the uneven support the Asquith Government had given to the Dardanelles Expedition.

In all Churchill's early life no event more clearly reveals the dichotomy of his mind than his decision to return to politics in May 1916. And it was a typically quixotic turn of fate that, within a few days, the Royal Navy's greatest battle of the war took place off the coast of Jutland, and a few days more his arch-enemy, Herbert Kitchener, had drowned in an armoured cruiser off Scapa Flow.

Already by March 1916 the quarrelsome murmurs of Whitehall were sounding louder in Churchill's ears than the artillery barrages of Ploegsteert. He returned on leave for the Naval Estimates debate, savagely attacked the Admiralty for its supine passivity, and – to the astonishment of every listener – demanded the recall of Fisher. Balfour replied with a very much more effective and balanced counter attack. It was a bad new start in politics for Churchill, and when two months later he resigned from the army he was able to recognize perhaps for the first time how few were his friends and numerous his enemies. Throughout the country he was deeply distrusted; even if Asquith had wished to do so, he could not have offered Churchill even a junior post in 1916. The Dardanelles fiasco hung over his political career like a dark shadow. 'Whenever I open my mouth in Parliament,' he complained to Hankey on 5 June (a few hours before Kitchener drowned), 'someone shouts out that I am the man who let us in for the Dardanelles mistake, and the papers are perpetually repeating it. My usefulness in Parliament is entirely ruined until my responsibility is cleared.'

It was the lowest period in Churchill's political life so far. 'I remain inactive & useless on the edge of the whirlpool,' he wrote miserably to Archibald Sinclair, his old friend and second-in-command of the battalion. He knew that he could never be reinstated in political esteem until his public reputation had been cleared. A great part of his time and talents was therefore now devoted to the unedifying but necessary task of gathering evidence to justify his actions while at the Admiralty. This was eventually accomplished, but with only partial success, by pressing the Asquith Government, itself in a state of terminal sickness, to set up a Commission of Enquiry into the Dardanelles campaign. This prolonged and exhaustive investigation led finally to the Dardanelles Report, which was debated in the House of Commons on 20 March 1917. In his own speech Churchill was critical of many points but did concede that it was 'an instalment of fair play'. With Lloyd George now Prime Minister, Churchill was back in office, as Minister of Munitions, four months later.

The Dardanelles Commission's final report was not published until November 1919, twelve months after the war ended. Churchill was not singled out for blame, but it was not the total vindication he sought and which he believed he needed to ensure his political future. He therefore decided to write his own account of his years at the Admiralty in peace and war, at first confined to two volumes but subsequently enlarged to become a history of the entire First World War. He wanted to use the title *The Great Amphibian*; his American publishers, Scribners, wisely insisted upon *The World Crisis*.

Churchill went about the task as if it were a military operation, gathering a team of subordinates about him with their special tasks, while he orchestrated the whole work, eventually into seven volumes. Reading *The World Crisis* today, self-justification, even special pleading, intrudes too evidently and accuracy is too suspect in the chapters covering the sea war up to May 1915. A more subtle hand could have made out a stronger case more convincingly and less intrusively. As to the rest of the narrative, it takes the reader through the war years at a fine pace, with much rolling of drums and fluttering of banners. It may not be standard history, but it is a good, rich read.

*   *   *

Just how damaging the Dardanelles failure had proved to be for Churchill became evident again when his first peacetime appointment was announced in January 1919. Lloyd George had reformed the Coalition Government which had at last brought victory and peace in the previous November. The Conservatives were still unforgiving of Churchill and his old enemy, the *Morning Post*, commented: 'We have watched his brilliant and erratic course in the confident expectation that sooner or later he would make a mess of anything he undertook. Character is destiny; there is some tragic flaw in Mr Churchill which determines him on every occasion in the wrong course.... It is an appointment which makes us tremble for the future.'

The appointment was to have been to the Admiralty again, which Churchill had indicated to Lloyd George would be his choice, and would offer him the best opportunity for reinstating his reputation with the navy. Instead, the one-time lieutenant of the North-West Frontier and Omdurman and brigadier and battalion commander in the Royal Scots Fusiliers took Kitchener's one-time office as head of the army – Secretary of State for War, which also involved responsibility for the RAF as Secretary of State for Air. In this second role Churchill ensured that the RAF, which was not yet a year old, remained independent of the other two services. But even at the War Office, where he took in hand the enormous problem of demobilizing a restless and even mutinous army in the shortest possible time, and became disastrously involved in counter-revolutionary activities in Russia, he also made his influence felt at the Admiralty.

Churchill's strengthening of the independence of the RAF also led to the unsatisfactory dual control by the RAF and the navy of the navy's aviation. The Royal Naval Air Service, which had come into being during Churchill's period at the Admiralty before the war, had become the largest and most advanced in the world. As Japan had earlier come to Britain for guidance on building her navy, so the now powerful Imperial Japanese Navy created its own air arm in the mould of the RNAS, importing British naval aircraft and using British aircraft carrier experience. Now with RAF control of aircraft flying with the navy over the sea from shore bases, and from carriers, the Royal Navy's air arm operated more as a poor cousin of the RAF than as the flying branch of the Senior Service. Only the enthusiasm and dedication of a small body of aircrew sustained morale through the difficult years until 1937. Then, too late for another world war, Churchill changed his mind, and the paper he prepared on the future of the Naval Air Service advocated the return of total control to the navy. In terms of the effect on the navy of Churchill's brief tenure of the War Office – 1919–21 – his critics' fears were realized. Beatty also, as First Sea Lord, at first supported the Smuts Plan which effectively destroyed the RNAS, and was blamed by the navy for doing so. He, too, changed his mind too late.

At the same time as the navy's air arm was being weakened by this dual control, faith in the battleship's future was being confirmed; and in the long-drawn-out battleship versus bomber debate Churchill believed there was 'an overwhelming case for the capital ship'. Stephen Roskill has written:

He wanted to initiate building programmes of four [battleships] a year for four or five years – just as he had done with Germany in view as the probable enemy in 1912. This was surely a case where his previous experience and his sense of history misled him badly, since in 1920 the circumstances were quite different. No possible enemy except the USA was in view, and all Ministers and service chiefs regarded war with that country as 'unthinkable'.

All this nonsense of international battleship competition, mainly between Japan, the USA and Great Britain, was ended at the Washington Naval Conference of 1921–2. But Churchill's faith in the battleship as the ultimate weapon of sea power remained until, and after, he came back to the Admiralty in 1939.

But whatever the eventual outcome of the battleship versus bomber contest, Churchill in 1924 found himself involved in one of the political somersaults which had punctuated his political life for twenty years. After losing office, and his seat in Parliament, in 1922, he was re-elected on 30 October 1924 as a pro-Conservative, crossing the floor of the House for the second time. This one was a double-somersault, for to his delighted surprise the new Prime Minister, Stanley Baldwin, offered him the Treasury.

As Chancellor of the Exchequer, Churchill saw it as his business to turn round on the Royal Navy and clip not just its wings but its men o'war too. It was a replay of 1908–9, with the important difference that he was now not merely a supporter of the Treasury's economy moves against the navy, but was the Chancellor himself.

In studying possible economies, the first task of any Chancellor, Churchill at once stated that more money might have to be found for the RAF, that the army's expenditure was already lean enough, and that the Admiralty was behaving extravagantly, as it had in 1908 but with the difference that there was no possible enemy on the horizon let alone within range. Beatty wanted more ships, wanted to make Hong Kong into a submarine base and Singapore into a full-scale base for a Far Eastern Fleet in the event of war against Japan. In Churchill's judgement this was all rubbish. Overlooking his recent advocacy of

four battleships a year (only two in all were laid down and completed
between the wars), he prepared a long document in the form of a letter
to the Prime Minister on the folly of increasing naval expenditure. How
would a stronger navy be financed? It was impossible to borrow the
money; there would be nothing for the taxpayer, nothing for social
reform. And who was this enemy we were rearming against? Germany
was bankrupt and impotent, Russia bankrupt, impotent and in political
turmoil. The Americans were our cousins; and Japan? 'A war with
Japan!' Churchill exclaimed. 'But why should there be a war with
Japan? I do not believe there is the slightest chance of it in our lifetime.'

Churchill also introduced the Ten-Year Rule, which operated on the
comforting assumption that there would be no major war for ten years.
this was not altogether unreasonable in 1924; but then the Treasury
made it into a 'rolling' ten-year assumption, every new year marking
the start of a fresh decade of peace.

Throughout this struggle Churchill remained puzzled, and sometimes
outraged, by the Admiralty's constant harping on the danger from
Japan. Even his long familiarity with the Admiralty had not taught
him that a navy has to have a theoretical foe. 'The Navy always needed
an "enemy",' Peter Kemp has written. 'At the turn of the last century
it was Russia, then until 1904 it was France, and after 1904 Germany.
Pretty well the whole Navy accepted Germany as the "enemy" mainly
because there was no one else (one or two admirals put forward the
USA as a possible but no one took them seriously).'

When the announcement had been made of his appointment to the
Treasury, Beatty had written a letter of congratulation, to which
Churchill had replied gracefully – 'I am one of your greatest admirers.'
Beatty was, according to Churchill, 'an inheritor of the grand tradition
of Nelson'. If only, claimed Churchill, 'I could have guided events a
little better and a little longer, Jutland would have had a different ring
if the plans already formed in my mind after the Dogger Bank for
securing you the chief command had grown to their natural fruition'.
So it appeared that but for the Dardanelles fiasco and Churchill's resignation, Jellicoe would have lost his command, probably less than a
year after he had been appointed to it.

Clementine Churchill, who was always inclined to take a more jaun-
diced view of her husband's admirals, certainly did not revere the one-
time heroic battle-cruiser comander. By March 1925, with the first
contest with Beatty over the estimates warming up, she wrote to her
husband urging him to

stand up to the Admiralty. Don't be fascinated or flattered or cajoled by Beatty.
I assure you the Country doesn't care two pins about him. This may be very

unfair to our only War Hero, but it's a fact . . . . Beatty is a tight little screw & he will bargain with you & cheat you as tho' he were selling you a dud horse which is I fear what the Navy is.

For once Churchill did not require advice from his wife. He knew very well how to stand up to Beatty. and as a mature politician he knew, like any legal advocate, the importance of keeping the fight on a professional level and avoiding personalities. Churchill's admiration and affection for Beatty never wavered, even at the height of the struggle over the Naval Estimates in 1925 and 1926. As for Beatty, he told his wife, 'I have had some bitter struggles in the past, but never so bitter as this – although there is no bad feeling about it. Winston and I are very good friends.'

Because the Washington Treaty had ruled out the construction of battleships and battle-cruisers, in the 'naval race' of the 1920s and early 1930s cruisers were the contestants, and the size and numbers of these the main bone of contention between the Treasury represented by Churchill and the admirals represented by Beatty. In the final count the compromise solution left the Royal Navy with an insufficiency of all classes of warships but numbers a great deal higher than if Beatty had not struggled so hard and for so long.

David Beatty was succeeded as First Sea Lord by Admiral Sir Charles Madden, a less belligerent and implacable leader, in 1927. By now the fire had gone out of the battle, and only glowing embers remained when Churchill left office two years later with the fall of the Baldwin Government. Ten more years were to pass – 'the wilderness years' – before he again became an active figure in the affairs of the Royal Navy.

At nine o'clock on the morning of Sunday, 3 September 1939, the British Government under the premiership of Neville Chamberlain despatched an ultimatum to the German Government of Adolf Hitler. It demanded that German troops which had invaded Poland must halt or Britain would declare war. Hitler was given three hours to comply. He did not trouble to reply. Germany had embarked upon almost six years of conquest, pillage, corruption, tyranny, mass murder and destruction – and final retreat – in a war that was to become many times more destructive than her earlier attempt to conquer and impose her will upon Europe.

No one had done more than Churchill to warn the timorous and supine British Governments of Stanley Baldwin and Neville Chamberlain of the dangerous and evil intentions of Nazi Germany.

No one had appealed more strongly for measures to defend Britain and the British Empire from this second threat within a quarter of a century from German paranoia, greed and militarism. An increasing number of people had listened to Churchill's warnings, but less than a year earlier the nation was united in joy and relief when Chamberlain returned from the last of several critical meetings with Hitler and informed the world that it was to be 'peace in our time'.

During those intervening months when the last British illusions dissolved in the heat of German threats and the last voices calling for further appeasement were drowned by the tread of German jackboots into Czechoslovakia and Lithuania, Churchill was increasingly recognized as the one man to lead the nation if war came again. He had never experienced such popularity since his return from South Africa almost forty years earlier. But the hatred and suspicion within the established hierarchy of the Conservative Party were as ferocious as in 1915, and Neville Chamberlain withheld office from Churchill until he was forced to appoint him under the threat of a backbench revolt with the support of millions outside Parliament.

It was not until after the ultimatum to Germany had expired that the Prime Minister asked Churchill to call on him. The country was already at war, the sirens – falsely as it happened – warning of the first air raid had already sounded out over London, when Churchill was offered a seat in the War Cabinet and the office of First Lord of the Admiralty again. Now, at the age of sixty-four and just a quarter century since he had been forced out of office, Churchill was confident that there would be no repeating of history, except that the Germans would again be defeated. He also believed that he would before long displace as Prime Minister the nationally discredited, weak figure of Chamberlain. And then he would recover not only his own reputation after past defeats and years in the wilderness, but that of his father, too. Robert Boothby, one of Churchill's most influential supporters, believed that it was within Churchill's power 'to go to the House of Commons tomorrow and break him and take his [Chamberlain's] place'. And Leopold Amery, himself a one-time First Lord, wrote in his diary: 'I think I see Winston emerging as PM out of it all by the end of the year.'

Meanwhile, early that evening Churchill arrived at the Admiralty to take over from Lord Stanhope, as weak and ineffective a First Lord as McKenna had been. Nothing could have done the navy more good, nothing could have raised higher its spirit, than Churchill's return to power at the Admiralty. Guy Grantham, at the time a captain and naval assistant to the First Sea Lord, got early wind of the news. 'I managed to get the buzz into the Admiralty, which led to the signal

"Winston is back !"' he recalls. 'It made our day, a great relief to every-one. The news shot round the fleet, everyone was cock a'hoop.' 'There was immense relief when Churchill became First Lord,' an officer in the Intelligence Centre recalls. 'A do-er was going to take over. I think the top brass knew Churchill was going to get them hard at it, and they said, "Well, never mind – it's a good thing".'

As a traditionalist, with a touch of the superstitious in his make-up, Churchill wanted everything to be as it had been left in 1915. 'It was very inconvenient,' recalls Sir Clifford Jarrett, Private Secretary to the First Lord for most of the war.

He wanted all his old furniture back and his notorious lampshade. This was an enormous affair of green silk with butter muslin to diffuse the light, and a long fringe of beads, the whole thing faded and filthy. Eric Seal [Churchill's Principal Private Secretary] had to find and dig out all these objects. After much difficulty, by some miracle he found the lampshade in the vaults of the India Office.

Churchill felt more comfortable and at home when everything was just as it had been, the old octagonal table placed immediately under the lampshade. Even some of the faces about him were the same as in 1915, notably and most important of them the First Sea Lord, Admiral Sir Dudley Pound, who had once been on Fisher's staff.

More ominously, a great many of the ships were familiar, too. All but three of the fifteen operational capital ships had been under con-struction or completed in Churchill's earlier period as First Lord. Some of the cruisers and many of the destroyers dated back to the First World War. Only the aircraft carriers provided an entirely new configuration.

To counter the threat from the air, all men o'war were now equipped with many more anti-aircraft guns than in 1915, and the 4.5-inch high-angle gun had been widely introduced. The eight-barrel two-pounder pom-pom, the 'Chicago piano', was a much-vaunted weapon against aerial attack, and multi-barrel machine-guns and, more recently, the Oerlikon 20-mm cannon, gave great comfort to those facing air attack. More than that, they induced a sense of false security, much as the quick-firers of the late nineteenth century were regarded as the battle-ship's complete answer to the torpedo boat. 'An air attack upon British warships, armed and protected as they now are,' Churchill had written earlier that year, 'will not prevent full exercise of their superior sea power.'

The truth was that the Royal Navy might have only a modest-sized battle fleet compared with 1914, but it was still battleship-minded. The battleship was still regarded as the final arbiter of sea power, and five

new battleships were under construction to meet the new German construction of battleships, just as if history had stood still in 1914 and
the torpedo-carrying plane and the heavy bomber and dive bomber
had never been invented. Churchill did not question these dated beliefs ;
he shared them, and wrote of a proposed new battleship as being 'absolutely proof against air attack'.

Neither did Churchill conflict with received 'battleship' opinion in
the navy that the answer to the U-boat had been found in Asdic, an
echo-sounding device which could locate submarines when submerged.
Some peacetime exercises seemed to confirm its reliability and accuracy,
just as anti-aircraft fire against slow, steadily moving targets at a moder-
ate height appeared to confirm that the bomber was not the menace
the 'fanatics' claimed it was. It made the admirals happy.

Jellicoe would have understood, and no doubt admired, the rewritten
Fighting Instructions prepared for the Fleet in 1938. This document
'was written on the basis that the naval war would be little different
from 1914–18', the Staff Officer Plans remembers. 'The war at sea would
be fought with battleships in line of battle', Admiral Dudley Pound,
one of the authors, insisted, envisaging war with Japan.

In action there would be A, B, C, or D formation with a line of scouting
cruisers ahead and a single signalling cruiser between them and the battle fleet.
Pound's fellow author, Admiral Charles Forbes, reluctantly agreed. The only
feature of these instructions which would have puzzled Jellicoe was that they
were triple-paged. Because the authors were at loggerheads and could agree
about nothing else [Admiral Grantham continues today], every time a passage
was drafted by one the other would turn it down, and if one approved the
other automatically disapproved. In the end the only way to cope was to print
the instructions three pages to a page, the third page being the compromise
conclusions in red ink of Terence Back and myself.

But on the whole the admirals, who had mostly been lieutenants
or lieutenant-commanders in the previous war, were of a higher quality
than the previous generation: 'those pleasant, bluff old sea dogs with
no scientific training ; endowed with a certain amount of common sense
but with no conception of the practice or theory of strategy and tactics,
who had spent their lives floating round the world showing the flag,
and leaving behind them a most admirable impression of the nature
of the British gentleman', as Stephen King-Hall has described them.
The younger officers were drawn from a broader – but still not broad
enough – spectrum of the nation's classes. There was still too much
class distinction, complacency and philistinism. A clever brain was more
respected than in 1912, but not much more.

The gunnery officer still ruled and other weapons were regarded as of secondary importance. There was no fault to be found in the spirit of the Senior Service, however, and the failure to destroy the German High Seas Fleet in 1914–18 in no measure clouded the RN's confidence that it would always beat the Germans in a straight fight – or with odds against it for that matter.

One department in which the navy was very advanced was in radar, unknown in the American or Japanese navies at this time; but radar was regarded as so secret, and also with so much suspicion, that its existence, with all its novel and fundamental implications, was not recognized in the *Fighting Instructions*.

The first task of the navy was to escort the new British Expeditionary Force to France where it would take up its position in the French defensive line, just as in 1914. A blockade of Germany had to be reinstated, and German commerce raiders loose on the oceans had to be rounded up. Perhaps, then, Churchill had been right to surround himself with the same objects and equipment, for the tasks ahead were almost identical. 'A few feet behind me, as I sat in my old chair,' he wrote, 'was the wooden map-case I had had fixed in 1911, and inside it still remained the chart of the North Sea on which each day, in order to focus attention on the supreme objective, I had made the Naval Intelligence Branch record the movements and dispositions of the German High Seas Fleet.'

Confirmation of the new spirit that was to run through Admiralty affairs was evident on that first night of the war when Churchill convened a meeting of the Board and senior Admiralty officials at 12.30 a.m. The Board Room rapidly filled, and Churchill took his old seat at the head of the long table. He was clearly deeply moved by the occasion, and by the words of welcome uttered by Dudley Pound. Like the host toasting his guests at dinner, he cast his eyes from officer to officer in turn, studying each face critically. Then he told them what a pleasure and honour it was to be there. 'There will be many difficulties ahead but together we shall overcome them.' Then he adjourned the meeting – 'Gentlemen, to your tasks and duties.'

There was a strong element of *déjà vu* in the opening moves of the Second World War, too. Scapa Flow, as was soon to be tragically proved, was insecure against U-boat attack. The German Navy showed as few qualms as before in attacking merchantmen without warning and, within a few hours of Churchill's appointment, the liner *Athenia* was sunk with the loss of 112 lives, including twenty-eight Americans. The German mine again proved superior to the British mine and, being activated by a magnetic mechanism, proved for a while to be highly lethal and difficult to contend with. Paralleling the air raid on Cuxhaven in 1914, twenty-nine aircraft of RAF Bomber Command attacked German men o'war with equally unsatisfactory results.

Churchill wasted no more time than in 1914–15 in starting his 'search for the offensive'. No one believed more strongly than he did that when not attacking the enemy you are offering him victories by stealth. A revived Baltic Project was the first major naval offensive operation Churchill proposed, just as if the ghost of Fisher could not be laid. He even proposed bombardment monitors of shallow draught for the operation combined with attacks on the Kiel Canal. It was the control of the Baltic Sea upon which Churchill had his eyes, and thus the cutting off of the important Swedish iron-ore traffic with Germany, rather than the landing of troops on the Pomeranian coast. But if all naval operations in the Baltic, other than by submarine, qualified for the realms of fantasy in 1914–15, their fatal nature in 1939–40 was multiplied many times over.

'I cd never be responsible for a naval strategy wh excluded the offensive principle', Churchill wrote in a memorandum to Pound, 'and relegated us to keeping open lines of communication and maintaining the blockade.' 'The entry of the Baltic', he wrote a few days later, 'for instance would soon bring the [German warship] raiders home and give us measureless relief.'

A great deal of Admiralty time was employed on proving the impracticability of Churchill's wilder schemes. The suspicion and natural distaste he felt for anything that could be described as negative was as strong as ever and Admiralty staff, many of whom were equally imbued with the offensive spirit, found it depressing to have to spend so much time finding reasons for not supporting certain positive Churchillian offensive operations.

Dudley Pound was the first target for 'Winston's ideas' or 'Winston's notions' as they were also called. 'His ideas poured out in a torrent, almost all impractical,' says Sir Clifford Jarrett. 'The Naval Staff and the technical departments became practised in seeing that the impractical schemes were abandoned. That there were great contests over these "notions" is not true; if the other services were also concerned they nearly always supported the Admiralty's objections.' Admiral Grantham also observed with fascination these counter measures. 'Churchill would blow into Dudley Pound's room exclaiming, "I've got an idea. Now ..." If Pound did not agree he always said, "I've noted that and will look into it right away." Then when he had got onto paper all the evidence he needed he would show it to Churchill.' That was usually the end of that.

The institution of convoys at the height of the U-boat war in 1917, two years after Churchill had left the Admiralty, had undoubtedly saved the Allied cause. But Churchill, like Jellicoe though for different reasons, did not care for the principle of convoy, which he regarded, quite wrongly, as a defensive practice. Contingency planning long before the war had decreed the immediate introduction of convoys in time of war, however, and Churchill did not attempt to interfere with this life-saving operation. What he did attempt to bring about, however, was what he called a 'loosening up' of the convoy system with a higher degree of risk by employing smaller convoys in order to segregate the faster from the slower ships. He was much concerned at the slowing up of trade which the convoy system caused.

He also wanted to employ in the Western Approaches small groups of anti-U-boat vessels in sweeps over likely areas rather than concentrating them all on patrol escort work. It was the old story of his military imagination visualizing groups of fast men o'war seeking out the enemy – on the offensive not defensive. But logic and experience showed that there was not one chance in a thousand of finding U-boats in this haphazard way. In the real world of U-boat war you protected your convoys and waited for the wasps to come to the honey and then swatted them, preferably before they had dipped in their mouths, or failing that after they had given proof of their presence. In mixing his terminology when advocating these groups – 'independent flotillas working like a cavalry division' – he revealed the confusion in his mind between military and naval practice which he had not been able to throw off after all these years.

The folly of offensive sweeps was demonstrated in the first month of the war when two precious aircraft carriers with destroyers were detached from the Home Fleet for anti-U-boat operations in the Atlantic. The new carrier *Ark Royal* was narrowly missed, the older *Courageous* sunk. Then, up at Scapa Flow, another U-boat succeeded in penetrating the defences and sinking the battleship *Royal Oak* with the loss of a further 833 lives.

The toll of U-boat sinkings of merchantmen rose, too, although it was not until 1941–2 that they became serious, just as the build-up of losses in 1914–15 was relatively slow. The depredations of German surface raiders again caused much anxiety, and it seemed for a time as if the old pattern of ill luck was again dogging Churchill as First Lord.

The most threatening and elusive of these raiders was the *Graf Spee*, appropriately named after the German admiral who had been hunted all over the Pacific in 1914. This vessel was one of Germany's 'pocket battleships' built under the restriction of a 10,000-ton maximum imposed by the Versailles Treaty, although this figure was secretly increased to about 11,700 tons. These were cleverly designed compromise men o'war, tough, fast (26 knots), carrying 11-inch guns and fuel to give a range of more than 10,000 miles. They were equipped with radar, which came as a nasty shock to the Admiralty, and two spotting sea-planes which greatly extended the range of vision. By contrast with 1914, the Royal Navy had only three old battle-cruisers with the speed and gunfire to ensure the destruction of one of these pocket battleships.

The *Graf Spee* began her operations in the southern hemisphere tow-ards the end of September 1939 and sank merchantmen in the Indian Ocean and South Atlantic. Now, however, almost all merchantmen were equipped with radio, and her movements could be followed by the signals sent out by her victims before they were silenced.

By clever calculation and anticipation, a force of three cruisers under the command of Commodore Henry Harwood intercepted the *Graf Spee* off the River Plate. The *Graf Spee*'s shooting was exemplary, quite as good as the *Gneisenau*'s and *Scharnhorst*'s in 1914, and early and destructive hits on the biggest British cruiser, the *Exeter*, gave warning of another possible Coronel disaster. But Harwood manoeuvred his three smaller ships cleverly and scored so many hits on the *Graf Spee* that she took refuge in neutral Uruguay waters in Montevideo.

Before and during this action Churchill remained in a frustrated fever of inaction in the War Room, some of the time in his flowing dressing-gown emblazoned with dragons, longing to despatch a series of signals to direct the battle. 'Why isn't he sending any signals?' he kept demand-ing of Pound. In fact, Harwood's signals had to be sent in cipher to the Falkland Islands, relayed to Gibraltar, then again to Cleethorpes w/t and finally to the Admiralty. The news was coming in faster from NBC in America, which infuriated Churchill.

Harwood was in tactical command from the start, and demonstrated brilliantly how the Royal Navy could have run the *Goeben* to destruction in 1914. It was Falklands luck again for the First Lord. By deceiving the German captain into believing that an overwhelming British force was assembling to greet him if he left neutral waters, the *Graf Spee* was scuttled and the German captain shot himself. The nation rejoiced, and the cry 'Good old Winnie!' sounded throughout the land.

(A photograph of the *Graf Spee* before she was sunk, published in *Life* magazine, was the first intimation to the British that Germany had ship-borne radar, too. Churchill tried unsuccessfully to buy the wreck from the Uruguay authorities in order to learn about this radar and recover the ship's code machine.)

In spite of his numerous and time-consuming 'notions', Churchill attracted little of the obloquy he had suffered from within the navy in the First World War. He was, by contrast, far more mellow, far less abusive and overbearing; no less tolerant of inefficiency but more susceptible to reason. There was none of the harsh setting of junior against senior, and he was altogether more human to work with. Small differences from that earlier period mattered out of all proportion. For instance, there was no conflict of working hours with Pound as there had been with Fisher: Pound worked almost twenty-four hours a day anyway, or so it seemed to those who worked under him, and besides, Pound was sane and selfless. The regime in the Admiralty could not by any means be called mellow, but it could be called less abrasive. And it was certainly as vibrant as ever.

You have only to read Churchill's memoranda (or his 'prayers' as they were called because demands so often began 'Pray, let me have without delay . . .') of 1939–40 to observe the reflected change from the forty-year-old First Lord. Churchill early made clear, for example, that he now wanted his ideas (*he* never called them 'notions') to form the basis for a discussion and not be regarded as the final word. For instance: 'The First Lord submits these notes to his naval colleagues for consideration, *for criticism and correction*, and hopes to receive proposals for action in the sense desired.' He would not have written in those terms in 1912.

In his brief period in office, Churchill succeeded in instituting a number of reforms. The most important with the greatest long-term effect were in welfare matters and in fighting the still significant elements of class distinction which impaired efficiency. He proposed an improvement in the roster of destroyer crews, who endured the toughest conditions at sea, in order to give them more rest. He instituted better leisure facilities at the bleak anchorage of Scapa Flow, where he installed a theatre and cinema ship. He ferreted out inequalities in the methods of appointing cadets, learning, for example, that three young bright men had been rejected because they came from a humble background, one with, horror of horrors, 'a slight cockney accent'! 'But the whole intention of competitive examination is to open the career to ability, irrespective of class or fortune.' All three made useful officers.

The war for the Royal Navy from September until the onslaught of April–May 1940 was by no means a 'phoney war'. The navy was the only service which saw continuous activity, and arduous activity in the submarine and destroyer branches. This greatly strengthened Churchill's power and influence in the War Cabinet, which he exploited to the utmost, and which later led to his additional appointment as Chairman of the War Cabinet's Military Co-ordination Committee. He was certain that Germany, having settled the fate of Poland and divided that unfortunate state up with the equally rapacious Russians, would swing round and attempt to devour France, the Low Countries and Britain itself. He fretted for offensive action and at the same time recognized that none would come from France, which he believed to be corrupt, politically unstable and militarily weak and ineffectual. It was not only the unprecedented cold of the European winter of 1939–40 that had the French shivering; it was fear of provoking the Germans into taking action against them. For the same reason the French War Government opposed any signs of positivism in her ally. When Churchill proposed floating mines down the River Rhine in retaliation for German indiscriminate magnetic mining in British waters, the French opposed the plan for fear of reprisals, and continued to do so until April 1940, which Churchill rightly found contemptible.

Another mining offensive proposed by Churchill was to be in Norwegian territorial waters. The German war machine drew considerable supplies of Swedish iron ore through the Norwegian port of Narvik, deep inside the Arctic Circle, and thence by freighter hugging the serrated Norwegian coast. By forcing this traffic outside the Inner Leads within the chain of islands, Churchill planned to capture the ships and close that route completely. The War Cabinet did not share Churchill's sense of urgency on this matter and the project hung fire while varying degrees of nervousness were reflected in War Cabinet opinion, from fear of offending neutrals to fear of counter measures by Norway. 'Oh, surely it's not as important as all that!' was the received opinion in the Cabinet.

But Churchill insisted that with the cutting off of all German iron-ore supplies from Sweden through 1940, Germany would suffer a blow 'at her war-making capacity equal to a first-class victory in the field or from the air, and without any serious sacrifice of life'.

Minor victories scored with the British people a success rating out of all proportion through that long, cold, drear, anti-climactic winter; a German plane shot down, a reconnaissance by a party of a dozen or so troops towards the German Siegfried Line on the Western Front, made headline news. The *Graf Spee* victory had caused great joy and satisfaction. Now, in the third week of February 1940, Churchill provided another display of good old-fashioned cheeky gallantry so beloved of the British people.

The Germany naval tanker *Altmark*, which had worked in company with the *Graf Spee* and had taken on board captured British seamen, succeeded in reaching Norwegian waters *en route* for Germany. But she was spotted by British aircraft and, when anchored, approached by the British destroyer *Cossack*, under Captain Philip Vian, who had been informed of her suspected cargo. The Norwegians proved intractable and refused permission for a British search of the ship, claiming falsely that they had already done so and there were no British on board. When Vian pressed the point, he was threatened with destruction by the two Norwegian gunboats present. Vian signalled for instructions. Churchill took the matter into his own hands, and without reference to the War Cabinet drafted a signal in his best uncompromising 1914 style – 'You should board *Altmark*, liberate the prisoners and take possession of the ship . . . . If Norwegian torpedo-boat interferes you should warn her to stand off. If she fires upon you, you should not reply unless attack is serious, in which case you should defend yourself . . .'

When negotiations with the Norwegians broke down, and the officer in command refused to accompany Vian on board the *Altmark* to confirm what Vian now knew to be the truth, Vian took his ship alongside the *Altmark* and boarded her in true Nelsonian style, killing four Germans who resisted while the rest surrendered or fled ashore. Below the hatches were 299 Britons facing what they had regarded as certain confinement for the rest of the war.

The *Altmark* affair raised mountainous excitement. King George VI, who like his grandfather but not his father greatly admired Churchill, sent him a personal letter of congratulation. Churchill replied: 'It is a vy gt encouragement & gratification to me to receive Your Majesty's most gracious & kindly message of approval . . .'

Churchill was prepared to go much further than this in risking good relations with Norway, and Sweden too. In early March he returned to the attack over the question of mining Norwegian waters and, taking a more dramatic step forward, proposed landing a force at Narvik to occupy the port and the Swedish iron-ore fields a short distance away across the frontier. Chamberlain opposed the concept. 'If we took such action, we should completely alienate the sympathies of Norway and Sweden at the very moment when they are feeling a sense of relief from the danger of being involved in hostilities.' The equally craven Lord Halifax, Foreign Secretary, also expressed his shock at such a suggestion. This, Churchill suddenly realized, was worse than the Asquith–Grey line-up of 1915 before the Dardanelles. 'It is', pleaded Churchill, 'the only hope of securing the iron ore and of thus shortening the length of the war, and perhaps obviating the slaughter . . . on the Western Front.' Shades of the Dardanelles indeed!

Worse still, there was even serious talk of a truce with Germany among some political elements, especially in the Foreign Office. Both Halifax and his Under-Secretary of State, R. A. Butler, were muttering about the desirability of coming to terms with Germany. The voice of the National Peace Council, articulated through the mellifluous voices of theatrical dreamers like John Gielgud, Sybil Thorndike and George Bernard Shaw, was heard in the land. And if they later claimed that they could hardly know that the plans for a Nazi spring offensive, including the rape of half of Europe, were already settled, a glance at the German record since 1933 might have suggested that the 'peace in our time' of the Prime Minister a year earlier was doomed and that it was 'tyranny in our time' unless something was done.

What little that was done was done, needless to say, by Churchill during the critical month of March when stronger and stronger rumours filtered out of Europe of German plans to assault the Netherlands, Denmark and Norway. He finally received War Cabinet authority to lay the minefields, with a strong landing force ready to sail if the expedition aroused German counter measures. The date of the mining was fixed for 5 April. And then, like the voice of Kitchener echoing down the years, the word 'No!' sounded out – this time, inevitably, from the French War Cabinet, expressing terror of German reaction. Three days passed, days as critical for the Norwegian operation as the days between 22 February and 10 March in 1915 when the 29th Division was forbidden to sail for the eastern Mediterranean. Then on 8 April the minelaying was carried out, the minelayers being escorted by destroyers and the battle-cruiser *Renown*. The assault troopships were still in harbour when the Germans struck. They were too late, by three days.

Churchill has recounted how, 'On the evening of Friday April 5, the German Minister in Oslo invited distinguished guests, including members of the Government, to a filmshow at the Legation.' The film, continued Churchill, 'depicted the German conquest of Poland, and culminated in a crescendo of horror scenes during the German bombing of Warsaw. The caption read: "For this they could thank their English and French friends."'

The party, according to Churchill, 'broke up in silence and dismay'. And with good reason; for virtually the entire German Navy, accompanying numerous troop transports and supported by a substantial proportion of the German Air Force – the Luftwaffe – had either already left German ports or were making last preparations for the invasion and occupation of Denmark and Norway. On the morning of 8 April the Norwegian Government was busy drafting protests to Britain concerning the mining off their coast, which had been announced at 5 a.m. in a broadcast from London. Late on that same day, German warships were seen approaching Oslo. Already reports were arriving of German attacks on other Norwegian ports. The defence of the Norwegian capital rested on a single 1,600-ton minelayer armed with four 4.7-inch guns, a pair of diminutive minesweepers and some aged shore batteries. The resistance was stout, in the finest tradition of Norse gallantry. The German cruiser *Emden* was disabled, two destroyers held off, and the new powerful German heavy cruiser, *Blücher*, like her namesake in 1915, was sent to the bottom, together with members of the Gestapo and the German staff intended to administer the conquered nation. It was a bad start for the German Navy. Oslo was taken later by German troops landed by air and from shore landings close by.

Elsewhere up the Norwegian coast, German forces landed at and occupied Bergen, Stavanger, Kristiansund, Trondheim and, evading British naval forces, at Narvik. Churchill remained optimistic in the face of this news, confident in the overwhelming superiority of the Royal Navy and relishing the crippling damage British men o'war now had it in their power to inflict: the German Fleet out and scattered far from its bases. 'The German forces which had been landed', Churchill noted, 'were commitments for them, but potential prizes for us'; and he predicted that 'we will liquidate them in a week or two'.

The Deputy Chief of the Naval Staff, Admiral Sir Tom Philips, 'Winston's blue-eyed boy' as he was called, was equally optimistic. Philips was a battleship man with a quick mind and good judgement; and Pound, though more cautious and thoughtful about the whole business, also calculated that the navy stood to gain a series of scattered victories. The C-in-C Home Fleet, Admiral Sir Charles Forbes, was as vigilant, eager and self-confident as his subordinates. Nowhere, on land or at sea, did there appear to be a revisionist realist like Herbert Richmond who recognized the deadly danger from shore-based aircraft to a fleet with inadequate air cover and inadequate air power to strike back effectively.

First contacts between the adversaries were, however, ship-to-ship actions which appeared to substantiate British confidence and optimism, and certainly British gallantry. The small destroyer HMS *Glowworm* chanced upon the 12,000-ton modern German heavy cruiser *Hipper* and two enemy destroyers. By brilliant manoeuvring, the *Glowworm* attacked the destroyers and, when the *Hipper* appeared, concealed herself behind a smokescreen and then emerged to ram, the only means she had left to damage the massively more powerful vessel. The *Glowworm* tore a forty-foot hole in the armoured side of the cruiser, then blew up and sank. The details of this action were not know for five years when a handful of survivors were released from prison camps. Lieutenant-Commander Gerard Roope was awarded the VC posthumously.

The next action was almost as one-sided, when the fast, modern battle-cruisers, *Scharnhorst* and *Gneisenau*, were sighted by the old Fisher-inspired and lightly armoured British battle-cruiser *Renown* in appalling weather off Narvik. In a brisk, brief exchange of fire the *Renown* scored a hit which temporarily put out of action all the *Gneisenau*'s main

armament. The two German ships, in marked contrast to their predeces-
sors of the same name with odds on their side, fled to the north, the
Gneisenau receiving two more hits before disappearing in snow squalls.
Admiral Lütjens, it seemed, was no Admiral von Spee.

In Narvik fiord on 10 April the Royal Navy, in spite of being overall
far superior in numbers to the German Navy, was again unfortunate
in facing severe adverse odds. Captain B.A.W.Warburton-Lee with
five destroyers made a surprise raid on the German-held port, sank
two more-powerful German destroyers, damaged three more and sank
a number of transports. Then he in turn was overwhelmed by superior
numbers, lost his ship and his life in a desperate battle which earned
him the vc posthumously. Another British destroyer had to be beached
and two more were damaged.

In describing this engagement to the House of Commons the next
day, Churchill said, 'I do not think we ought to have a kind of mealy-
mouthed attitude towards these matters. We have embarked on this
war and we must take our blows.' He also used the occasion, recalling
Norway's anti-British behaviour over the *Altmark* and the constant
traffic in war-sustaining iron ore inside Norwegian waters since the war
began, to remind the House that 'It is not the slightest use blaming
the Allies for not being able to give substantial help and protection
to neutral countries if they are held at arm's length ... until those
countries are actually attacked ...'

If he had waited a day or two longer, Churchill could have
recounted in his marvellously orotund delivery the annihilation of all
eight German Narvik destroyers, together with a U-boat, by a British force. George vi, noting Churchill's increased responsibilities as
Chairman of the Co-ordination Committee on Defence, added: 'I
would like to congratulate you on the splendid way in which, under
your direction, the Navy is countering the German move against
Scandinavia.'

German naval losses continued over the following days. British submarines found the pocket battleship *Lützow* and put her out of action
for many months; another found the cruiser *Karlsrühe* and damaged
her so badly that she had to be sunk. But the fact remained that the
Germans were there in Norway, strongly established, within a few days
of the invasion, with powerful elements of the Luftwaffe which made
difficult any blockade of the Norwegian ports. As Churchill admitted
to Pound, 'We have been completely outwitted.' He began his memorandum: 'The Germans have succeeded in occupying all the ports on
the Norwegian coast, including Narvik, and large-scale operations will
be required to turn them out of any of them .... It is now necessary
to take a new view .... We must ... concentrate on Narvik, for which

long and severe fighting will be required ...'

The failure of the navy, with its superiority over the enemy greater than at any time during the First World War, to intercept and destroy the German invaders was raising old doubts about Churchill's ability to lead the navy effectively. He counterattacked stoutly but the truth could not be denied. 'Everyone must recognise the extraordinary and reckless gambling which has flung the whole German Fleet out upon the savage seas of war,' he told the Commons. '... This very recklessness makes me feel that these costly operations may be only the prelude to far larger events which impend on land ...'

For the present at least, the events on land continued to be confined to Norway and their shape began to assume more and more closely that of the Dardanelles. The De Robeck of 1940 was Lord Cork, Admiral of the Fleet the Earl of Cork and Orrery, who had been brought out of retirement by Churchill at the outset of the war and placed in an office in the Admiralty to work on the proposed Baltic operations, like Admiral Wilson in 1914. Now, at the age of sixty-five, he was appointed Flag Officer, Narvik, to command naval forces in the recovery of that vital iron-ore town. The General Hamilton of this latter-day Dardanelles was Major General Pierse Joseph Mackesy, whose main base was Harstad, a short distance from Narvik. He was not the most aggressive of soldiers; moreover his supplies, like General Hamilton's in 1915, had been wrongly loaded, leaving him short of artillery and ammunition. Although the Germans occupying the town had been badly shaken by the mutilation of their naval forces, Mackesy refused to attack with what he regarded as his inadequate forces.

'The similarity between De Robeck's signals from the Dardanelles and Cork's signals from Norway twenty-six years later is quite remarkable,' Martin Gilbert has commented. On 20 April Lord Cork began bombarding the German-held forts with the *Queen Elizabeth*'s sister ship *Warspite*. 'Starting harassing fire today,' he reported to Churchill. 'HMS *Warspite* much appreciated. Intend her to engage pill-boxes at point-blank range ...' Greatly encouraged by this positive attitude, Churchill answered, 'It seems to me that you can feel your way and yet strike hard'; and put Cork in overall command.

By this time the War Cabinet, and Churchill, were forced to concede that, in spite of all their supply problems and the elimination of a large part of their Fleet, the German control of the air, almost without a break from Oslo to Narvik, was making the liberation of Norway impossible. French and British troops put ashore farther south in the Trondheim area were being constantly harassed by German fighters and bombers, and it was not until RAF fighters could be put ashore near Narvik that an assault on the town could be contemplated, such was the recent rapid build-up by the Luftwaffe. But the 'larger events' predicted by Churchill were now about to break. On 10 May 1940 the German blitzkrieg burst upon the frontiers of Holland, France and Belgium, and the last pretence that Hitler was interested in only a phoney war was shattered in the scream of Stuka dive bombers, the silent descent of paratroops and the swift advance of Panzer divisions.

Narvik was later occupied by Allied troops only in order that installations could be destroyed, and the evacuation of Norway, the first of so many evacuations over the coming months and years, was carried out with the same consummate skill and efficiency which had marked the evacuation of the Dardanelles by the navy.

Misfortune and good fortune alike accompanied this retreat. The three surviving German heavy men o'war, the cruiser *Hipper* and the battle-cruisers *Scharnhorst* and *Gneisenau*, chanced upon one transport, fortunately empty, and a tanker, which were sunk. Then the battle-cruisers, steaming farther north, caught sight of the distant chunky silhouette of the aircraft carrier *Glorious*.

Besides her naval planes, the *Glorious* carried a squadron of RAF Hurricane fighters, whose pilots had just been obliged to make a deck landing without arrester gear or experience of any kind. The pilots had little time to congratulate themselves. The 11-inch shells set the carrier ablaze, and she went down shortly after.

The glory of this operation was provided by the officers and crew of the two escorting destroyers who laid smokescreens and then attacked the massive ships at point-blank range. One torpedo struck the *Scharnhorst* right aft doing damage which put the ship out of action for many weeks. Only a handful of survivors from the *Glorious* were picked up; they included the RAF squadron commander, who enjoys life to this day.

The damage to the *Scharnhorst* led the German force to abandon its efforts to intercept any further convoys to the north, and it returned to Trondheim harbour, thus missing the opportunity which otherwise would have been wide open to the battle-cruisers to destroy the cruiser *Devonshire*, a mere hundred miles distant, which was carrying the entire Norwegian royal family to Scotland.

The *Gneisenau* was later badly damaged by the submarine *Clyde*. As Churchill has written, 'From all this wreckage and confusion there emerged one fact of major importance potentially affecting the future of the war. In their desperate grapple with the British Navy the Germans ruined their own, such as it was, for the impending climax ... the supreme issue of the invasion of Britain.' The Royal Navy had suffered some grievous losses, but at the end of the Norwegian campaign the German Navy had almost ceased to exist. It could call immediately on just one heavy cruiser, two light cruisers and four destroyers.

By contrast with the First World War, the German Navy had been handled recklessly and had paid a terrible price. Nor had it shown the same skill and courage as the *Kriegsmarine* of 1914–18, and from the Norwegian campaign was born Hitler's later disillusionment with his surface fleet. As for the Royal Navy, it had been forced within a few weeks and at a high cost to face the realities of sea power in the age of the bomber. Ships on both sides had been sunk by dive bombers and high-level bombers, the first to suffer this fate in war. And in spite of the presence of British anti-aircraft cruisers bristling with guns, the navy had to accept that it could not survive and perform its functions in combined operations without control of the air. Where this was acquired, as briefly at Narvik, the army could operate successfully. Where it was lacking it was virtually helpless. The threat of an invasion of Britain was still some weeks away, but already Churchill could see with prescient eye that the survival of the country for the time being must depend primarily on the RAF and only secondarily on the Royal Navy.

Treated as a real-life exercise, the Norwegian campaign was of priceless value. The same mistakes had been made as at the Dardanelles. The Admiralty had many times interfered with operations, with dire results. Looking back, for example, on the Admiralty's cancellation of a potentially successful attack on Bergen, Churchill wrote that 'I consider the Admiralty kept too close a control upon the Commander-in-Chief, and after learning his original intention to force the passage into Bergen we should have confined ourselves to sending him information.' Once again, as at the Dardanelles, Churchill, lacking full information, was urging a course of action which could prove fatal to those on the spot.

The decisive, underlying fault which led to the disasters and miscalculations of the Norwegian campaign rested in pre-war Naval Staff Planning which established to its complete satisfaction that Norway could not be successfully invaded and held by German arms while the British Fleet at Scapa Flow dominated the North Sea. Churchill had seven months in office in which to question this accepted view. He did not do so and fell comfortably and uncharacteristically into the illusion that the nature and function of sea power had changed little.

The chief blame, however, lies with the Admiralty, blinkered and still living between the wars as if nothing had been changed by the First World War. The Germans knew better. The German planning Staff had had their eye on Norway for years. In *Die Seestrategie das Weltkrieges* Vice Admiral W. Wegener had advocated an attack on

Norway and the establishment of bases along the long saw-toothed coast.

England could then no longer maintain the blockade lines from the Shetlands to Norway but must withdraw approximately to the line of the Shetlands–the Faeroes–Iceland. But this line was a net with very wide meshes . . . . Moreover [it] was hard for England to defend, for in the first place it lay comparatively near to our [new Norwegian] bases and, above all, as the map shows, we should considerably outflank the English strategic position to the north.

This influential and authoritative book was readily available before 1939. No one at the Admiralty appears to have read it.

It remains the greatest blessing and good fortune for Britain – and for the USA and the whole free Western world – that, far from hounding Churchill out of office after his second Dardanelles, the disastrous Norwegian campaign led to his becoming Prime Minister on 10 May 1940.

How could Churchill be 'disentangled from the ruins' a later Prime Minister, Harold Macmillan, recalled when writing about the parliamentary debate on Norway. But he was. And it was at Neville Chamberlain not Churchill that the finger was pointed and 'the terrible words', as Churchill called them, were uttered: 'Depart, I say, and let us have done with you. In the name of God, go !'

8
'As naval people . . .'

There was little surprise in the White House, and generally in Washington, when the words, 'In the name of God, go!' appeared in the American newspapers the following day. Roosevelt had been President for almost eight years and had been observing events in Europe with growing concern. This was not shared by most United States citizens, who generally were anxious to keep out of any overseas conflict and felt safe and remote from it. Roosevelt had met Churchill only once, and briefly, in the summer of 1918 when Churchill had been Minister of Munitions and Roosevelt was among several speakers at a dinner in London. After that, the only contact between the two men occurred when Churchill inscribed and sent to Roosevelt a copy of the first volume of his life of Marlborough. To Roosevelt's surprise, the inscription wished him well in his New Deal programme. It was October 1933 and Hitler had been dictator of Germany for eight months.

Roosevelt watched Churchill's ever increasing fear for the future of Europe, from his speech in the House of Commons on 7 April in the same year, when he had warned of the dangers of a German militaristic dictatorship. By the early summer of 1939, when all the world could recognize the near inevitability of renewed war, there is no doubt that Roosevelt also recognized the likelihood that Churchill would at some future time lead Britain in another Anglo–German conflict.

Roosevelt had earlier greatly admired Churchill's performance as First Lord and deplored his resignation over the Dardanelles. At this time Roosevelt himself was serving in an appointment effectively parallel to Churchill's as Assistant Secretary of the Navy under the kindly, ineffectual Josephus Daniels. The two men had much else in common. Both were patrician figures with aristocratic backgrounds; both were romantically attached to their navies; both had entered politics early and progressed with remarkable speed; both were politically concerned with the welfare of the underprivileged, Roosevelt as a Democrat, Churchill as a Liberal.

But while Churchill's background and experience were strictly military, Roosevelt had inherited a love and instinct for the sea. As small boys, Churchill played with lead soldiers while Roosevelt mucked about with boats. As political naval men, they both wished to reform and strengthen their service. But Roosevelt's methods were much less aggressive and abrasive than Churchill's. Roosevelt would never have ridden roughshod over his admirals; he admired them almost unreservedly. During his long term of office with the United States Navy he endured patiently the pacifism and procrastinations of his saintly but maddening boss, Josephus Daniels, and succeeded with guile and deviousness in circumventing numerous policies and decisions with which he did not agree. To accomplish all this and still end up loving the man was beyond Churchill's powers.

Roosevelt's term of office in the Navy Department ended with the fall of President Wilson in 1921. Within months Roosevelt had succumbed to the dread disease of polio, and for a time it seemed that his career was finished. Also in that same year the Washington Conference to stem the flow of renewed naval competition was convened. It was widely believed in American naval circles that the outcome of this conference was as crippling to the navy Roosevelt had done so much to enlarge and strengthen as his disease had crippled Roosevelt himself. Under the Wilson administration the US Navy had been on the way to becoming the largest and most modern in the world. But under the terms of this treaty over 600,000 tons of capital ships under construction were to be scrapped. 'Here was a magnificent potential of sea power,' Commodore Dudley W. Knox has written, 'upon which we had already spent upwards of 300,000,000 dollars, tossed overboard in a magnanimous gesture for international goodwill and peace, neither of which was subsequently realised.'

During the following decade, while Roosevelt fought his disease and courageously re-entered the arena of politics, the US Navy – 'his' navy as he always regarded it – maintained a fine spirit and prepared itself for the imminent naval revolution of the mid-twentieth century. In 1932 it was, like the British Navy, still a battleship navy with tactical concepts based on the line of battle and the big gun. And, because of the Washington Treaty, the American battle fleet was an ageing instrument of war. All but one of the fifteen battleships had been laid down during or before the First World War. Even the much-reduced British battle fleet had nothing as ancient as the 12-inch-gunned *Arkansas* or the 14-inch-gunned *New York* and *Texas*. A modernization plan was under way but no new battleship construction was contemplated. The destroyer flotillas, too, were all obsolescent, being made up largely of the simple and rapidly-built 'thousand-tonners' and 'flush-deckers' of the war years.

On the material side, however, the US Navy was, like the Royal

The German pocket battleship *Graf Spee*, named after the defeated admiral at the Battle of the Falkland Islands in 1914, repeats history twenty-five years later and lifts the spirit of the nation and empire.

'Winnie is back!' Churchill returns from 'the wilderness' to Whitehall and the Admiralty, 4 September 1939.

Churchill's 'Dardanelles' of the Second World War, the Norwegian campaign, led to heavy losses on both sides. This is one of the two British destroyers attempting to protect their charge, the carrier *Glorious*, from the *Gneisenau* and *Scharnhorst*. While failing to do so and being sunk at point-blank range, the *Acasta* so damaged the *Scharnhorst* that the Germans missed a rich convoy.

Admiral Sir Dudley Pound (top left), First Sea Lord during the difficult and dangerous first years of the war: Churchill learned to love and respect him. Vice-Admiral Sir Tom Philips (top right) enjoyed Churchill's respect as Vice Chief of Naval Staff and was mourned when he went down in the *Prince of Wales*, a battleship admiral to the end. Admiral Sir Bruce Fraser (bottom left), one of the greatest seagoing commanders of the war, commanded the Home Fleet when the *Scharnhorst* was sunk, Christmas 1943, later commanding the Eastern Fleet in the Pacific. 'A.B.C.' Admiral Sir Andrew Cunningham (bottom right), 'valiant in action and in facing adversity . . . staunchly loyal to his superiors and generous to his equals' – the Nelson of the Second World War, but later less happy in the Admiralty.

Atlantic meetings: a solemn and moving moment at Sunday service on board the *Prince of Wales* at the first Atlantic meeting, August 1941. Fourteen weeks later the United States was at war and the *Prince of Wales* sunk by the Japanese. Below: a less solemn greeting.

Pearl Harbor: Day of infamy, and day of stupidity for the Japanese who did relatively little damage for rousing the most powerful nation to arms. The fate of the Imperial Japanese Navy was sealed before the last planes returned to their carriers.

Some of the team who won the war in the Pacific, with unprecedented skill and remarkably low loss of life. Top left: Fleet Admiral Chester W. Nimitz, Commander-in-Chief Pacific Fleet, who had just been decorated with the Order of the Bath, Knight Grand Cross, by Admiral Bruce Fraser. Top right: Admiral Nimitz (left); Admiral Ernest J. King, in dark trousers, who was Commander-in-Chief United States Fleet, in Washington, where he was suspected of hating every-one and everything, especially the British; and Admiral William 'Bull' Halsey, who commanded in the south Pacific. Below left: Admiral Raymond Spruance, the shrewdest of them all, who was chiefly responsible for the epochal victory at Midway and later commanded the Fifth Fleet. Below right: Frank Knox was Secretary of the US Navy during the early years of the war.

As in the First World War, the U-boat came close to winning the Battle of the Atlantic, and later suffered grievous losses without any failure of morale. Below: Japanese torpedo- and dive-bombers attack the carrier *Yorktown* at the crucial Battle of Midway, the new shape of naval warfare.

In the closing stages of the Pacific war at sea, the Japanese employed suicide 'kamikaze' pilots, but by now American superiority was so massive and anti-aircraft fire so effective, that damage was limited.

In one of the few big-ship actions of the war the mighty *Bismarck* opens fire on the *Hood* and *Prince of Wales*, sinking the former and damaging the second. But it took the intervention of air power in the form of a torpedo hit to disable the German ship before she was finally sunk by gunpower and more torpedoes.

The grand alliance has brought the Allies close to victory in Europe, and at Yalta the shape and power structure of the post-war world is arranged, to the benefit of Soviet Russia, thanks to the ailing Roosevelt.

Navy, blessed with a skilled and enthusiastic air arm. Back in Roosevelt's time – May 1919 – the General Board had made a report 'to insure air supremacy'. This supremacy was 'to enable the United States Navy to meet on at least equal terms any possible enemy, and to put the United States in its proper place as a naval power, fleet aviation must be developed to the fullest possible extent. Aircraft must become an essential part of the fleet.' By 1929 two giant aircraft carriers were operating on fleet exercises along with the much smaller pioneering carrier, the *Langley*.

An indirect benefit of the Washington Treaty was the ban on the development by the USA of further Pacific naval bases. Much criticized by senior officers at the time, but a blessing none the less, this restriction forced the navy to consider more closely the art of amphibious warfare conducted across the vast spaces of the Pacific. By 1933 a Fleet Marine Force had been established and landing-craft, supply problems and joint action with the army were all being considered. It was still only a small seed ; but it was to grow into the vast and remarkable amphibious task forces and self-sustaining fleet trains of the Pacific war in the early 1940s.

Although the Washington Treaty provided for a US Navy of roughly the same size as the Royal Navy – and two-fifths larger than the Japanese Navy – the Americans possessed one marked advantage over their past and future allies, the British. The US Navy was a classless service which had never been in need of the selection reforms introduced by Fisher and Churchill and others – none of which, incidentally, was wholly successful. Advancement on merit and merit alone was many times more effective in the US Navy than the Royal Navy. The US Navy suffered none of the Royal Navy's Victorian–Edwardian class prejudice and lingering distaste towards brains and the lower orders which kept down so many good men right up to the early years of the Second World War.

From the American Naval War College there emerged every year some seventy graduate senior officers. These were the men who fought and won the greatest naval war in history with extraordinarily low casualties.

The arrival in the White House of Franklin Roosevelt in November 1932 had a similar effect on the US Navy as Churchill's arrival at the Admiralty on the Royal Navy seven years later. Everyone in the service knew how attached to the navy was the one-time Assistant Secretary and now Commander-in-Chief. And like Churchill in 1940, Roosevelt appointed as civil head of the navy – Secretary of the Navy – a man who would do his bidding. Senator Claude Swanson was 'a benign old Virginian who wore high, wing collars and a frock-coat' whose appointment 'indicated that Roosevelt would be his own Secretary of the Navy'.

Few of the fears of what would happen to the nation under Roosevelt percolated into the navy. 'I was just bustin' to see that smile in the White House and to shake your hand,' wrote Captain Harold R.'Betty' Stark, a future Chief of Naval Operations. 'If I should try to say any or all that I feel, it could be but a poor attempt in the first place, and an inroad on your time in the second. I know you are too busy now ... for social calls but some time ... I just want to see you in those surroundings where we have so long wanted and needed you.'

Three months later this same officer referred in a letter to the President to the new building programme – 'a veritable Godsend' he called it. 'Few people realize how far below treaty strength and relative strength we have sunk, and also how badly, in some instances, we need replacements ...'

The new building programmes between 1933 and 1941 reflected more than the worsening of international relations. They reflected the urgency and determination with which Roosevelt tackled the neglect and inadequacies suffered by the navy since he had ceased to be Assistant Secretary. In battleships alone the 1936 programme included two, the 1938 programme called for four more, and in 1940 eleven mastodons of 45,000 to 58,000 tons were ordered or projected, together with six battle-cruisers, American's first. This scale of rearmament made Britain's most extravagant programmes look puny indeed. (In fact a number of these ships were never completed.)

Naval aviation expansion was not so massive, and not massive enough to meet war needs as it turned out, but was still given great new impetus during Roosevelt's early years at the White House, two 20,000-ton carriers being laid down in 1934, and then in increasing volume until some dozen were under construction by the time of Pearl Harbor. The same number of 8-inch-gun cruisers were ordered between Roosevelt's inauguration and the end of 1941 ; and huge programmes of light cruiser, destroyer and submarine construction were put in hand.

Scarcely a day passed when Roosevelt did not involve himself in some aspect or other of the workings of the navy. Like Churchill, Roosevelt was always preoccupied with the design of new men o'war. In June 1934 we find him proposing to Swanson the construction of 'flying deck' cruisers, hybrids which combined the firepower of a heavy cruiser with flying-off and flying-on facilities, a configuration which the Russian Navy exploited fifty years later. The General Board in fact advised against these vessels. 'As we already have three airplane carriers, flying deck cruisers are not needed at this time.'

Recalling the desperate need for large numbers of anti-U-boat patrol vessels in the First World War, Roosevelt wrote to his naval aide in 1937 for plans to be prepared 'for a wooden vessel which can be turned out in about six weeks and can be built by many shipyards throughout the country'.

Roosevelt also prepared a memorandum suggesting the laying down of two 8,000-ton cruisers armed with four 11-inch guns 'plus as many 5-inch dual as possible'. He wanted a ship with 'a good chance of standing up against the German pocket battleship type'. Like Kaiser Wilhelm II, Roosevelt designed ships in his sleep; and, like that ex-emperor, many of his designs were sound and some prophetic.

The President and C-in-C took just as much interest in the minutiae of his navy: in promotions, new training schemes, defence of bases, performance of new navy aircraft, the movements of ships. 'I am inclined to agree with the recommendation', he wrote to Swanson on 28 June 1935, 'that a heavy cruiser be kept as the flagship of the C-in-C Asiatic Fleet. Will you therefore either keep the *Augusta* on her present assignment, or relieve her with another heavy cruiser, preferably one of the older ships of this class . . .' Hearing of German progress in alternative forms of marine engine, Roosevelt calls for a paper on the merits and demerits of 'dieselization'. Then again he calls for the most detailed intelligence available on the new Japanese battleships. Unfortunately Swanson replied, 'I am satisfied that Japan will use 16-inch guns,' when to the dismay of the US Navy later they turned out to be of 18-inch calibre.

Roosevelt was never happier than with the Fleet at sea and he made as many and as long visits as the responsibilities of the White House allowed. Personnel at all levels loved it. 'Your visit to the Fleet has had a very stimulating influence upon its entire personnel,' writes Swanson (3 December 1935).

Between 1938 and 1941 Roosevelt's wartime team was formed. Swanson died in July 1939. 'Claude loved you more than anyone I knew,' his widow wrote to Roosevelt. Frank Knox, a tough, shrewd Chicago newspaper publisher, was appointed Secretary of the Navy to replace Swanson's successor, Charles Edison, in June 1940.

Harold Stark, now an admiral, was appointed Chief of Naval Operations in March 1939. 'I do not have to tell you how much I appreciate your confidence,' he wrote to Roosevelt, 'nor that you will have all the loyalty and effort I can give; you know that. My hope is that my service to the navy, where you are placing me, will measure up to what you expect and to the benefit of our sea-going forces which we both so love. I assure you I will do my very best.'

Among others who were to figure prominently in the US Navy hierarchy during the coming war was James Forrestal, in the post

Roosevelt had occupied as a young man, who succeeded Frank Knox when he died in 1944. At sea Admiral Ernest King was C-in-C Naval Forces, later to replace Stark as Chief of Naval Operations after March 1942 ; the naval aviation wizard Vice Admiral William 'Bull' Halsey and other aviation specialists, Vice Admiral Frank 'Black Jack' Fletcher and Vice Admiral Raymond 'Electric Brain' Spruance ; the future Commander of the Eighth Fleet, Vice Admiral Henry Kent Hewitt. These senior officers, and so many others who were to become household names after Pearl Harbor, contributed to the quality of the US Navy at war, without doubt the best team of leaders in any naval war in history.

Within a week of Churchill's assuming office again as First Lord of the Admiralty, Roosevelt wrote a letter to him which initiated a remarkable exchange of communications, by letter, telegraph and telephone which were to cover every aspect of the war until Roosevelt's death on the brink of Allied victory in April 1945. Read in sequence, these communications reflect in sharp detail the course of the war as seen from the White House and 10 Downing Street, from the time when Britain and the British Commonwealth and France declared war on Nazi Germany, through the cold, unreal winter of 1939–40, the crushing blitzkriegs of the spring and early summer of 1940 which left Britain alone, and Italy a new enemy. Then the second and third phases : the spreading of the conflagration with the German attack on Russia, the Japanese attack on the USA, until every ocean and every continent except the Americas experienced the flames and suffering of war.

Roosevelt had frequently employed the informal approach of a personal letter in his conduct of diplomacy and foreign affairs. Churchill controlled the navy which traditionally secured the eastern flank of the Americas. However hostile United States public opinion might be towards involvement in another European war, the survival of Western democracy in Europe was of vital concern to the American Government. And a quick totting up in *Jane's Fighting Ships* showed that the German Fleet, supported by the surrendered Fleets of France and Britain, could total a force greatly superior to any that America could muster. It therefore seemed both natural and sensible to establish an informal line of communication with Churchill in London. The consequences of Roosevelt's wise step were incalculable.

'It is because you and I occupied similar positions in the [First] World War', Roosevelt began, 'that I want you to know how glad I am that you are back again in the Admiralty. Your problems are, I realise, complicated by new factors, but the essential is not very different. What I want you and the Prime Minister to know is that I shall at all times welcome it if you will keep me in touch personally with anything you want me to know about.' Then, referring to Churchill's first volume of his life of his ancestor, Marlborough, sent to him six years earlier, Roosevelt said how glad he was that Churchill had completed the work 'before this thing started'.

Churchill, after consulting the Prime Minister and members of the War Cabinet, drafted a reply to this welcome letter and despatched it through the US Embassy by diplomatic bag. The subject of Churchill's letter was German surface raiders and the anxiety they were causing.

At an Inter-American Conference in Panama City on 23 September the delegates had adopted a so-called 'Declaration of Panama' designed to safeguard the republics of the Americas from the consequences of the European war. It was Roosevelt's idea, with domestic politics in mind, to create a deep zone extending from 300 to 1,000 miles, from the Canadian border to the Argentine, in which hostile acts by the belligerents would be prohibited. It was internationally illegal and impossible to enforce but it seemed to make everyone feel happier, including Churchill.

In his reply to Roosevelt's first letter, Churchill wrote (5 October 1939) that the prohibited zone would make easier the tracking down of German surface raiders on the assumption that the zone would be properly policed by the US Navy. 'The more American ships cruising along the South American coast the better, as you, sir, would no doubt hear what they saw or did not see. Raider might then find American waters rather crowded, or may anyhow prefer to go on to sort of trade route where we are preparing'. Churchill concluded his first telegram with his tongue firmly in his cheek: 'We wish to help you in every way in keeping the war out of Americas.'

The suggestion that American sighting of German raiders might benefit the Royal Navy in its searches was not presumptuous. Even before the Second World War, secret consultations had taken place in London between Royal Navy and US Navy representatives concerned especially with the maintenance of security of the North Atlantic trade routes in time of war.

The first direct naval co-operation between Roosevelt and Churchill took place by transatlantic telephone even before Roosevelt received Churchill's telegram of reply. The subject was the sinking of the *Athenia*, about which Hitler was furious. The very last thing he wanted to do at this stage was to arouse American fury as the sinking of the *Lusitania* in 1915 had done. He therefore ordered it to be made known that a bomb had been planted on the ship at Churchill's orders in order to cause an outcry in America. The statement was followed by a bogus enquiry by the German Navy, the outcome of which was made known to the American naval attaché in Berlin. On 16 September this officer noted in his diary that he had been summoned by Grand Admiral Erich Raeder, who told him that the previous night he had received negative reports from the last of the submarines which could possibly have torpedoed the *Athenia*. 'He asked me to report the matter to my embassy, which I did.'

To add verisimilitude to this story, Raeder gave out a warning over the German radio to America that a similar bomb had been planted in the American merchantman *Iroquois*, then in mid-Atlantic out of Cork, implying that German intelligence had got wind of Churchill's second plot. Roosevelt at once put through a telephone call to Churchill in London.

Churchill was dining with naval company at the time and told the butler that he could not answer the telephone. But the butler pressed him to come and Churchill reluctantly did so, discovering that he was talking to the White House and that the subject was an urgent one. Roosevelt took Churchill's advice and had the ship thoroughly searched – nothing was found – and then publicized the whole plot, discrediting German intelligence and making plain to the world that the *Athenia* must indeed have been the victim of a U-boat. Direct co-operation between the President and future Prime Minister had started well.

The Royal Navy found the last of the big German raiders, the *Graf Spee*, unassisted by the patrols of the US Navy, and Roosevelt – and the whole American people – followed the action and the aftermath with excitement and admiration. Knowing how interested the President would be in the technical and other details of the action, Churchill wrote on Christmas Day 1939 ('Sir, all the compliments of the season') to tell him that these would be coming at once by air mail. 'Damage to *Exeter* from eleven-inch guns was most severe and ship must be largely rebuilt. Marvel is she stood up to it so well.' It was an action such as this, with smaller cruisers attempting to tackle a German pocket battleship, that Roosevelt had in mind when he proposed 11-inch-gunned American heavy cruisers; and Roosevelt was grateful for the 'tremendously interesting account of the extraordinarily well fought action of your three cruisers'.

The naval battle off the River Plate had, however, led to protests to Britain from several South American states, claiming that the British warships had penetrated the non-combatant zone recently set up, and the United States felt obliged to add her voice. Churchill in his Christmas Day message regretted this and other incidents, but pointed out that

as a result of action off Plate whole South Atlantic is now clear ... of warlike operations. This must be a blessing to South American republics [Churchill's

telegram continued], whose trade was hampered by activities of raider ....
In fact we have rescued all this vast area from war disturbances .... Trust
matter can be allowed to die down and see no reason why any trouble should
occur unless another raider is sent which is unlikely after fate of first. South
American States should see in Plate action their deliverance perhaps indefinitely
from all animosity.

Friction at sea continued, with the United States increasingly upset
by Britain's search and detention of American ships suspected of carrying contraband to the enemy – shades of the War of 1812 when Britain
and the United States had last fought one another! 'At the time of
dictating this [1 February 1940],' Roosevelt wrote coolly, 'I think our
conversations in regard to search and detention of American ships is
working out satisfactorily – but I would not be frank unless I told you
that there has been much public criticism here. The general feeling
is that the net benefit to your people and to France is hardly worth
the definite annoyance caused to us.'

'The United States was cooler than in any other period,' Churchill
has written of this unsatisfactory state of relations. 'I persevered in
my correspondence with the President, but with little response.'

As the United States naval attaché in Berlin noted, 'It appears that
Great Britain is clamping on the blockade of Germany much more
drastically than it did in 1914.' The cause of American annoyance was
British insistence in bringing American merchantmen into the danger
zone drawn by the United States around British shores in order to
ensure that they were not carrying contraband goods destined for
Germany. This practice had ceased since a system had been devised
for clearing these merchantmen before leaving American ports, and
Churchill replied, firmly but courteously, that this was now operating
satisfactorily – 'no American ship has been brought by the navy into
the danger zone' – but that one large American line was advertising
that they don't have to bother about these niceties. 'You can imagine
my embarrassment,' Churchill remarked.

Roosevelt replied on 5 March 1940 :

To the Naval Person from the President
Upon my return to Washington, I received your message. I deeply appreciate
your efforts. I am having the situation thoroughly studied and will communicate
with you further as soon as possible.
Roosevelt

But the 'search and detention' friction continued, arousing further
anger in the United States and anxiety in Britain. Lord Lothian, British
Ambassador in Washington, wrote to Lady Astor, the American-born

Member of Parliament for Plymouth: 'You will have seen from the papers that poor old Britain has had "the heat turned on" against it recently by the State Department. It is a nuisance because, as you know well, once the American public begins to feel that Great Britain is treading on its corns, it gets easily inflamed because of old memories.'

It was not until American sentiment towards Britain mellowed after Dunkirk and the Battle of Britain and the subsequent bombing of London and other cities that the blockade resentment diminished.

Criticism in America of the Royal Navy and Churchill was aroused on entirely different grounds in April and May 1940. Recalling how the many-times-larger German High Seas Fleet of 1914–18 could not break British dominance of the North Sea, the US naval attaché in Berlin wrote of the failure of the Royal Navy to halt the invasion of Norway, 'The immediate reaction, among Americans and foreign naval attachés was where in hell was the British Navy? They got caught flat-footed.' Roosevelt was in despair. He had all his life admired the skill and prowess of the Royal Navy and he felt personally affronted that the Germans had been able to carry out this devastating operation seemingly without serious opposition. 'The thing that has made me hopping mad', he was heard to remark, 'is where was the British Fleet when the Germans went up to Bergen and Oslo? It is the most outrageous thing I have ever heard of.'

No communication has been recorded between the President and Churchill during the difficult and anxious weeks after the Scandinavian invasion, except the despatch to Washington by Churchill of the official account of the Battle of the River Plate. But by that time the Royal Navy had lost much of the kudos it had gained in that distant action.

The date of 15 May 1940, five days after Churchill took over the premiership, marks a fundamental change in the relationship and communications with Roosevelt. Churchill is sixty-five years old, Roosevelt fifty-eight; Churchill is leader of His Majesty's Government, Roosevelt as head of state and head of government combines the roles of sovereign and prime minister in Britain; Churchill at all times recognizes this distinction, as eyewitnesses observed when he gave a little bow at their first meeting on board the *Augusta*, and by the frequent use of 'Sir'. On 15 May Churchill, in a long telegram, becomes simply and appropriately 'Former Naval Person', following his earlier-coined title 'Naval Person', and signs himself 'With all good wishes and respect'. Since their earlier tiff about the British blockade, the European continent has shuddered under the shock waves of a massive blitzkrieg which has shattered the puny defences of Denmark, Norway, Belgium and Holland. The Wehrmacht has stormed into Luxembourg and France, crushing all before it. Open cities are being torn apart by high-level and screaming dive bombers. The warning signs from across the Channel are clear for all to see ; and Churchill in this first telegram of the new era warns the President, 'You may have a completely subjugated, Nazified Europe established with astonishing swiftness.' Then, closer to home, 'We expect to be attacked here ourselves, both from the air and by parachute and air borne troops in the near future . . .'

This telegram reflects a very different view of Britain's position after the German breakthrough at Sedan and the swift retreat in the west from the robust and defiant tone of Churchill's radio broadcasts of this period. There is no hint of compromise or surrender to Germany – 'we shall continue the war alone and we are not afraid of that'– but there is a note of urgency, of almost desperate urgency, which would have shocked the British people if this 'most secret and personal' communication had been made public, especially the statement that 'The weight may be more than we can bear'. This was not a consideration at British breakfast tables at the time.

Churchill's first 'shopping list' was a formidable one : the loan of forty or fifty destroyers, several hundred of the latest type of aircraft, anti-aircraft guns and ammunition, steel in unspecified quantity but sufficient to make up loss of supplies from Sweden, Spain and North Africa. More breathtaking was the suggestion that the United States should proclaim non-belligerency in order that it could provide all help 'short of actually engaging armed forces'. And finally, Churchill while pledging to 'paying dollars as long as we can' hoped that when they ran out 'you will give us the stuff just the same'.

At this time Roosevelt and his chiefs of staff had no conception of the danger and imminence of defeat in the west. Military minds were still conditioned by the pace of military action of 1914–18, and there was a strong tendency to view Churchill's *cri de coeur* as false, political or hysterical. Cry wolf ! Roosevelt replied the next day, but he offered little and did not comment on the extremely hot issue of a proclamation of non-belligerency. It was far ahead of what he could even consider politically.

Churchill was already viewing with dismay the rapid disintegration of French resistance and endeavouring to put some steel into the heart of Britain's ally. He was facing the threatened entry of Italy into the war, and was deeply preoccupied with preparing the nation's defences against invasion. Roosevelt's seeming procrastination was almost more than he could bear. In a brief telegram (18 May 1940) he told Roosevelt that 'We must expect ... to be attacked here on the Dutch model [bombing and airborne troops] before very long' and 'if American assistance is to play any part it must be available soon'. Two days later, a second telegram presented in uncompromising terms what might happen if 'the present administration were finished and others came in to parley amid the ruins'. Who could blame a new government for temporizing and using the British Fleet as a bargaining counter to obtain 'the best terms they could for the surviving inhabitants'? Of course we will fight on to the bitter end, Churchill stressed. And then: 'Excuse me, Mr President, putting this nightmare bluntly.' Was it a nightmare, or was it blackmail? Worse was to come.

Lord Lothian was making no better progress in Washington. 'The truth about USA is that it is dominated by fear of war – which is exactly what Hitler wants. Oh for Theodore Roosevelt!!' he wrote to a friend. The Ambassador expressed his exasperation to Lady Astor: 'Your countrymen are very volatile. When the allies get a success they say, "Well, that's fine. They can win without us." When Hitler is winning they say, "It's all over."' Now, on the vexed and urgent question of the destroyers, he suggested to Churchill a formula which might produce results. This was to weaken American intransigence by offering certain rights on British-owned or -controlled territory which would further secure American defences, for example leasing certain air and naval bases in Newfoundland, Trinidad, Bermuda and the West Indies. America's appetite for bases was, he reckoned, limitless.

Churchill opposed this suggestion unless something firm was slapped down on the counter in exchange. He had been much offended when, months earlier while he was still at the Admiralty, American defence chiefs turned down his suggestion that the British secret of Asdic should be exchanged for the American revolutionary Norden bombsight. In fact the US Navy was not too impressed by what they had heard of Asdic, and agreed with the Germans who 'hold the British listening gear in contempt'. He had also refused a US Navy request to appoint observers in British men o'war, and commented on proposed interchanges of technical information: 'Generally speaking I am not in a hurry until the United States is much nearer to the war than she is now.'

At a War Cabinet (27 May) Churchill complained bitterly that the United States had 'given us practically no help in the war'. First, so Churchill thought, America had considered that Britain was presenting a false black picture; 'and now they saw how great was the danger, their attitude was that they wanted to keep everything that would help in their own defence.'

But it was Roosevelt's failure to respond to the appeal for destroyers that most infuriated Churchill. Even before the evacuation at Dunkirk, the Royal Navy had lost 30 per cent of its destroyer strength. There were more than 100 First World War 'flush-deckers' laid up in east coast American yards, rusting, unwanted for two decades, and the President had the effrontery to write that America's own defence requirements precluded the navy disposing 'even temporarily' of these destroyers. Furthermore, the authorization would, he said, require congressional approval (which it did not, as was later shown) and 'I am not certain that it would be wise for that suggestion to be made to the Congress at this moment'.

Roosevelt's difficult political and defence position was not a subject much in Churchill's mind during this supreme crisis. Only much later could he acknowledge the President's dilemma in facing broad isolationism throughout the land, and the defence staff's opposition to diverting supplies to a doomed belligerent when their own needs were so desperate. For example, General George V. Strong, chairman of the war plans division, advocated no further aid to Europe, as 'a recognition of the early defeat of the Allies'. Private manufacturers should be prohibited from accepting orders from Britain ; and if necessary British and French possessions in the Western Hemisphere should be occupied to keep them out of German hands.

On behalf of the army, General George Marshall, and Stark for the navy, deprecated sending anything more to Europe. They were supported by the Foreign Relations Committee, whose chairman, Senator Key Pittman, replied to Churchill's renewed plea, as 'a matter of life and death' (15 June), with a demand that Churchill should send the entire British Fleet to American waters immediately to preserve it from falling into German hands. 'It is no secret that Great Britain is totally unprepared for defense and that nothing the United States has to give can do more than delay the result,' reported the Senator ; and he hoped that the plan to transfer the British Fleet 'will not be too long delayed by futile encouragement to fight on'.

The voice of Henry Morgenthau, Secretary of the Treasury and close confidant of Roosevelt, was almost the only voice, and unheard, in advocating urgent aid. 'Unless we do something to give the English additional destroyers, it seems to me it is absolutely hopeless to expect them to keep going.'

American intervention to help Britain during and after Dunkirk and the fall of France was certainly not helped by the American contingent in London, with the exception of courageous newspapermen like Ed Murrow and Drew Middleton who sought to tell the truth about Britain's plight and needs. The Ambassador, Joseph Kennedy, made clear that Britain had no chance of survival, even before the attack in the west, and persevered in his hostility until he quit some months later, when Roosevelt commented, 'I never want to see that son of a bitch again as long as I live. Take his resignation and get him out of here.' 'It seems to me that if we had to fight to protect our lives we would do better fighting in our own backyard,' Kennedy wrote in one despatch to Roosevelt. And in another: 'The United States will have plenty to worry about in their own country. The cry should be to prepare for anything right there.'

On Joseph Kennedy as ambassador; on his alarmist, even hysterical tendencies and general unhelpfulness, Roosevelt and Churchill spoke with one voice – although strictly not aloud for the other to hear. Churchill's distrust of the man was total. 'Joe always has been an appeaser and always will be an appeaser,' Roosevelt complained to Morgenthau. 'If Germany and Italy made a good peace offer tomorrow Joe would start working on the King and his friend, the Queen, and from there on down, to get everybody to accept. He's just a pain in the neck to me.'

There is no telling how many lives were lost as a direct result of Kennedy's strong and persistent hostility to sending any American aid to Britain in 1940. Roosevelt attempted to justify his retention as ambassador by claiming that he at least 'knew his man' and could discount much that was contained in his despatches, an unconvincing and uncharacteristically negative policy. In fact he was politically afraid of his vast wealth and influence.

Another even more dangerous if covert American figure in London at this time was a code clerk in the American Embassy named Tyler G. Kent. He was so strongly opposed to any American aid for Britain that he copied and smuggled out of the Embassy, for enemy eyes, Churchill–Roosevelt messages. He was arrested and spent the remainder of the war in a British gaol.

Joseph Kennedy was the most influential opponent abroad to despatching old American destroyers to Britain; at home in the United States, Admiral Stark's voice was loudest and most convincing in professional defence circles, in spite of his close affinity to Roosevelt whom he knew to be, in principle and at a price, sympathetic. Stark not only believed, politically, that any deal over American destroyers would create outrage in Congress; but also that the 'mothballed' ships would be vital for America's defence when France and Britain capitulated, which he believed to be inevitable and imminent. In that event America would then be facing a hostile navy two-thirds the strength of the US Navy in the Pacific, and a combined British, German, French and Italian navy in the east more than twice as powerful as the total American battle fleet. The United States would then be crushed as swiftly as France.

The destroyers-for-Britain controversy laboured on through the cataclysmic summer of 1940, the chief contestants being the two national leaders, their ambassadors and service chiefs. Around 15 June Churchill seems to have lost confidence in the personal approach and left Lothian and the War Cabinet to get on with the struggle. It was not until the last day of July that Churchill renewed his pleas. In emphasizing the need for destroyers among other urgent requirements, Churchill wrote : 'The Germans have the whole French coast line from which to launch U-boats, dive-bomber attacks upon our trade and food, and in addition we must be constantly prepared to repel by sea action threatened invasion . . .' He then gave the names of eleven more destroyers which had been sunk or knocked out in the past ten days. 'Mr President, with great respect I must tell you that in the long history of the world, this is a thing to do now.'

A few days earlier Roosevelt had told Secretary Knox that Congress was in no mood to allow any form of sale. 'You might, however, think over the possibility at a little later date of trying to get Congressional action to allow the sale of these destroyers to Canada on condition that they be used solely in American hemisphere defence.' That represented the President's line of thinking on 22 July. But this most recent appeal of Churchill's struck home, a bull's eye. Immediately on receiving it Roosevelt got on to Secretary of the Navy Knox with instructions to see Lothian and put to him the proposal for a deal, a deal based on destroyers in exchange for British bases. Lothian was 'almost tearful in his pleas for help and help quickly', Knox reported later after putting the proposition to the British Ambassador. As early as 24 May Lothian had put up the idea of a similar *quid pro quo* to Churchill, who had peremptorily dismissed it. Now, more than two months later, Churchill and the War Cabinet were prepared to be less fastidious. Churchill later justified the exchange of fifty 'antiquated and inefficient craft' for an indefinite lease on a string of Atlantic and Caribbean bases by suggesting that 'the strategic value of these islands counted only against the United States. They were, in the old days, the stepping-stone by which America could be attacked from Europe or England. Now, with air power, it was all the more important for American safety that they should be in friendly hands.'

Through the first half of August Roosevelt struggled to turn American opinion in favour of such a deal, rallying all the forces he could muster. These included the national hero of the First World War, General John J. Pershing, who made a radio appeal on behalf of Britain and of America supporting her cause in any way possible – 'We have an immense reservoir of destroyers left over from the other war . . .' Progress remained slow, so slow that Roosevelt resorted to the law. Did he really have to get congressional approval? Did he not have the right to act on his own initiative? Lawyers of renown and distinction busied themselves in the library of the New York Bar Association ; a prominent letter above the names of distinguished and nationally famous lawyers appeared in the *New York Times*.

Strengthened by the law, and by a rising chorus of voices in the nation calling for help for the beleaguered British, Roosevelt decided to act on his own. The decision to go ahead was communicated to Churchill on 13 August 1940. The Battle of Britain was at its height and the hard-pressed squadrons of Fighter Command were holding off the Luftwaffe challenge. The spirit of the British people had never been more unified and determined to survive. It was a deadly dangerous if beautiful summer.

'It is my belief', ran Roosevelt's message, 'that it may be possible to furnish to the British Government as immediate assistance at least 50 destroyers . . .' The bases to be leased were specified, and the earlier condition about the Royal Navy in the event of successful German invasion toned down at the insistence of Churchill. It now read : 'Assurance on the part of the Prime Minister that in the event that the waters of Great Britain become untenable for British ships of war, the latter would not be turned over to the Germans or sunk, but would be sent to other parts of the Empire for continued defense of the Empire.'

Roosevelt liked to use the expression 'As naval people . . .' As naval people, the relief of Churchill and Roosevelt was mutual and heartfelt. 'I need not tell you how cheered I am by your message,' Churchill signalled Roosevelt, 'nor how grateful I feel for your untiring efforts to give us all possible help.' The fifty 'flush-deckers' themselves – terrible sea boats, old, requiring extensive modification before being fit for duty, disliked by those who manned them – did fulfil some sort of role in due course. But to Churchill the material consequences of the American decision were far less important than the effect on enemy, and British, morale, and on neutral opinion. The deal was, Churchill informed the War Cabinet, 'a long step towards [America] coming into the war on our side'.

Back in May, before France fell, Roosevelt had given the order that the army should send to the French a number of fighter planes that were urgently required. The American Army would just have to wait. 'After all,' Roosevelt had told Morgenthau, 'we will not be in for 60 or 90 days.' Those ninety days had passed, and in spite of the destroyer deal and Churchill's optimism about an early American entry into the war, the bomb and torpedo explosions of Pearl Harbor, which eventually brought America into the war, were still more than a year away.

But Roosevelt's Columbus Day message for 1940 was a stirring one. As bombs fell on a dozen darkened British cities, he told his audience, 'The men and women of Britain have shown how a free people defend what they know to be right. Their heroic defence will be recorded for all time .... Our course is clear. Our decision is made. We will continue to pile up our defence and our armaments. We will continue to help those who resist aggression far from our shores.'

On 2 August 1940 the interventionist American Secretary of the Interior, Harold L.Ickes, wrote to Roosevelt, favouring the destroyer-for-bases deal, and at the same time planting in Roosevelt's mind a fanciful parallel that would justify to the American public a radical idea that the President was brooding over. Britain was, quite simply, going broke. Her industry had already turned over to war production on a far more comprehensive scale than German industry, which was still manufacturing consumer goods for export and home consumption which had long since ceased to be produced in British factories. Under the American Neutrality Law war materials could only be supplied on a 'cash and carry basis' and the cash had all but run out. At the same time the American administration now recognized that Britain intended to fight it out to the end and that the defeat of Britain would leave the United States in a grave situation. 'Never before since Jamestown and Plymouth Rock has our American civilization been in such danger as now,' Roosevelt warned in his 'Fireside Chat' over the radio on 29 December 1940.

'It seems to me,' wrote Ickes, 'we Americans are like the householder who refuses to lend or sell his fire extinguishers to help put out the fire in the house that is right next door although that house is all ablaze and the wind is blowing from that direction.' This provided the kernel for Roosevelt's later 'lending the garden hose' phrase, the analogy being just right for the American people.

While cruising in the USS *Tuscaloosa* in early December 1940, Roosevelt had received the longest telegram – over 4,000 words long – from Churchill. It summarized the war situation and prospects for the future. Following a list of the dangers the nation faced, Churchill wrote, 'In the face of these dangers, we must try to use the year 1941 to build up such a supply of weapons, particularly aircraft, both by increased output at home in spite of bombardment, and through ocean-going supplies, as will lay the foundation of victory.' The outstanding orders for war materials from the US were already worth $4\frac{1}{2}$ billion dollars. How was this bill to be met? It was far beyond the resources of the customer.

Before the United States entered the First World War, Roosevelt could recall, when he was a youthful, bustling Assistant Secretary of the Navy, in order to evade rather than break the law, he had proposed that American merchantmen should be armed with guns 'loaned' from the Navy Department. Now the idea began to form in his mind of using this principle, on a vastly greater scale and seemingly without long-term cost to the nation, in order to solve Britain's payment problem. It was at least better than building up an unrepayable loan of the kind that had bedevilled Anglo–American relations since the First World War.

At a press conference at the end of his winter cruise, Roosevelt, after telling his audience that 'there was no particular news', presented the notion that the immense orders from Britain were great for America. They were, he said, 'a tremendous asset to American national defense, because they create, automatically, additional facilities. I am talking selfishly, from the American point of view – nothing else.' What he was trying to do was 'to eliminate the dollar sign'. Lending money to Britain was 'banal'.

This was the moment he chose to bring in the hose and neighbour analogy. 'I don't say . . . "Neighbour, my garden hose cost me 15 dollars ; you have got to pay me 15 dollars for it." I don't want 15 dollars – I want my garden hose back after the fire is over . . .'

In short, Roosevelt told his riveted audience of hard newspapermen, America would take over British orders and lease them to Britain 'on the general theory that the best defense of Great Britain is the best defense of the United States'.

Thus was born 'lend-lease', 'the most unsordid act in the history of any nation' as Churchill later described it, a startling and momentous blend of altruism and realism which was to solve the worst of Britain's financial problems and which Britain was later to apply to war materials for Russia on a similar giant scale. There was a long, bloody fight ahead before Roosevelt got the approval of Congress but, together with the recently concluded destroyer deal, it marked the end of a brief and distant friendship between the President and the Former Naval Person and the beginning of a courtship that would culminate in the ceremonial in Placentia Bay eight months hence.

The threat of the French Fleet was a subject that worried and preoccupied Roosevelt almost as much as it did Churchill, and within the limits imposed upon him, he supported all the British steps to neutralize the great number of powerful vessels remaining in French and French colonial ports after the French defeat and surrender of June 1940. In the first days of July Churchill, the War Cabinet and the Admiralty jointly agreed that firm steps had to be taken to deal with the most powerful concentration of French warships at Oran in North Africa. 'Force H', consisting of the battle-cruiser *Hood* – the biggest warship in the world – two battleships, a modern carrier, two cruisers and supporting craft, was ordered to head for the port and deliver an ultimatum to the French authorities.

The entire French force, of roughly the same strength, was instructed either to join the British force to 'continue to fight for victory', sail to a British port with a promise that the crews would be repatriated, or sail to a French port in the West Indies, or to an American port, to be demilitarized. After prolonged negotiations the French rejected all these alternatives. There was then applied what Churchill referred to as 'the deadly stroke', with aerial attacks and a ten-minute bombardment by Force H. One of the French heavy ships escaped, but the remainder were crippled or blown up, with grievous loss of life.

It was a hateful task but absolutely necessary. Other benefits accrued. 'Here was this Britain,' as Churchill wrote, 'which so many had counted down and out, which strangers had supposed to be quivering on the brink of surrender to the mighty power arrayed against her, striking ruthlessly at her dearest friends of yesterday and securing for a while to herself the undisputed command of the sea.'

Roosevelt's reaction, conveyed through Lord Lothian, was wholly favourable, and American public opinion was impressed. In due course, the United States succeeded in neutralizing, without resorting to violence, French men o'war stationed in the West Indies. The two most deadly thorns in Britain's flesh were the new and immensely powerful 15-inch-gun French battleships *Jean Bart* and *Richelieu*, the first of which lay in Casablanca harbour, without her main armament, at the time of the fall of France; the *Richelieu* was operational and had now reached Dakar on the West African coast.

Early in November Churchill learned that the French Government planned to bring these two ships to Toulon. 'It is difficult to exaggerate the potential if this were to happen,' Churchill notified Roosevelt on 10 November 1940, 'and so open the way for these ships to fall under German control.' Roosevelt reacted swiftly and firmly, and informed Churchill that the American chargé d'affaires in Vichy, seat of Marshal Pétain's puppet French Government, was seeking confirmation of this report. If this was confirmed,

the Chargé d'Affaires has been instructed to convey to Marshal Pétain an expression of the grave concern of the Government and to point out that the Government of the United States ... believes that if it is necessary ... to move the units in question the French authorities will not transfer them to any port inconsistent with the ultimate interests of the United States.

Roosevelt added that he had told the French that he would gladly buy the battleships 'if they will dispose of them to us'. Churchill said that he was 'deeply obliged for the promptness of your action'.

The American offer was not taken up by the French authorities – they would have been prohibited from doing so by their masters in any case – and the *Richelieu* at Dakar remained a serious threat. Towards the end of September Lothian informed Roosevelt that Churchill was planning a naval attack on Dakar in order to land a force of General Charles de Gaulle's Free French and take over the town, the port and the *Richelieu*, which had been disabled by an aerial torpedo attack from a carrier. This would have the further advantage of denying the strategically important port to the Germans as a future U-boat base.

When Lothian told London of Roosevelt's approval, Churchill telegraphed (24 September) his appreciation and, ever anxious to persuade the United States Navy into a demonstration of unified action, suggested Roosevelt might care to send men o'war to nearby West African ports, which could then call at Dakar when the port was captured. Roosevelt was given no time to respond to this idea for the very next day Churchill signalled Washington that 'I much regret we had to abandon Dakar enterprise'. The French defenders, not for the first or last time, had demonstrated a will to fight their fellow countrymen and recent allies which had not been consistently evident during the German attack on the homeland. They defended the port and town so effectively, and with the declared intention of continuing to do so to the last man, that the operation was called off. One of the main reasons for the French success was the *Richelieu*, which used her 15-inch guns to great effect but was herself damaged.

Roosevelt much regretted this set-back but did not in any way blame the Royal Navy as he had done over Norway. Meanwhile, he gave comfort to Churchill by continuing to apply pressure on Vichy France through the Ambassador in Washington. 'The fact that a government is a prisoner of war of another power does not justify such a prisoner in serving its conqueror in operations against its former ally,' he told the Ambassador firmly, and reported this to Churchill (24 October). Roosevelt added a thrust to the heart by hinting that 'when the appropriate time came' the United States would see to it that France would not recover her old overseas possessions.

In spite of the Dakar failure, and the presence of powerful French men o'war in Vichy-controlled Toulon, Churchill felt that the damage done to the *Richelieu* removed her as a threat. With the neutralization of other French units caught at Alexandria, he was now easy in his mind about the future of the French Fleet.

For the present the threat of the German surface Fleet, savaged in the Norwegian campaign, was restricted to the battle-cruisers *Scharnhorst* and *Gneisenau*, the pocket battleship *Scheer* and one or two heavy cruisers whose condition was uncertain. There was no reason for any complacency, but the Admiralty was confident that superior forces could rapidly be brought to bear if any of these men o'war came out to attack North Atlantic shipping.

With the entry of Italy into the war and the elimination of the French Fleet, Britain was, however, faced with massive new naval considerations in the Mediterranean. Churchill despised Mussolini and his Government, their bombast and sycophancy towards Hitler. 'People who go to Italy to look at ruins won't have to go so far as Naples and Pompeii again,' he muttered threateningly to his secretary early on the morning of 10 June. Nor did he have a high regard for them militarily. As for their fleet ...

The Italians had for long been regarded as better builders of ships than sailors. In 1940 the Italian Fleet was of about the same strength as the now scattered or defunct French Fleet had been. The ships were certainly the most beautiful and the swiftest in the world. A number of Italian cruisers could make over 40 knots and could comfortably outpace the standard British biplane torpedo bomber when steaming into a stiff wind. It was mockingly said before the war that the Italians needed this speed to run from the enemy, and this proved to be the case.

This Italian Fleet remained a menace, however, and was dealt with severely and swiftly on the night of 11 November 1940. Twenty lumbering Swordfish biplanes, guided by flares, made a low-level torpedo-dropping attack on the Italian Fleet in Taranto harbour and knocked out three of the six battleships there in a miniature prototype of Pearl Harbor a year later. With the loss of two planes in all, it was the most cost-effective operation of the war, and its success was closely noted by the Japanese. Reconnaissance was provided by a squadron of American-built planes operating from Malta, a point which Churchill did not miss in his report to Roosevelt.

With the virtual elimination of the French Fleet and the temporary crippling of the Italian Fleet, Churchill was relieved of two grave anxieties. By contrast, the future of the United States Fleet occupied his thoughts and entered into his calculations every day. A vast amount of time was spent in working out ways of involving units of the American Atlantic Fleet in the shooting war – the never-ending war of the U-boats and German bombers whose toll of shipping was developing into as critical a danger as in 1916–17. Between May and December 1940 3,239,190 tons of British, Allied and neutral shipping had been lost due to enemy action. By contrast with the First World War when bases on the west and south-west coasts of Ireland were available, Britain was deprived of these and also of the use of French Atlantic ports, which were now 'nests of hornets', which saved the U-boats the long passage round Scotland or the dangerous passage through the English Channel.

Admiral Karl Doenitz, C-in-C of the German U-boat Fleet for the entire duration of the war, established his headquarters in France and his still-small, highly efficient force operated mainly from St Nazaire, Lorient, La Pallice and Brest. New techniques included night attack and, later, 'wolf-pack' tactics, which had been tried out in 1918. The Royal Navy found difficulty in countering them. Between ten and twenty U-boats operated together under shore command, at first fanning out until a convoy was located, when it was shadowed usually by a single U-boat during daylight. The 'wolf-pack' then came under local command for a tightly organized series of night attacks, made on the surface before submerging to avoid counter action. The same procedure would be followed the next night, and again for perhaps three or four nights running.

'You will have seen what very heavy losses we have suffered ... to our last two convoys,' Churchill signalled Roosevelt on Trafalgar Day (21 October) 1940. '... We are passing through an anxious and critical period.' A week later Churchill refers again to 'the U-boat and air attacks upon our only remaining life line, the north-western approach'. In his long telegram of 7 December 1940, Churchill listed the additional difficulties in the fight against the U-boats the Royal Navy now faced, lacking 'the assistance of the French Navy, the Italian Navy and the Japanese Navy, and above all', he added pointedly, 'the United States Navy, which was of such vital help during the culminating years [of the First World War]'.

Roosevelt faced the situation resolutely, confident in his own unsurpassed political skill and sensitivity to the beat of the public pulse. No one in the nation recognized the danger as clearly as he did. As Sam Morison has written:

President Roosevelt, considerably in advance of public opinion, apprehended the threat to American security contained in the German seizure of the Atlantic Coast of France, and the strong possibility of a German invasion of Great Britain. For three centuries the British Navy could always be depended upon to prevent any power dominant on the European Continent from obtaining control of the Western Ocean sea lanes. In expectation that Britain could do it again, the United States Navy since 1922 had been largely concentrated in the Pacific, to watch Japan. Now we were faced with a possible pincer movement from across both oceans.

In addition to the informal talks between the two navies which had been taking place for some time, in July 1940 Roosevelt asked Stark to select a naval delegate for a three-man defence team to fact-find in London. Stark selected Rear Admiral Robert L.Ghormley. From the start, Churchill was determined to give the team priority attention and a warm welcome, and ensure that frankness was the keynote of the conversations. 'What arrangements are being made to receive this important United States mission?' he demanded. 'I should see them almost as soon as they come, and I could give them a dinner at No. 10.'

Ghormley's impressive and favourable reports led to a highly important memorandum on defence policy which Stark drew up and handed to the Navy Secretary on 12 November 1940, a time of savage shipping losses in the Atlantic. Stark's document had historical importance because for the first time it stated baldly that the US Navy might have to involve itself in combined operations with the Royal Navy in the Atlantic. It was also many months ahead of any seriously considered defence policy in envisaging that eventually the United States would have to 'send large air and land forces to Europe or Africa, or both, and to participate strongly in this land offensive. The naval task of transporting an army abroad would be large.'

Although by the end of 1940 Roosevelt was reconciled to the eventual American involvement at Britain's side, he still believed that it might be restricted to air and sea support – perhaps on a massive scale, but without the necessity of sending great armies across the seas. Six months later, with the German attack on Russia, he was confirmed in his view that 'it will mean the liberation of Europe from Nazi domination'.

Meanwhile the wheels had been set in swift motion to bring the US Navy into direct involvement in the Battle of the Atlantic. At the end of January 1941 secret staff conversations began in Washington between American, Canadian and British delegations from the three services, Admiral Ghormley, recently returned from London, leading for the US Navy. Rear Admiral Roger Bellairs, who had been on Jellicoe's Staff when Churchill was First Sea Lord in 1914, and Rear Admiral Victor Danckwerts, who in the same year, serving in the *Kent*, took part in the destruction of two of von Spee's cruisers, the *Nürnberg* and *Dresden*, represented the Royal Navy. As a symbolic gesture of unity, on the day the talks began in the USA, in Britain Roosevelt's recent political opponent, Wendell Wilkie, handed to Churchill an affectionate letter from Roosevelt. It included the Longfellow verse, 'Sail on, O Ship of State/Sail on, O Union, strong and great! ...' Churchill telegraphed that he was deeply moved and that he was going 'to have it framed as a souvenir of these tremendous days, and as a mark of our friendly relations'.

It was an auspicious start to the Washington negotiations, which resulted in a number of historic decisions and principles. These included the decision, in a shooting war, to beat Germany first 'as the predominant member of the Axis powers' and also because of the fear that German scientists might invent new and terrible secret weapons, unlikely to emerge from Japan. The Atlantic Ocean and Europe were defined as the decisive theatre. In the event of America entering the war, a Supreme War Council would be formed (it was, as the Joint Chiefs of Staff), and meanwhile staff conversations would continue; the blockade of Germany would be rigorously enforced; Italy knocked out of the war by a concentration of naval power in the Mediterranean; and concentration of American and British troops in Britain to prepare for an invasion of the Continent.

This time, the delegates determined, there would be none of the chaos and lack of co-ordination which delayed the effect of America's entry into a European war, and which had cost numberless lives in 1917 and 1918.

But of more immediate moment was the agreement that 'the United States Navy would take over the prime responsibility for protecting transatlantic merchant convoys, as soon as the Atlantic Fleet was in a position to do so'. This was the second stage in the unstated American 'short of war' policy, and a much more effective and important stage than the destroyer deal. This American Support Force, as it was termed, would be made up from parts of the Atlantic Fleet and would initially consist of three destroyer squadrons and a dozen long-range flying-boats.

Initially, the US Navy provided convoy escort from Argentia in Placentia Bay, Newfoundland, where bases were under urgent construction, to Iceland, which had been occupied peacefully during the Battle of France by British forces. The relief of pressure on the Royal Navy was valuable. It was hoped that soon further American involvement in the desperate struggle with the U-boats and bombers would tip the scales more heavily in favour of eventual victory. This was to happen, but it was going to take more than two years, and full American participation, before the U-boat was mastered.

While these profitable talks were proceeding in Washington, Harry Hopkins was in England, seeing a great deal of Churchill, forming an imperishable new friendship with the Premier, and writing to his old friend at the White House with vivid descriptions of life in Britain and with lists of urgent needs for survival. One evening at Chequers, after a strenuous day inspecting bomb damage in the West Country with Churchill, Hopkins produced a box of gramophone records. They were, Churchill's Principal Private Secretary, John Martin, recalled, 'all American tunes with an Anglo–American significance. We had these until well after midnight, the PM walking about, sometimes dancing a pas-seul, in time with the music. We all got a bit sentimental & Anglo–American under the influence of the good dinner & the music.'

With down-to-earth Anglo–American military and naval talks in Washington proceeding swiftly and amicably, and sentimental Anglo–American dancing at Chequers in England, how was it possible that the final sealing of the bonds be long delayed, and that they should be indivisible?

No one in Washington, and no one in London, enjoyed a good naval battle more than the nations' two leaders. In May 1941, while US Navy convoy work was building up, a new threat to Atlantic trade was developing, and this time no number of American destroyers, or ex-American destroyers, could help very much.

At the beginning of the war, the German Navy had under construction two formidable battleships, each more powerful than any battleship the Royal Navy could muster. The *Tirpitz* and *Bismarck* were to be over 45,000 tons and armed with eight 15-inch guns. Like the German dreadnought battleships that opposed the Grand Fleet at Jutland, they were so strongly protected and built that they were virtually unsinkable by gunfire alone. Their completion was awaited anxiously by Churchill and the Admiralty. The first to go into service was the *Bismarck*, and this giant battleship was known to have left the Norwegian port of Bergen on 21 or 22 May 1941 in company with a heavy cruiser, the *Prinz Eugen*, herself a match for any cruiser in the Royal Navy. It was evident that the two ships intended to engage in raids on North Atlantic convoys, with French Atlantic ports as bases upon which eventually to fall back, and reinforce the battle-cruisers *Scharnhorst* and *Gneisenau* and the heavy cruiser *Hipper* which were already at Brest. There were no fewer than eleven convoys at sea or about to sail, including a pricelessly valuable troop convoy from Canada and a large convoy out of Liverpool for the Middle East. The German surface fleet had suddenly become menacing again.

When the news of this break-out arrived at Chequers, Averell Harriman was Churchill's guest, on a fact-finding mission as Roosevelt's Special Envoy. He became deeply involved in the pursuit and engagements that followed. In Washington, Roosevelt was kept almost as well informed, and in equal suspense, from the moment the telegram arrived from Churchill: 'We have reason to believe that a formidable Atlantic raid is intended.' In recounting what steps the Royal Navy was taking to answer this threat, Churchill added, 'Should we fail to catch them going out your Navy should surely be able to mark them down for us . . . . Give us the news and we will finish them off.'

Churchill and his guests stayed up until 2.30 a.m. on the morning of Saturday 24 May in the hope of news. The old battle-cruiser *Hood* and the new battleship *Prince of Wales*, so new as to be imperfect in any action, supported by heavy cruisers, were in full pursuit, guided by radar.

At seven o'clock the next morning Harriman was awoken by the presence of Churchill at his bedside, dressed in a short nightshirt and yellow sweater. 'Hell of a battle going on,' announced the Premier. 'The *Hood* is sunk. Hell of a battle.' Harriman asked about the *Prince of Wales*. 'She's still at her,' he was told cheerfully, leading Churchill later to remark that 'it costs nothing to grin'. Churchill then returned to his room, and to sleep, to be awoken by his Principal Private Secretary at half past eight. 'Have we got her?' Churchill asked him. John Martin answered, 'No, and the *Prince of Wales* has broken off the action.'

'This was a sharp disappointment,' Churchill wrote later. 'Had then the *Bismarck* turned north and gone home?' It would have been the German ship's best course, returning home in triumph after destroying Britain's greatest warship, especially as the smaller and out-gunned *Prince of Wales* had scored several hits with 14-inch shells, one of which had pierced a fuel tank. This injury led to a continuous and serious loss of oil and, equally serious, to an indelible stain to mark her track as she sped south-west towards the convoy routes.

Churchill may have spared a grin for Averell Harriman but his mood at Chequers that weekend was grim, and he was led to remark that the past three days 'had been the worst yet'. He was furious that the *Prince of Wales* had broken off action and, according to one of his secretaries, he 'keeps saying it is the worst thing since [Admiral] Troubridge turned away from the *Goeben* in 1914'. The navy was suffering casualties in the Mediterranean at this time, too, where the army had been driven out of Greece and was about to be driven out of Crete as well. Churchill did not have a good word for anyone – the faithful Dudley Pound in the Admiralty or Admiral Andrew Cunningham, the C-in-C in the Mediterranean – 'he must be made to take every risk'.

After the shadowing cruisers lost contact with the *Bismarck*, the pursuit turned into a nightmare – a nightmare suffered in four nations: in Canada, where it was known that thousands of her troops were now at grave risk *en route* to Britain; in the USA and Britain, now jointly responsible for the defence of countless ships and men in the Atlantic; and in Germany, where the Admiralty knew of the *Bismarck*'s damage and that the raid had now become a race for survival with the French port of Brest as the haven.

It was a near million-to-one chance and dramatically appropriate that the quarry was at length spotted by an American-built plane manned by an Anglo–American crew. The long-range Consolidated PBY amphibian, named 'Catalina' by the RAF, had only recently been delivered to Britain in small numbers and was already proving valuable to Coastal Command for U-boat hunting. It had an enormous range and carried depth-charges as well as defensive machine-guns. The US Navy had, only weeks earlier, decided to send some seventeen experienced Catalina pilots to Britain to teach the RAF how to fly them, and to learn in exchange how Coastal Command was operating in the Battle of the Atlantic. Ensign Leonard ('Tuck') Smith was one of those who volunteered, a farmer's son from Higginsville, Missouri, aged twenty-six. He had been assigned to Catalina Z of 209 Squadron based on Oban on the west coast of Scotland, as co-pilot with Flying Officer Dennis Briggs, RAF.

The crew of Catalina Z were aroused at 2 a.m. on 26 May 1941 and ordered out to search for the escaped battleship. They had been in the air for over six hours when, flying at 500 feet below low cloud, Smith suddenly caught sight of a distant dark shape on the sea. Briggs, who had just taken over the controls, climbed into cloud and emerged again directly over the ship. It was enormous, and it was without doubt the *Bismarck*, ablaze from end to end – or so it seemed – with the flash of anti-aircraft guns. The Catalina's radio operator managed to transmit their position as the big amphibian was thrown about the sky evasively. And the pursuit was on again, with the odds in favour of the *Bismarck* making it safely to France.

But air power did for the *Bismarck* in the end, as air reconnaissance had found her. A single torpedo from an 80-knot biplane costing a few thousand pounds caught the *Bismarck* in the extreme stern, jamming her rudders. And then, with awesome inevitability, the armada of battleships, battle-cruisers and heavy cruisers despatched to run down the enemy, closed round the hapless giant, 14-inch and 16-inch shells tearing to pieces her upper works and hull at point-blank range, just as Beatty's battle-cruisers had shattered the *Blücher* twenty-six years earlier, with the *coup de grâce* delivered by torpedoes.

Churchill was able to announce the dramatic news of the end of the *Bismarck* in mid-speech in the House of Commons on 27 May. The news was at once flashed to Washington, and on the following day Churchill promised to send Roosevelt 'the inside story of the fighting with the *Bismarck*'. The *Bismarck* had been, he added, 'a terrific ship and a masterpiece of naval construction .... The effect upon the

Japanese will be highly beneficial,' Churchill surmised. 'I expect they are doing all their sums again.' No one mentioned, until long after the end of the war, that it had been an American on combat patrol in an American warplane who had found the *Bismarck*. The American Neutrality Act had been flagrantly violated, and the whole affair was 'a very hot political potato', at home and abroad.

The rest of the naval news in that summer of 1941 was less palatable, and Churchill had little of a favourable nature to report to Roosevelt. The losses in the eastern Mediterranean, especially of destroyers and cruisers, were very serious. In the Battle of the Atlantic, the loss of around half a million tons of shipping monthly in the early summer fell in July and August but later rose again to unacceptable levels in spite of greater American intervention.

The German attack on Russia on 22 June, which Churchill believed would lead to a speedy triumph for Germany while Roosevelt held the opposite view, certainly offered no relief for the hard-pressed Royal Navy. On the contrary, the support of Russia by every means, which became Churchill's instant policy, led to further stretching of naval resources with convoys to Murmansk via the Arctic and within range of German bombers as well as U-boats from Norway.

Churchill would have valued highly some spectacular piece of good news to mark the meeting with Roosevelt in August at Placentia Bay. Nothing occurred to lighten the darkness. But it was one of Churchill's great qualities that he could recover himself and rise above the worst news. He was difficult, even dangerous, company at Chequers during the awful weekend of uncertainty over the *Bismarck* and the fate of Crete. But by the following Tuesday, in the makeshift premises to which the House of Commons had had to retreat when the chamber was bombed into uninhabitability, Churchill was speaking with buoyancy and optimism even before the news was passed to him that the threat was over and the giant battleship was at the bottom of the Atlantic.

On 25 July Churchill signalled Roosevelt, 'Am looking forward enormously to our talks, which may be of service to the future.' Roosevelt was equally excited and was already relishing the cloak-and-dagger deception he was about to practise. He was also deeply curious to meet the war leader he had admired since he became Assistant Secretary of the Navy almost thirty years ago. Roosevelt was suspicious of Churchill's imperial attitudes, hostile to his nineteenth-century views on colonialism and especially India. But how could he fail to be impressed by the manner in which he had held his country together and inspired its martial spirit in spite of a series of stunning blows? Roosevelt recognized that without Churchill's leadership Britain might have given in as rapidly and cravenly as had France little more than a year earlier.

Many facets of Churchill's character, judged from afar, still remained a mystery to the President, and he would have benefited greatly if an assessment by one of Churchill's closest and cleverest lieutenants had been available in the White House as it was at Chequers on the weekend before Churchill sailed. General Sir Claude Auchinleck, the Commander in the Middle East, was at Chequers that weekend, and was going to be relentlessly grilled by Churchill in connection with his offensive plans in the western desert. 'The Auk' was unfamiliar with Churchill's methods and provocative style of dealing with his commanders. It was of inestimable value, therefore, that Major-General Hastings ('Pug') Ismay, as Chief of Staff to the War Cabinet closer to Churchill than almost anyone, was also at Chequers. Ismay was an old friend of Auchinleck and was therefore anxious to brief him and make him aware of what sort of man his host and political boss was.

Ismay later wrote down 'the gist of what I said' in his memoirs :

Churchill could not be judged by ordinary standards ; he was different from anyone we had ever met before, or were ever likely to meet again. As a war leader, he was head and shoulders above anyone that the British or any other nation could produce. He was indispensable and completely irreplaceable. The idea that he was rude, arrogant and self-seeking was entirely wrong . . . . He was certainly frank in speech and writing, but he expected others to be equally frank with him . . . . He was a child of nature. He venerated tradition, but ridiculed convention. When the occasion demanded, he could be the personification of dignity ; when the spirit moved him, he could be a *gamin*. His courage, enthusiasm and industry were boundless, and his loyalty was absolute. No commander who engaged the enemy need ever fear that he would not be supported . . . . He was not a gambler, but never shrank from taking a calculated risk. His whole heart and soul were in the battle, and he was an apostle of the offensive.

When Churchill stepped on board the *Prince of Wales* at Scapa Flow on that morning of 4 August 1941, he knew that he had much to learn about the President he was to meet. Since the overture he had received from Roosevelt almost two years earlier, he had pondered on the nature and policies of the American leader. Churchill understood American politics infinitely better than Roosevelt understood the British parliamentary system and the convoluted processes which had caused it to work since 1688. He admired the style and subtlety – to say nothing of the immense courage – that had taken this dreadfully disabled man to the White House and kept him there for almost nine years. He admired his ruthlessness and was comforted by the certain knowledge

that they possessed in common a charm of manner and quality of patrician leadership which would make communication straightforward.

Churchill had admired Roosevelt's New Deal and the way he had
dragged the United States out of the terrible recession following the
stock market crash of 1929. He had admired his radical politics at home,
but was puzzled by the naïvety of Roosevelt's radical foreign policy.
For a man who had approved so wholeheartedly of America's colonial
exploits at the turn of the century, and after, as conducted chiefly by
his kinsman Teddy Roosevelt, the President's antipathy for British and
French colonialism appeared ridiculously inconsistent.

Churchill better understood American mercenary tendencies, which
he had inherited himself through his mother, and was less outraged
than some of his Cabinet members by the cash-on-the-nail attitude towards arms supplies when France fell and the survival of democracy
in Western Europe rested on a small British air force and a much-
battered navy. In December 1940, when London was suffering some
of its worst bombing raids, Washington was pressing for Britain's gold
reserves in South Africa to be released and despatched to America
pending approval of the proposed Lend-Lease Bill by Congress. There
was even the suggestion that the US Navy might be used as mailman.

On 28 December Churchill drafted a telegram addressed to Roosevelt
which began,

We are very anxious to tide over the interval of payments until you have declared policy of United States to Congress. But I am much puzzled and even
perturbed by the proposal now made to send a United States battleship to
collect whatever gold there may be in Cape Town .... It is not fitting [he
continued] that any nation which is fighting under increasingly severe conditions
for what is proclaimed to be a cause of general concern .... I should not
be discharging my responsibilities to the people of the British Empire if, without
the slightest indication of how our fate was to be settled in Washington, I
were to part with this last reserve, from which alone we might buy a few
months' food.

These were the strongest and certainly the bitterest words ever written
by Churchill to the President. But Roosevelt never read them. Time
and again Churchill gained much-needed relief in putting to paper his
thoughts on the crisis of the day, modifying them repeatedly and then
either despatching the final draft in a more considered or milder form,
or thrusting the paper aside, for good. On this occasion sound judgement
told him that he should await Roosevelt's next broadcast to the nation,
the end-of-the-year 'Fireside Chat'. In the event, this presidential
message proved to be the most outspoken warning of the need of the

American people to guard against the danger they faced: 'Never before since Jamestown . . .' and the clarion cry, 'We must be the great arsenal of democracy.'

Ever since the fall of France, Churchill had accepted that Britain's will and means to prevail depended, more than any other factor, on the cultivation of close relations with Roosevelt until – as day follows night – the United States would be drawn into the conflict. On the Atlantic voyage, between and during the games of backgammon with Harry Hopkins, Churchill learned more about the man who regarded Hopkins as his closest confederate. Churchill increasingly liked what he heard; and even accepted with good grace that it would be fruitless and unwise to press the President about American intentions to become involved militarily in the war.

With the warm handshake between the two leaders on the deck of the *Augusta*, a new phase in the relationship between the Former Naval Person and the C-in-C of the United States Navy opened. It was a brief phase, more an overture to the Wagnerian crash of bombs and torpedoes at Pearl Harbor and in the South China Sea four months later. These catastrophes marked the beginning of a new era of joint command and total co-operation – inhibitions, reservations, domestic political considerations, all sunk along with the battleships both nations lost in those early days of December 1941.

9
Day of Infamy

Harry Hopkins lunched with Roosevelt in the Oval Room of the White House on Sunday, 7 December 1941. 'We were talking about things far removed from the war,' Hopkins recalled, when the telephone rang. It was Secretary of the Navy Knox on the line. He informed the President that an air raid was taking place on Pearl Harbor, according to a broadcast from Honolulu. No, it was not an exercise – 'no drill'. Hopkins thought that there must be some mistake ; he could not conceive that the Japanese could be so foolish. But the President 'thought the report was probably true and thought it was just the kind of unexpected thing the Japanese would do' – breaking up a peace discussion with a surprise all-out attack.

Two Japanese diplomats were at that time in Washington, Kitchisaburo Nomura and Saburo Kurusu, ostensibly to preserve the peace with the United States by negotiation of differences. They were due shortly at a further meeting with Secretary of State Cordell Hull. Roosevelt now called up Hull, told him the news and asked him to hold the meeting, 'to receive their reply formally and coolly and bow them out'. It was heard later that the Secretary of State added a touch of rich language to his formal statement to the diplomats. Admiral Stark then called up from the Navy Department to confirm the news from Hawaii and inform the President that there had been damage and loss of life.

In England, Churchill had two Americans as guests for the weekend at Chequers, the Ambassador John Winant, and Averell Harriman. Churchill was low and depressed at dinner, almost as if he were on the verge of a 'black dog', the occasional moods that had assailed him since his early political days. Shortly after nine o'clock he switched on the little American portable radio Hopkins had once given him. The news bulletin had already begun, and at the end of a number of items about the fighting in the western desert and Russia, there was a brief mention of reported Japanese attacks on American shipping at Hawaii and British shipping in the Dutch East Indies.

The potential enormity of the news had not yet sunk in when

Churchill's butler entered. He had listened earlier and more attentively to the news and confirmed the report of these Japanese attacks.

'We looked at one another incredulously,' Winant recounted later. 'Then Churchill jumped to his feet and started for the door with the announcement, "We shall declare war on Japan." There is nothing half-hearted or unpositive about Churchill – certainly not when he is on the move.'

And 'on the move' Churchill certainly was. Within minutes he was talking to Roosevelt at the White House. 'Mr President, what's this about Japan?'

'It's quite true. They have attacked us at Pearl Harbor. We're all in the same boat now,' Roosevelt replied. And then told Churchill that on the following day he intended to go to Congress 'to declare a state of open hostility'.

'This certainly simplifies things,' said Churchill before handing the telephone over to Winant. 'God be with you.'

Winant and Harriman, according to Churchill, 'took the shock with admirable fortitude', while Churchill did his best to hide his elation. War between Germany and the United States was now inevitable. Everything towards which Churchill as Prime Minister had been working for eighteen difficult and dangerous months had now, suddenly and spectacularly, taken place. From that moment he knew that the sinister and evil empires of Japan and Germany, as well as Mussolini's seedy regime, were doomed. There could be only one result now; the imponderables were: how long? and at what cost? 'No American', wrote Churchill, 'will think it wrong of me if I proclaim that to have the United States at our side was to me the greatest joy .... So we had won after all!'

The reaction in the White House to the news was mixed and more complicated. The pain and the tumult from which Roosevelt was suffering was evident to Cabinet members who entered the Oval Room, urgently summoned for conversations. There were three chief emotions at play, and at conflict, in the President's mind: shame for the United States Navy, which was almost a part of his being and on which he had lavished such pride for all his conscious life; anguish and pity for those who had already suffered and would suffer in such numbers in the future; and there was relief that the uncertainty which had hung ever more heavily over the considerations and debates of the past months was at last over.

Now the decisions would be clear-cut, unequivocal, pragmatic, military. The leader of the nervous, squabbling mob was now the commander on the parade-ground barking orders to the disciplined ranks. But for this instant there was the pain of disillusionment, there was no doubt of that. What had the navy been doing to be unprepared when so many warnings had been issued and war was clearly so imminent? In one hour, it was now clear, Japanese planes had crippled the US Pacific Fleet, the battleships neatly berthed in a row like fairground targets.

The Secretary of Labor recalled the scene in the Oval Room as Roosevelt spoke. 'His pride in the Navy was so terrific that he was having actual physical difficulty in getting out the words that put him on record as knowing that the Navy was caught unawares, that bombs dropped on ships that were not in fighting shape and not prepared to move, but were just tied up.'

All that would have to be investigated. For the present the anguish must be overcome. For, just as – in Roosevelt's coined phrase – this had been 'a day of infamy', so also was it a day of destiny for the man who ruled the most powerful nation on earth. In spite of the rain of blows that had fallen upon his country, and would continue to fall for certain, Roosevelt had supreme confidence in America's strength as soon as it was mobilized. For, if the Japanese had surprised the navy with the speed and effectiveness of the Pearl Harbor operation, this was no greater than the surprise experienced in Washington at the diplomatic ineptitude of the Japanese military leadership. The Japanese, with their reputation for guile and craftiness, had opened hostilities in a manner guaranteed to unite the enemy instantly and inspire it with a will and determination that could have been achieved in no other way.

There must, in the end, be victory in the Pacific. And as for Germany, inevitably an enemy, too, now – well, she might be a more difficult nut to crack. But here again there was no lack of confidence in the President's mind. What had Stark told him recently? A close friend of the Chief of Naval Operations, Colonel Etherton, who had been educated in Germany and knew Hitler well, recalled Hitler saying, 'There is only one man in the world whose picture when I look at it, makes me think he would be a pretty tough opponent, and that is President Roosevelt.'

Hitler was, indeed, the first enemy, as had already been agreed with Britain, and only three days were to pass before Germany and Italy declared war. But for the present and without neglecting the needs of the bitter and everlasting Battle of the Atlantic, it was the naval situation in the Pacific that had to be corrected. There were only two battleships out of eight fit for action at Pearl Harbor after the Japanese attack, and there were, proportionately, as few planes left fit to fly. All over the Pacific, Malaysia to Timor, from Wake Island west to Hawaii to Guam to the Solomon Islands, the Japanese crack task forces of battleships, carriers and cruisers were on the attack.

On the credit side, however, the most important relief was that not a single carrier had been at Pearl Harbor at the time of the attack. By great good fortune all were absent on various duties, and as the Imperial Japanese Navy had just demonstrated, the capital ship of the future *was* the carrier, its armament not the 14-inch guns of the *Oklahoma*, lying capsized at the bottom of the harbour, but bombing and torpedo aircraft with a range far beyond that of any gun and with an accuracy only a gun at point-blank range could match. It was also noteworthy that none of the sunk battleships was less than twenty years old. There were more than that number, modern, brand new, already completed or completing in home shipyards. The Japanese, then, had aroused the fury and fire of the United States by destroying an obsolete battle fleet made up of an obsolete type of man o'war. They had not even killed many people – few more than the civilians killed on a bad night in the bombing blitz on Britain.

Unharmed at the end of this 'day of infamy' were the considerable carrier and submarine forces of the US Navy, and these were the ships that would win the war in the Pacific. On every count except proof of the effectiveness of the Japanese air arm, Pearl Harbor was a Japanese disaster. At the time there was, understandably, grave anxiety. It was undeniable that Japanese skill and weapons had been gravely underestimated. This was confirmed by the Japanese victory in the South China Sea three days later. In a remarkable feat of arms, Japanese planes operating at an unprecedented range and armed with torpedoes of unprecedented destructive power, sank the *Prince of Wales* and the battle-cruiser *Repulse* in short order while at sea. Both ships were equipped with what was considered adequate anti-aircraft protection, but lacked the fighter aircraft cover now recognized as essential.

Inevitably, heads rolled for the Pearl Harbor fiasco. Admiral Husband Kimmel, C-in-C Pacific Fleet, was first for the guillotine, although 'responsibility for the debacle was in fact spread so widely through governmental and service organisations that individual error other than excusable human fallibility was not pinpointed'. He was relieved of his command on 17 December and at once applied for retirement. To Roosevelt's sorrow and chagrin, Stark had to go, too, after criticism at the enquiry that he had not kept Kimmel sufficiently informed of the imminent danger to the base. Stark was, however, merely transferred, and in March 1942 was made C-in-C US Navy Forces in the European theatre of operations. He remained a close friend and confidant of the President to the end.

Stark had served in the Navy Department in Washington for many years, latterly as Chief of the Bureau of Ordnance. He was preeminently a desk admiral. He was, in the eyes of Robert E. Sherwood, 'able to consider the political as well as purely military aspects of the global situation . . . . He had exceptional qualities as a staff officer, but lacked the quickness and the ruthlessness of a decision required in war-time . . . his contribution to the formation of Grand Strategy was immeasurable.'

Stark's successor, Ernest J. King, was a very different man, with none of Stark's refinements of diplomacy, 'a stern sailor of commanding presence, vast sea-knowledge and keen strategic sense'. At first judgement he appeared a dour, uncompromising figure, and very often at second judgement, too. He never ceased to want the Pacific war to take priority and preference, was deeply suspicious of Britain as an ally, dubious about the quality of the Royal Navy and fought off for as long as he could any British or other Allied support in the Pacific war. Between the wars he was much concerned with the development of naval aviation and commanded a carrier for two years before taking a Naval War College course. At the time of Pearl Harbor, after gaining his wings at the age of forty-nine, he was the only American officer of high rank with specialized experience and knowledge of undersea, surface and air warfare.

'Ernie' King was in command of the Atlantic Patrol Force before coming to Washington. He was, it has been said, 'a man of strong will and hot temper: but he also possessed an innate sense of justice which allowed him to pardon failure in those whom he knew to have done their best'. On his appointment as C-in-C US Fleet and Chief of Naval Operations, he stated as his policy: 'It is time to toss defensive talking and thinking overboard. Our days of victories are in the making – we will win this war.' His determination to make the US Fleet win the war in the Pacific unaided was caused, it was said, 'by the need he felt for wiping out the memory of the disaster at Pearl Harbor'.

Ernest King was vindictive, irascible, overbearing, hated and feared. He had no time for his contemporaries, regarding General Marshall as stupid, General 'Hap' Arnold as Marshall's yes-man and Admiral Leahy as a fixer. On the British side, he liked Pound and admired Portal, but mistrusted Churchill and loathed General Alan Brooke [Chief of Imperial General Staff].

King drank too much, seduced his fellow officers' wives, was a poor sport. So how did it come about that Roosevelt, who knew about the drink problem, appointed him to supreme command when King was sixty-three and already reconciled to going 'to the scrap heap'? Only a part of the answer can be found in the fact that he was by chance in Washington at the time of Pearl Harbor when everyone was in a state of panic and became convinced that the tall, handsome, stern King would sort things out.

King himself, with engaging frankness, explained his appointment: 'When they get into trouble they send for the sons of bitches.'

On the Joint Chiefs of Staff Committee, set up to plan and supervise the direction of the war, Admiral King was regarded as difficult, and sometimes quite intractable: 'a tough sixty-three-year-old salt of strong views and uncompromising temper who had grown up with the American Navy and was intensely jealous of its independence'.

Churchill found King trying for his obstinacy and inflexible views. In the closing stages of the war when Churchill, far ahead of the American administration, sought to limit Russian intransigence and penetration into Eastern Europe and the Balkans, King lined up with the radical and suspicious American view of British motives. Better a communist revolution, and a communist regime in Greece, for example, than give assistance to Churchill and the Greek Government. King refused the use of American ships to help transport the British division ordered there by Churchill. Roosevelt was prevailed upon to cancel King's order, but only after much acrimony.

As the catastrophe of Pearl Harbor brought King to Washington to replace Stark, Admiral Chester Nimitz owed his position as C-in-C Pacific for almost the entire war to the judged failure of Admiral Kimmel to prepare that base for the attack. Chester Nimitz was more agreeable company than King. 'Nimitz won the respect and affection of sailors of all nationalities who came under his command,' *The Times* stated on his death. 'He was that rare person in any fighting service – a leader of exceptional presence who was yet naturally and entirely modest.' It was also stated that 'whenever a British ship called at Pearl Harbor he found time to board her and . . . would walk round the decks informally, chatting to officers and men in the most winning and intimate manner'. Referring to King, but without naming him, Admiral Bruce Fraser, C-in-C British Pacific Fleet, once remarked, 'The warmth of Nimitz's welcome was in marked contrast to the attitude of those American naval men who had not wished to see the English return to the Pacific.' Morison's considered judgement was that 'Nimitz probably inspired a greater personal loyalty than did any other admiral in the war' – and it is hard to beat that compliment. Roosevelt felt closer to Chester Nimitz than any other of his admirals.

As the fighting crept close to the Japanese homeland and the US marines captured the key island of Iwo Jima against fanatical resistance, Roosevelt received from Nimitz a copy of a triumphant photograph which was to become famous. Roosevelt thanked him for 'that very fine picture of the Flag being raised on Mount Suribachi by the Marines. I am delighted to have it for my collection.' It was signed by Nimitz, Admirals Turner and Spruance, and the Marines General Smith.

Admiral Richmond Kelly Turner had by this time become 'the leading practitioner of amphibious warfare in the Pacific', a fine officer who had recovered from an early set-back and a near deadly dose of malaria to form an imperishable partnership with Raymond Spruance.

Admiral Spruance personified the whole philosophy of conduct of the gigantic Pacific campaign, which rested upon caution and steadiness, minute planning and a proper traditional regard for full back-up and consolidation of supplies before a further advance with the minimum losses of men and material. His nickname 'Electric Brain' derived less from his early specialist training in electrical engineering than from his quick thinking in a crisis. Most authorities agree that he possessed the best tactical mind of any naval commander in the Pacific; and Morison has commented that he was 'a happy choice indeed' for command at the Battle of Midway, 'for Spruance was not merely competent; he had the level head and cool judgement that would be required to deal with new contingencies and a fluid situation: a man secure within'.

Spruance was, it has been said,

a man of quiet and modest personality but possessed of great powers of organization and outstanding resolution in moments of crisis ... a master of the complexities and uncertainties of large-scale amphibious warfare. If it was Nimitz who created the supremely successful Pacific strategy, it was Spruance and Halsey who translated the energy into action.

William F. 'Bull' Halsey was a strongly contrasting character to Spruance, a flamboyant fire-eater and probably the most popular commander with the lower deck in the Pacific Fleets. Halsey proved the exception to the rule of caution which generally governed the naval war in the Pacific, and on several occasions paid a heavy price for the risks he took, but he was a brilliant director of naval aviation. Halsey, according to Morison, will

always remain a controversial figure, but none can deny that he was a great leader, one with the 'Nelson touch'. His appointment as Commander South Pacific Force at the darkest moment of the Guadalcanal campaign lifted the hearts of every officer and bluejacket. He hated the enemy with an unholy wrath, and turned that feeling into a grim determination by all hands to hit hard, again and again, and win.

Halsey, from long association with Roosevelt in the Admiral's destroyer days, was very close to the President, too. But Roosevelt's nature, his feeling for the sea and his lifelong love for the American Navy, gave him an affection for all his admirals. Besides King, Stark, Nimitz, Turner, Spruance and Halsey, Roosevelt felt an all-embracing affinity with Admirals Daniel Barbey and Theodore Wilkinson, Admirals Wilson Brown and Frederick Sherman, Admirals Richard Conolly, Thomas Hart, Thomas Kinkaid, Marc Mitscher and many others.

From the outset of the Pacific war Roosevelt was blessed with an exceptional Secretary of the Navy, a very different man from Josephus Daniels of the First World War, and by no means the cipher whom Churchill had chosen as First Lord when he became Premier. William Franklin Knox was a Bostonian with a fine fighting record as a younger man. He was born in 1874 and fought in the Rough Riders in the Spanish–American War and as a colonel of field artillery in France in 1918. His careers between the wars were as newspaperman first and Republican politician a close second. By 1936 he was nominated Vice-President on the Republican ticket, and was publisher of the Chicago *Daily News*. Roosevelt brought him into his administration in July 1940 during the infiltration exercise of his opponents before the 1940 presidential election. He was not known for any special interest in the navy but he was a first-rate administrator, and tough besides. He needed all his strength to deal with Admiral King, who loathed and despised him and came close to reorganizing the administrative structure of the navy in 1942 in order to strip to almost nothing the civilian influence in naval affairs. It took Roosevelt's intervention to prevent this step towards a total King dictatorship.

For his part, Knox was always trying to get King out of Washington and into the Pacific and a seagoing command. He never succeeded. And the incessant sniping from King certainly contributed to Secretary Knox's premature death on 28 April 1944. On hearing of Knox's death – from a heart attack – Churchill signalled, 'His Majesty's Government and especially the Admiralty feel his loss acutely, for no one could have been more forthcoming and helpful in all our difficult times than was this distinguished American statesman and War Administrator.'

The excellent and efficient Knox was succeeded by James V. Forrestal, Knox's number two, who had done much useful liaison work in Britain before Pearl Harbor. Roosevelt admired him as much as he had admired the dogged Knox. Again far too much of the Secretary's time was taken up dealing with King and his temperament. Forrestal was cooler with him than Knox had been. 'Forrestal's temperament seemed to have been more annoying to King than the admiral's mannerisms were to Forrestal,' Forrestal's biographer suggested.

With both his Secretaries of the Navy Roosevelt maintained smooth-running relations, but they were political relations that lacked the special quota of warmth he reserved for his admirals – even for King to whom he showed a tolerance far beyond what this irascible and non-co-operative admiral deserved.

*   *   *

And now, what of the Pacific Fleets, Japanese and American, and the course of the mighty and long-drawn-out campaign, for American tribulation 'Mid toil and tumult of her war ...'? With the elimination of the American battle fleet at Pearl Harbor and, three days later, the *Prince of Wales* and *Repulse* off Singapore, the Imperial Japanese Navy could lay claim to control of the central and western Pacific Ocean. All that remained to the west was the weak American Asiatic Fleet under the command of Admiral Thomas C. Hart, and a mixed force of American, Dutch and British cruisers and destroyers under the command of the Dutch Rear Admiral Karel Doorman based on Surabaya. The Japanese had been disappointed to find no carriers at Pearl Harbor, but were confident in their own superiority in skill and material if the American carriers should ever emerge to challenge them.

The Imperial Japanese Navy was a superbly efficient fighting machine, highly professional, dedicated and skilful. Their ships and equipment were first class. Their two newest battleships dwarfed even the German *Bismarck*, their 18-inch guns were the biggest ever fitted to a battleship, their carriers fast and efficient and the planes they carried, supported by a fine shore-based maritime air force, superior to anything the Americans possessed. Their 'Long Lance' 24-inch torpedoes were propelled by liquid oxygen which gave them unprecedented speed and range. Carrier plane torpedoes could be dropped from a height which amazed the men of the *Prince of Wales*. Although they had no radar, their night-fighting methods had been taken to a peak of efficiency, aided by enormous night binoculars – which had deceived pre-war pundits into the comforting illusion that they were confirmation of oriental myopia.

The C-in-C of the Combined Fleets, Isoroku Yamamoto, had justifiable confidence in the superiority of Japanese arms at the end of 1941. He had also voiced his belief that victory must come to Japan within one year, or it would never come. He was aware of the vastly greater industrial capacity of the United States when it was switched to war production, enlarged and speeded up. On the evidence of the first few months, it looked as if Yamamoto's time limit for America's defeat would be met.

The US Navy deserved Roosevelt's pride and admiration. The hard-core professionals were a fine body of sailors, but with the accelerating growth of the Fleet they were relatively few in number and the called-up reservists and new recruits required to man the new ships coming from the yards lacked the experience of the peacetime men. The carrier air-crew and the submariners in particular were outstanding in their specialist trades. The newer ships, too, were first class. The 16-inch-gunned

new generation of battleships now joining the Fleet were as stoutly
protected and built as their German counterparts, could make 30 knots
and could take massive punishment. Not one was to be lost in almost
four years of war in the Pacific.

The greatest equipment weakness was in the navy's torpedoes, which
were slow and unreliable and not in the same class as Japanese torpedoes. Time and again in those early months of war destroyers and submarines were courageously brought within close striking range of the
enemy only to be frustrated by inefficient torpedoes. Inadequate anti-
aircraft protection bedevilled the ships of every fleet in the world, none
more so than the British and American. Many months passed and many
ships were damaged or sunk by bomb or torpedo before sufficient anti-
aircraft batteries were fitted. Then the screen of metal and high explosive
made penetration to the target almost impossible, even by kamikaze
suicide pilots.

But it is quality of personnel that counts in the end as much as quality
and output of material. The Japanese professionals of 1941 were unsurpassed in any navy. But as the war took its toll, and Yamamoto's first
year passed without a conclusion, hastily trained replacements were
no match for the old professionals. American training facilities were
many times greater than the enemy's and with every passing month
the tens of thousands and finally hundreds of thousands of civilian sailors
became more accomplished, learning as fast as Americans always have
learned. By 1945, when the carrier fleet had increased from five to
over ninety, new battleship construction had replaced the Pearl Harbor
losses many times over, and cruisers, destroyers, auxiliaries, transports
and landing-craft numbered many hundreds, the US Navy was not only
the biggest fleet the world had ever seen but its skill and efficiency
were remarkable by any standards.

But while the US Navy recruiting office queues were still forming
in the early weeks of 1942, the Japanese task forces and invasion forces
ranged far and wide and almost unopposed. Doorman's international
heterogeneous force was destroyed piecemeal in the Java Sea. Vice
Admiral Chuichi Nagumo's 1st Air Fleet, exultant after Pearl Harbor,
swept west and south, smashing into submission Wake Island, Rabaul
and Amboina, bringing war to Australia for the first time by devastating
Darwin and its shipping. Then west into the Indian Ocean, challenging
British control of these waters and the small mixed fleet of Admiral
Sir James Somerville. Two heavy cruisers, a carrier and her escort were
all sent to the bottom by dive bombers, and Colombo and the British
naval base of Trincomalee were given the same treatment as Darwin.

The task force returned home on 18 April 1942. It had been an amazing cruise across a third of the world, triumphing from Pearl Harbor

to Ceylon, 157° west to 80° east. They had all but destroyed the American Battle Fleet, crippled the British Eastern Fleet and caused devastation wherever they steamed. If ever there has been an invincible fleet, this was it – five carriers against the two most powerful navies in the world. And not one of the carriers had been attacked, let alone damaged.

How could the Japanese High Command succeed in the equally difficult next task : to restrain themselves and their admirals from over-confidence and ambitions beyond the bounds of wisdom? Malaysia, Singapore, the whole Malay barrier were safely in their hands; the Philippines and Borneo would soon be theirs, and Burma, with India directly threatened. To the north, part of the long string of the Aleutians was soon to be under their control, threatening the west coast of Canada and the United States.

Succumbing to what came to be known as the 'victory disease', voices in the high command demanded an acceleration of the long-laid plans for total victory in the Pacific, with surrender of their enemies – Australia and New Zealand in the south, India in the west, China (almost accomplished), and finally the North American nations, when war-weariness and disillusionment would lead Canada and the United States to seek terms.

Under the heady fumes of saki toasts, it all seemed not only possible but inevitable. The contemptible Americans had revealed the hollow-ness of their past claims of invincibility ; the British had sent their best battleship and, like their much-vaunted eastern base of Singapore, it had succumbed at once. Now, disregarding the age-old military adage of securing your supplies and supply lines before further advance, the Imperial Japanese Navy thrust for Midway Island, from which they could assault and capture the Hawaiian islands, south towards the New Hebrides, the Fijian Islands and the Solomons to cut the communica-tions with Australia, and New Guinea on the northern doorstep of Australia. It was a breathtaking programme of conquest for a nation which had emerged from secretive isolation only eighty years earlier.

Six months to the day after the Pearl Harbor attack, the invincibility of the Japanese at sea was put to its first full test, almost on Australia's doorstep, in the Coral Sea. It was an operation like none other before it in the history of sea warfare, in which electronics and aviation played the major roles and the ships' roles were limited to search and the carriage of aircraft. In the course of the two-day battle on 7–8 May 1942 no ship on either side sighted the enemy, and the presence of a battleship would have been a hindrance rather than an advantage.

The battle taught both sides lessons which were applied in all subsequent operations in the Pacific war. Commanders learned that pilots tended to exaggerate the size of enemy ships and claims of damage inflicted on them ; they learned to keep back some fighters for the protection of their carriers when despatching an attacking force ; they learned to resist laying on an attack until confident of the enemy's position. Scouting and reporting by destroyer and by aircraft were unsatisfactory ; and for the Americans radar played a significant part for the first time. American intelligence also benefited greatly from its code-breaking ability, which was a heavy advantage through all the Pacific operations. This was supplemented by the valiant work of so-called 'coast-watchers', the Allied spies who operated with short-wave radios from concealed observation points on Japanese-held islands.

Coral Sea was a long-drawn-out and indecisive engagement during which the Japanese lost a small carrier and Admiral Fletcher one of his large carriers. But for the Australians and Americans it was an encouraging and exhilarating experience which proved that the Japanese could be halted, on this occasion frustrated in their amphibious attack on Port Moresby. Also for the first time, the Japanese planes proved relatively vulnerable, and the American fighter pilots in particular shot down with consummate skill enemy bombers in considerable numbers.

Weather, radar, deception, initiative, luck, all played their part in this fascinating contest. The long-revered art of gunnery was practised only by the men manning the anti-aircraft guns, who were to prove key figures in the campaigns ahead, and the fighter pilots.

Superior intelligence played a vital role in the next Japanese move. Foiled in the southward offensive, Admiral Yamamoto now thrust east again, hell-bent on the capture of Midway Island, the key to the door to the Hawaiian Islands and the eastern Pacific. The Japanese C-in-C knew that he was engaged in a logistical race as well as the widest-ranging naval campaign in history. He knew that before the end of 1942 the American Pacific Fleet would have been reinforced with the men o'war being rushed to completion in American yards. He must attack now, without delay, shrugging off the set-back at Coral Sea, ignoring the evidence of American and Australian will to fight.

By 10 May Admiral Nimitz at Pearl Harbor had every reason to believe that his opponent would be attacking Midway within fourteen days. And he possessed only two operational carriers. Admiral Nagumo alone had twice this force of these new capital ships. In the Pearl Harbor dockyard men worked round the clock to repair a third carrier, the *Yorktown*, badly damaged at Coral Sea.

While the code-breakers worked their magic skills, providing Nimitz with a clear picture of Japanese plans, even, finally, the precise date of the attack, he despatched his only two carriers, under the command of Admiral Spruance, to intercept Nagumo's carriers as they advanced, strongly supported by a battleship task force, from the north-west. By prodigies of industry, the *Yorktown* was repaired in three days, emerged from dry dock and was at once on her way to join Spruance's two carriers at a rendezvous on the ocean cheerfully code-named 'Point Luck'. Admiral Fletcher flew his flag in the *Yorktown* and was in overall command.

The Japanese pilots were bursting with self-confidence, the fresh replacement pilots as buoyed up by the record of this task force at Pearl Harbor and off Ceylon. 'We were so sure of our own strength that we thought we could smash the enemy fleet single-handed, even if the battleship groups did nothing to support us,' Commander Fuchida boasted. Admiral Nagumo, ever the realist, was not so sure. He had no idea of the whereabouts of the American carriers. If he had possessed the detailed knowledge vouchsafed to Fletcher and Spruance, this critically important operation might well have led to a Japanese victory.

If Coral Sea was the overture to a new age of sea warfare, Midway confirmed this historical fact. Many Japanese and American airmen died on that fourth day of June 1942. Several squadrons were decimated by fighter and anti-aircraft fire. American torpedoes were as ineffective as they had been earlier; Japanese torpedoes as effective. Attacks by torpedo bombers and dive bombers which should have been synchronized were hopelessly unco-ordinated. But at the end of the two days, all four Japanese carriers were at the bottom of the sea or fatally damaged while only one American carrier succumbed to the furious Japanese assault.

Besides four carriers and a heavy cruiser, the Japanese lost around 250 naval aircraft and their aircrew – most of them the irreplaceable, highly trained professionals of the Pearl Harbor triumph. The Imperial Japanese Navy was still by no means crippled but it was never to regain the ascendancy of earlier days. In the fierce fighting around the Solomon Islands which followed Midway, the Japanese showed themselves superior in night fighting and the Americans and Australians suffered heavy losses, this time mainly in gun duels and destroyer torpedo attacks. The Battle of Savo Island was a clear Japanese victory, and at Santa Cruz Islands in October 1942, the Japanese committed more damage than they received and won a tactical victory.

But within a year of Pearl Harbor and the termination of Yamamoto's time limit for Japanese victory, the Japanese were not only being held on every quarter but the United States Navy had become a many-headed hydra and the most herculean efforts by the Japanese could no longer prevail. The whole Bismarck Archipelago was under American control, and General Douglas MacArthur could start on the long and bloody route back to the Philippine Islands from which he had been ejected in the early typhoon-like Japanese offensives.

The Pacific war in 1943 and 1944 resolved itself into attacks on Japanese island bases in the central and western Pacific by task forces of carriers, like queen bees, protected by battleships, cruisers, destroyers and submarines. Japanese positions would be bombarded by surface ships and bombarded from the air before assault forces went ashore and secured possession. The US 5th Fleet, under the overall command of Admiral Spruance, was made up of a number of these task forces, supported by fleet trains of transports and landing-craft – by mid-1943 an armada consisting of over 200 ships and some 1,500 aircraft.

Admiral Nimitz's overall plan, worked out at his Pearl Harbor headquarters and in conjunction with Admiral King and the Joint Chiefs of Staff, was to repossess the Pacific islands methodically to a set timetable and at a cost of as few lives as possible. With ever-weakening relative material resources, the Japanese strength of determination appeared to increase with every island-hopping step towards the Japanese mainland. Japanese occupying troops fought to the last man without air support or hope of reinforcement. As the last Japanese carriers were sent to the bottom under the impact of enormous American air fleets, kamikaze suicide pilots, mere boys who could scarcely take off on their one-way missions, hurled their bombers at American men o'war. Even the battleship *Yamato*, largest in the world, was reduced to committing a form of naval *hara-kiri* by steaming to her inevitable end at the hands of hundreds of American torpedo and dive bombers.

In the Battle of Leyte Gulf on 25 October 1944 the Japanese Navy was virtually wiped out, and little defence was left to the crushed and constricted empire which had sought to conquer half the world. After Midway, the outcome was inevitable, given a continuing American will to win and the vast industrial resources at her command. The first credit for eventual victory must go to the officers and men who out-fought, often against odds, the Japanese in the first year of the Pacific war. It was men like Admirals Spruance and Fletcher, Halsey and Thomas C. Kincaid, R. Kelly Turner and Aubrey Fitch, under the overall command of Nimitz ('Cincpac' as his title was compounded) who took the first waves of the storm and held steady, who are the first heroes of the Pacific war. It is quite wrong, however, as some historians have suggested, that the later victories were straightforward and inevitable. They were nothing of the kind. The Japanese sailor remained a formidable foe to the end, and it is a sound commander who takes the fewest risks and prevails with the fewest possible casualties and smallest losses of material.

There has been no more decisive victory at sea than that achieved by the US Navy (latterly assisted by Allied navies) between 1941 and 1945. The atom bomb may have saved millions of Japanese lives, and many thousands of Allied lives, and it is one of God's mercies that it did so. But in terms of naval warfare the fight was over by then, and all that remained was to secure a bloody hold on the Japanese islands and crush the last life out of the wretched, misled nation.

Today there are a number of older people who can recall Roosevelt on naval business in his last years. They will all testify to the enthusiasm, interest and affection he always demonstrated, at sea or in the White House or Hyde Park. Just as Peter Kemp believes that Churchill would have made a superb fighting admiral if he had spent his life in the navy, no one can doubt that Roosevelt would have enjoyed a career at sea and been a supremely good captain of a ship, and fleet commander.

10

Premier's Team

Churchill's naval team after he became Premier was of much higher quality than any he could have mustered in the First World War. As Prime Minister and Minister of Defence, he had no intention of having a powerful or independent-minded civil head of the navy in succession to himself. He intended to run the war and all three services at the highest level through the Chiefs of Staff, and the office of First Lord of the Admiralty was to be demoted almost to extinction.

With the fall of Chamberlain as Prime Minister, the Government which Churchill now led (10 May 1940) was a coalition one, with Labour Party members in the offices of Labour and Economic Warfare, a Liberal as Secretary of State for Air, the leader of the Labour Party, Clement Attlee, as Lord Privy Seal. After consultations with Attlee, Churchill offered the post of First Lord of the Admiralty to the Labour member, A. V. Alexander.

No one could have made a stronger contrast in the Admiralty with Churchill himself. Albert Victor Alexander had been First Lord in Ramsay MacDonald's 1929 Labour administration which Churchill regarded as sufficient reason for putting him back into the Admiralty. He was 'a thick-set, chunky man with a square face and looked rougher and tougher than he really was'. He got through paperwork well and was well liked. Guy Grantham found him 'a pompous little man' and Peter Kemp says 'he was nothing more than a cipher really. But he was a very nice, simple man who was brought up in the Co-Operative Movement. Whenever he came to see me after the war he always took his hat off when we passed the local Co-Op shop.'

Anything of a highly confidential nature was kept from A. V. A., as he was called, or 'Wide Mouth' for his indiscretions. In October 1940 Churchill, who was almost obsessively security-minded, gave instructions that Alexander's name should be added to the circulation list of Enigma decrypts (intercepted and decoded German signals) 'who of course must know everything known to his subordinates'. But the instruction was never carried out, and Alexander went through the entire war largely ignorant of the pricelessly valuable work done at

Bletchley by 'Ultra', the collective code word for decrypts obtained by the Enigma code-breaking machine. Dramatic events were therefore constantly surprising Alexander, like the certain intelligence, derived from decoded German signals, that the *Bismarck* had turned to seek refuge in France. But he never seemed to take offence. A.V.A. was a splendid orator, and Sir Clifford Jarrett, his Principal Private Secretary for four years, regards his speech-making up and down the land on behalf of the navy as his greatest war contribution.

With Churchill's promotion, Dudley Pound's power and responsibility increased greatly, although Churchill was never distant from his shoulder. Dudley Pound was sixty-two years old, unimpressive in manner, wholly dedicated to the service, and without much sense of humour – in fact not unlike Sir Arthur Wilson, Churchill's first First Sea Lord. But Pound had a shrewder and more flexible mind than 'Tug' Wilson. 'I've never seen anyone who worked so hard,' says Admiral Grantham, his Naval Assistant. 'He was at work at 6.30 a.m. I was always bad in the morning. When I reported before breakfast I always gave the wrong answers, which had to be corrected later in the day. At length, Pound said to me, "You don't seem to be very good before breakfast."' In fact, Pound soon acquired the reputation for being a sleeper at meetings and people said that he ought not to start work before dawn. Churchill noticed this quite early on in their relationship; he also observed that if any subject relating to the navy came up, he would not only at once be alert but appeared not to have missed a single word of the proceedings. 'Nothing slipped past his vigilant ear, or his comprehending mind,' Churchill recalled. In fact, Pound was never out of pain from an arthritic hip, and later from the tumour that killed him.

Admiral Pound's one weakness was for shooting. 'He would drop everything at the chance of going shooting,' says Admiral Grantham. Another officer remembers when Pound was C-in-C of the Mediterranean Fleet that he used to arrange the Fleet flagship's programme to include Albania for the duck shooting and the Greek islands for partridge. 'He organized shoots with a large number of sailor beaters headed by his coxswain, with a whistle and red, green and white flags . . .'

Pound was half American, on his mother's side, and Pierpont Morgan was his uncle. Morgan wanted Pound to join the bank, but there was never any possibility of that in Pound's mind. Apart from his shooting, the navy was his whole life.

Recalling his relationship with earlier First Sea Lords, Churchill had at first contemplated the prospect of Dudley Pound as his partner with some reservations. 'I had strongly condemned in Parliament the dispositions of the Mediterranean Fleet when he commanded it in 1939 at the moment of the Italian descent upon Albania,' Churchill wrote. 'Now we met as colleagues upon whose intimate relations and fundamental agreement the smooth working of the vast Admiralty machine would depend. We eyed each other amicably if doubtfully. But from the earliest days our friendship and mutual confidence grew and ripened.'

Guy Grantham can all too clearly remember his working routine after the too-early start, the first part of the afternoon at the Admiralty again, then a Chiefs of Staff meeting which would go on until dinner. Grantham would then have all the dockets ready for his return around midnight when they would go through them, and the brief his Assistant had prepared, until about 1.15 a.m. 'I slept in my office at this time,' Grantham recalls, 'and one night when Pound had not returned at 1 a.m. I turned in, to be awoken sharply by the message that the First Sea Lord wished to see me. There he was, at his desk. "Come on," he said, "get down to it. And never do that again."'

Arthur Marder perceived the real qualities of Pound, unlike Captain Roskill whose misjudgement and prejudice in his official history of the war at sea has led to a grave miscarriage of historical justice.

In a short time [Marder has written] Churchill formed a close attachment to, and trust in, Pound. He was impressed with the admiral's energy, keen intellect and analytical mind, and mastery of his profession. He respected this officer of unimpeachable character who was able to state his case to ministers in a dry and factual manner and without ever losing his temper, and to stand up firmly when necessary to the prodding of the arch-prodder. Pound feared neither God, man, nor Winston Churchill. Churchill had no great opinion of the planners ('masters of negation' he once called them), but he was ready and willing to accept Pound's judgement, which he trusted. On his part, Pound recognized that Churchill's qualities of leadership were so exceptional as to justify extraordinary effort to co-operate with him and to support him. He accordingly quickly developed an intense loyalty towards Churchill. He was never heard to criticize him or to complain about him. 'I have the greatest admiration for W.C., and his good qualities are such and his desire to hit the enemy so overwhelming, that I feel one must hesitate in turning down any of his proposals.'

Like Jellicoe, Pound's one great weakness was an inability to depute. He wanted to be in on everything, and Churchill was not in a position to correct this fault. The one massive blunder for which Pound must be held responsible was the near destruction of the massive PQ17 convoy of war materials to Russia in the summer of 1942. Fearing attack from a powerful German force of armoured ships, Pound ordered the convoy to scatter, depriving it of almost all its escort vessels and leaving the merchantmen the helpless victims of bombers and U-boats. Only eleven of the thirty-five ships that had sailed reached their destination.

'Dudley Pound should never have intervened – you can't run a battle from the Admiralty,' asserts Admiral Grantham. 'Like Churchill, he felt that in any operation that was taking place he should have his say.' On the other hand, Pound's great asset was that he could and did stand up to Churchill when it was important to do so. Churchill 'had a deep respect for Pound and his judgement and for all naval wisdom', and when his health started to fail in August 1943 Churchill expressed deep concern. Pound suffered a stroke later that month while in Washington, was brought back home and died, appropriately, on Trafalgar Day, 21 October. 'A very gallant man who literally went on working until he dropped,' Field Marshal Alanbrooke, his brilliant opposite number at the War Office, wrote in his diary. 'He was a grand colleague to work with.'

Roosevelt agreed, and on Pound's death telegraphed his Ambassador in London :

US joins with Great Britain in mourning the death of the former First Sea Lord who directed the operations of the fleet through four critical years and whose sagacity and wide experience made him a pillar of strength .... I was privileged to count Sir Dudley Pound among my friends and his passing brings a deep sense of personal loss.

In the early stages of the war, the officer who had even more influence on Churchill was Admiral Sir Tom Phillips, the Vice Chief of Naval Staff. Like Sturdee in the First World War, Tom Phillips was regarded as an intellectual with a rapid and astute mind. This view was better justified in the case of Phillips. 'He was a very clever man,' says Admiral Grantham, who knew him well at the Admiralty, 'but a traditionalist.'

Shortly before Pearl Harbor, and against the strong advice of Dudley Pound, when Churchill determined to despatch two powerful capital ships out to the Far East in the belief that they would act as a deterrent to Japanese ambitions, it was Tom Phillips who was selected to command this Force Z. It was a curious choice. 'It shook me when Tom Phillips was chosen,' Admiral Grantham recalls. 'It is terrible to send a Staff officer to sea when the war has been going on for a long time ; he has got out of touch with what it is like. For instance, Phillips was a two-watch man [watch on, watch off as opposed to the less taxing three-watch] which was too much for men month after month. Sitting in the Admiralty he had not learned that sort of thing.'

As all the world was soon to learn, the despatch of Force Z led to a major disaster. Churchill wrote of it later :

I was opening my boxes on the 10th [December 1941] when the telephone at my bedside rang. It was the First Sea Lord. His voice sounded odd. He gave a sort of cough, and at first I could not hear quite clearly. 'Prime Minister, I have to report to you that the *Prince of Wales* and the *Repulse* have both been sunk by the Japanese – we think by aircraft. Tom Phillips is drowned.' 'Are you sure it's true?' 'There is no doubt at all.' So I put the telephone down. I was thankful to be alone. In all the war I never received a more direct shock .... As I turned over and twisted in bed the full horror of the news sank in upon me.

It is far easier to get a positive picture of British admirals of the Second World War through Churchill's eyes than of American admirals through Roosevelt's eyes. The reason for this lies in Churchill's sharply critical view and distrust of the breed of admirals in general by contrast with Roosevelt's natural tendency to relate with his admirals. It is not that the President took a bland or uncritical attitude towards the senior officers of his service. On the contrary, he followed their progress keenly and endeavoured as far as was possible to see that the right man was installed in the right command. In this he was much more successful than Churchill. Once there, he let them get on with the job, confident in his own judgement and the judgement of his Chiefs of Staff. Here was evidence, if such were needed, of his self-confidence, steadiness and sense of security.

Churchill was not only fundamentally insecure, remaining so even when he became the greatest public hero since Wellington and Nelson, but he was also a victim of megalomania. He distrusted admirals from his experiences with them from 1911 to May 1915. With a few exceptions he regarded the professional hierarchy of the Royal Navy of the First World War as tradition-bound, unadventurous and underendowed with initiative and intelligence. Some he believed quite simply lacked courage. He judged Cradock to be insubordinate, stupid and rash; Milne and Troubridge stupid and cowardly; Carden craven and weak; De Robeck little better; even Jellicoe lacking in positivism.

It is easy to see the origins of Churchill's over-regard for aggression in his admirals: the Mediterranean experience, when the *Goeben* escaped as a result of timorousness and ineptitude; then there were Carden and De Robeck at the Dardanelles; and also the demonstration of negativism and stupidity at the Battle of Dogger Bank, which should have been a major not minor victory. After he had left the Admiralty, Jutland confirmed his belief that the Nelson spirit was all but extinguished. It was kept flickering only by the younger generation, and one or two go-getters. Of these Roger Keyes remained a friend

and supporter during all the years between the wars, an officer in whom
'all the old offensive spirit of the Navy was personified'. As a Member
of Parliament from 1934, Keyes was a keen supporter of Churchill in
the wilderness. Earlier, in 1924, when Churchill was not only out of
office but out of Parliament, Keyes tipped him off about a safe and
promising seat where he might be welcome, warned him unsuccessfully
of the Japanese threat the following year, cruised with him in the Mediterranean, pushed for him to be Minister of Defence in 1936 and First
Lord again in 1937 and 1938.

Keyes was not terribly bright, but he was as brave as a lion and
loyal as a gundog. When Churchill became Prime Minister he made
Keyes head of a new fighting branch, Combined Operations. In this
capacity, after service in Norway and elsewhere, Keyes had many spar-
ring matches with other services and with politicians. Recalling his skill
and gallantry at Zeebrugge in the First World War, Churchill backed
Keyes in his proposal to attack the small Italian island of Pantellaria
in December 1940. It came to nothing, opposed by steadier calculations.

'Churchill was personally fond of Keyes,' Sir John Colville has written
recently, 'whose courage at Zeebrugge he admired, but this fondness
was not shared either by Churchill's colleagues, or by the Chiefs of
Staff or by General Ismay, who found his demands to be Chairman
of the Chiefs of Staff Committee and even, at one stage, Deputy Prime
Minister, wholly ridiculous.' 'Keyes was the Fisher of World War 2,'
comments Captain John Litchfield. 'He was brought back when he was
past it.' Still determined to be in the thick of action after his retirement
if he ever got a chance, Keyes became an unofficial observer with the
US Fleet. At the Battle of Leyte Gulf, while flying too high without
oxygen after being gassed by a toxic smoke-screen, his heart was so
strained that he died soon after, a very decent and very gallant naval
officer.

Keyes's appointment in 1940 reflects Churchill's inordinate regard
for admirals of action. Admiral Harwood was another example. He
had fought gallantly against odds at the Battle of the River Plate and
brought the navy great kudos. 'So Churchill made him C-in-C Mediterranean,' Peter Kemp recalls, 'a very different job. He was a failure
and never recovered from it. Harwood was a good fighting admiral
with very little stuff up top. He was an example of Churchill's over-
admiration of the positive in commanders.'

If Harwood at the Battle of the River Plate demonstrated to Churchill
that the fighting spirit of the navy was more Nelsonian in 1939 than
in 1914, Admiral Sir Dudley North gave evidence a few months later
of the old sloppiness and lack of grit that had (in Churchill's judgement)
broken the Dardanelles offensive. North was Flag Officer Commanding

North Atlantic Station at Gibraltar at the time of the ill-fated Dakar expedition in 1940. North was considered in the service as 'a courtier sailor', a favourite of the palace, full of royal yacht service and periods as senior equerry, and highly conscious of the honours that had been heaped upon him.

North had taken up this shore-based 'safe' appointment when he was fifty-nine years old, chiefly because, considering his royal connections, he had to be given something to do and he could not do too much harm there – at least in the context of November 1939. But by the summer of 1940, with the fall of France and the fate of the French Fleet and French colonies in the balance, FOCNA assumed vastly greater responsibilities, for which he was to prove himself unfit.

'I have a distinct recollection', wrote Sir Clifford Jarrett, 'that people at the top in the Admiralty were becoming fed up ... with the readiness with which he appeared to find reasons for inaction or delay.' His inaction on 9 September proved fatal to his career, and of serious consequence to the Anglo–French force ordered to establish the Free French in Dakar in West Africa. On that day North learned from a reliable French intelligence source that a powerful Vichy French force of three cruisers and three *contre-torpilleurs* (exceptionally powerful destroyers) might leave Toulon and force the passage of the Straits of Gibraltar. North did nothing, and although there were redeeming facts in the Admiral's favour, the consequence was that the men o'war passed through into the Atlantic at high speed without interference and headed for Dakar, where their presence was of great comfort to the Vichy French and great influence in the disastrous outcome of the expedition.

The Dudley North affair became a naval *cause célèbre*. Except for Dudley Pound, who sacked him, there was scarcely an admiral who did not consider that this likeable flag officer had been made a scapegoat by Churchill for the failure of the whole expedition. Churchill always had to have a scapegoat for his disasters, so ran senior naval opinion. Look how he had blamed the French for the failure at Antwerp in 1914, and everyone but himself for the Dardanelles! In fact, as Peter Kemp confirms today, 'This was very much an Admiralty business and nothing to do with Churchill.' But the navy's admirals had not forgotten Churchill as First Lord in 1914–15 any more than he had forgotten them, and this stigma stuck right up to North's death in 1961, when *The Times* wrote ridiculously of him as the Admiral Byng of the Second World War.

Without doubt the greatest British seagoing admiral of the Second World War, and of the twentieth century, was Andrew Cunningham, 'A.B.C.'. His performance in the Mediterranean, sometimes against what seemed to be hopeless odds, and against the full might of the

Luftwaffe when he had virtually no air power of his own and quite inadequate anti-aircraft defences, was a lesson in cool judgement, fine example, imperishable courage and masterly handling of his Fleet. 'A.B.C. was absolutely superb,' Peter Kemp affirms today, 'despite the losses he suffered.' He had a terrible time in the eastern Mediterranean during the Greek and Crete evacuations, and took some heavy criticism for losing so many ships. But the wonder was that he did not lose the lot under the circumstances, and the navy's success in keeping all but airborne troops out of Crete led to the permanent crippling of Germany's airborne forces as a result of their savage losses.

Cunningham, writes Kemp,

was the epitome of the fighting admiral. Not a great deal of 'brain' but one of the few admirals who chose a good staff and used it intelligently and to the full. He loathed 'yes-men', got rid of them as quickly as he could, and expected his staff to stand up to him if their opinions differed from his.

With the death of Dudley Pound, Cunningham was brought home as First Sea Lord, which he did not enjoy. Nor at first did Churchill much enjoy his company: he had wanted another, more pliable, admiral. 'In this role A.B.C. was fortunate in following Pound who bequeathed him an Admiralty which was working like a well-oiled and remarkably efficient machine. So it didn't matter that he was a bit out of his depth.' Churchill had sometimes shown exasperation and impatience with Cunningham the fighting admiral, particularly if he was not showing bared-teeth aggression. In Whitehall, paradoxically, he was later immensely kind and patient with him 'and eased him through the political difficulties of trying to stand up to the other (very strong) Chiefs of Staff'.

Andrew Cunningham's arrival in the cos [wrote Alan Brooke in his diary] was indeed a happy event for me. I found in him first and foremost one of the most attractive of friends, a charming associate to work with and the staunchest of companions when it came to supporting a policy agreed to amongst ourselves, no matter what inclement winds might blow. I carry away with me nothing but the very happiest recollections of all my dealings with him. His personality, charming smile and heart warming laugh were enough to disperse at once those miasmas of gloom and despondency which occasionally swamped the cos.

A.B.C. never failed to give credit for the great debt Britain owed to the USA, and to Roosevelt in particular, in the two-and-a-quarter critical years before Pearl Harbor.

I find it difficult [he wrote] to see how Britain could have survived without assistance from the other side of the Atlantic before the formal entry of the United States into the war after the Japanese attack upon Pearl Harbor on December 7th, 1941. Indeed, we have so much for which to be everlastingly grateful to the United States of America that it cannot be expressed in words. Much of that gratitude is due to Franklin Delano Roosevelt and his advisers for their wisdom and foresight in bringing home to the mass of their countrymen that after the fall of France, Britain, bleeding, and impoverished, stood alone as a buttress against the Nazi domination of the civilized world.

I knew nothing of President Roosevelt as a politician. To me he was a man of great wisdom, charm of manner, humanity and simple kindness. He took a profound interest in the Navy, and in the days of his affliction collected stamps as a hobby and a relaxation. His quiet, unforgettable voice in those 'fireside talks' over the radio must have lifted the hearts of millions all over Britain and the Empire just as they did in America. I think it is right to say that our admiration and affection for the President of the United States of America were second only to the feelings we treasured for our own great leader, Mr Churchill.

Cunningham, the Nimitz of the Mediterranean and immensely popular with the Fleet, was 'a man of florid and smiling countenance with the blue eyes of the born sailor and the genial manner of one whose naval career had been passed chiefly in small ships'.

The other admiral who also performed wonders, in his case with the Home Fleet, was Bruce Fraser. From May 1943 he carried the responsibilities of protecting the Russian convoys, of keeping the Atlantic free from the German surface raiders (appropriately sinking the *Scharnhorst* in the navy's last classic big-gun action) and then took over in the Pacific. He remained a popular bachelor totally dedicated to the service. 'Everyone liked Fraser and admired him,' says Admiral Grantham. 'Equally important, he stood up to Churchill when it was necessary to do so. He feared nobody.'

Admiral Sir John Tovey, Fraser's predecessor as C-in-C Home Fleet, also had a mixed relationship with Churchill, and held his own against him with equal resolution. He was the admiral with the most celebrated First World War record, performing with great gallantry in his destroyer *Onslow* at the Battle of Jutland. Until July 1943 he led a life of anxiety and action, as demanding as Cunningham's in the Mediterranean; the *Bismarck* chase and destruction, the PQ17 convoy disaster (in which he was fatally overruled by Dudley Pound), the worst U-boat convoy battles – all these occurred during his time.

Admiral Grantham describes Tovey as a 'tall, impressive man, always immaculately dressed, a strong character and a committed churchman (he became a Church Commissioner). He had a strong sense of discipline and was a fine example to all serving him. At the same time, he seemed rather remote to all those who did not know him well.'

Admiral Philip Vian was the flag officer most decorated for bravery and most admired by Churchill for his super-aggression, from the boarding in real Nelsonian style of the German ship *Altmark* to the *Bismarck* business, when he commanded the harassing destroyers; to the beating off of an immensely superior Italian force in the Mediterranean, including a modern battleship and heavy cruisers, at the second Battle of Sirte. Churchill loved him. During the Normandy invasion in 1944 Vian commanded the naval forces covering the British landings. After Churchill visited the front line in Normandy on 10 June, he embarked in Vian's destroyer *Kelvin*. It had been a surprisingly quiet day and Churchill suggested a bombardment to waken things up.

'Since we are so near, why shouldn't we have a plug at them ourselves before we go home?' He said, 'Certainly,' and in a minute or two all our guns fired on the silent coast. We were of course well within the range of their artillery, and the moment we had fired Vian made the destroyer turn about and depart at the highest speed . . .

If Vian saw the most action Admiral Sir James Somerville was the most intelligent flag officer of the war, and he, too, was enormously popular. Somerville also possessed an ingenious scientific mind, had invented a form of ship sounding gear, the predecessor of sonar, and was De Robeck's Fleet Wireless Officer at the Dardanelles. Due to a wrong diagnosis of an illness by naval doctors, he was retired before the Second World War, but bullied his way back in again and was in the last ship to clear Calais during the Dunkirk evacuation. It fell upon Somerville, as Flag Officer Force H, to bombard and cripple the French Fleet at Oran. He never really forgave Churchill for making him carry out this distasteful task; but his war career prospered.

Perhaps the most remarkable of his successes [writes Peter Kemp] came after the Singapore disaster when he was made C-in-C East Indies with a scratch fleet made up in the main of the old R-class battleships. Morale was at a very low ebb after the loss of the *Prince of Wales* and *Repulse*, and this was a scratch fleet which must have known it was completely outclassed by the Japanese. Yet by the time he got it out into the Indian Ocean, he had built it up to a state of extraordinarily high morale. He was that kind of man.

When Churchill made Lord Louis Mountbatten, Keyes's successor at Combined Operations, Supreme Commander in the Far East in 1943, the first question Mountbatten asked Dudley Pound (according to

Mountbatten) was whether he was allowed to sack Somerville, twenty-three years his senior, for whom he had conceived a powerful dislike. Once out in the East Mountbatten found it difficult to find an excuse for ridding himself of such an efficient and liked flag officer. However, at a fleet inspection Mountbatten considered that he had been treated with a lack of respect appropriate to his rank, and that was the end of the seagoing career, in August 1944, of one of the finest fighting admirals of the war.

Churchill's attitude towards the admirals who served the Royal Navy in his time was mercurial: 'excellent, when he thought they were shooting!'; appalling, when he perceived procrastination or plodding. When Mountbatten was promoted in 1941 we can see why and can follow the pattern of his progress with a fair measure of accuracy. Cunningham had no use for him as a leader. Churchill had promoted his father to the navy's top job because he had the valuable advantage of access to the palace, was satisfactory to work with and was a good, brainy administrator. His son, Lord Louis Mountbatten, was a cousin of the King, too, was personable, had shown his qualities in peacetime and had supported Churchill during the wilderness years when Mountbatten was a mere captain in his thirties. Now, in war as a destroyer flotilla commander, he rapidly showed a degree of aggression and positivism to satisfy even Churchill's highest standards. The beam of favour settled upon this already privileged and boundlessly ambitious young officer, and in view of his dash nothing now could halt the speed of his progress. When Mountbatten succeeded in safely bringing home his destroyer which had been damaged, not for the first or last time, Churchill said that he ought to get a DSO. 'Dudley Pound said "Not yet, it is too early." But Churchill insisted, and that was that.' By early October 1943 Mountbatten, a favourite of Roosevelt too, was on to higher things, appointed Supreme Commander South-East Asia – '... to feel that it had fallen upon me to be the outward and visible symbol of the British Empire's intention to return to the attack in Asia'.

Captain Roskill has written of Churchill's 'love–hate' relationship with his admirals. There is a deeper measure of truth in this than is at first apparent. He was indeed in love with the navy but like an aspiring candidate for a club who knows he will never be elected for membership, Churchill was always jealous of the committee members – the admirals – who were there in power. He resented their skills and ability to command and manoeuvre great fleets and perhaps change the destiny of a nation with massive broadsides from their guns. The romance of sea power never faded and this was why he was at heart a traditionalist, like so many of the admirals who served under him. At the same time, and in apparent contradiction, he was an innovator, welcoming new brains and new ideas, and propounding a good many – sometimes too many – himself. Such a lot of contradictions!

The Royal Navy was outmanoeuvred and outwitted in April 1940 at the time of the Norwegian invasion because Admiralty thinking, and Churchill's thinking, were still conditioned by a past age of naval warfare. When it was learned that the German Fleet was out, it might have been the Grand Fleet leaving Scapa Flow to meet the High Seas Fleet. Heavy German units, according to Admiralty reckoning, were about to attempt the breakthrough into the Atlantic to prey on British shipping – 'a purely naval affair', as Sir Ian Jacob of the War Cabinet Secretariat described it. Troops already embarked in British men o'war, themselves destined for an intervention at Stavanger and Bergen, were put back ashore, without anyone in Whitehall being informed, and the ships put to sea only to learn too late that it was a full-scale German invasion.

But now Churchill reacted with speed and decision to correct the sorry miscalculation, and although the situation was never recovered at least the German surface fleet lost heavily and was temporarily crippled. Churchill, who for years had been warning Britain of the growing strength of the Luftwaffe, had at the same time misunderstood the deadly effect it would have on naval operations unsupported by air-power. To be both a traditionalist and an innovator did lead sometimes to confused thinking, and to tragedy. The Force Z affair – the despatch of the *Prince of Wales* and *Repulse* to the Far East – was a prime example of muddled conception. A carrier was to accompany them to provide air cover, but when this was not forthcoming, against all Admiralty advice he ordered them to carry on alone, confident in their ability to defend themselves against air attack. But if Admiral Tom Phillips, once at Singapore, had not sought to attack the Japanese invasion fleet, which was his undoing, he would have been a prime target of Churchill's abuse.

It was as well that the really 'big' British admirals – notably Andrew Cunningham, Bruce Fraser and James Somerville, and of course Dudley Pound in the Admiralty – were capable of withstanding the quaint, puzzling, misguided, hectoring and sometimes abusive messages des-patched to them. They knew their man, overcame their resentment and got on with the job. When Cunningham was at the most delicate stage of his negotiations with the French admiral commanding the French fleet in Alexandria after the fall of France, Churchill despatched impatient and critical signals – '. . . Do not, repeat NOT, fail.' There was only one place for this sort of rubbish, and in it went, without acknowledgement.

Lacking Roosevelt's trust and confidence in his admirals, Churchill's antennae were forever extended, sensitive to the slightest hint of his admirals' failure to live up to his exacting standards of forcefulness and offensive-mindedness; and was at the same time highly resentful of any tendency towards counter criticism: unlike Roosevelt, he was never at ease with them. Once, when Secretary Knox was complaining of an American admiral's decision to turn back from an offensive operation in the Pacific and asked Churchill's advice – 'What would you do with your Admiral in a case like this?' – Churchill replied with, one imagines, a shrug of resignation, 'It is dangerous to meddle with Admirals when they say they can't do things. They have always got the weather or fuel or something to argue about.'

Martin Gilbert has said, 'Churchill felt closer to people than they felt to him.' This shrewd, simple generalization can be applied to his admirals. The trouble was that if they did not come up to the mark (in his judgement) he felt all the worse about it and over-reacted accordingly, almost as if slighted.

All said and done, it was an odd relationship but it did not work too badly thanks on the one side to Churchill's unsurpassed image of bulldog heroism and national reputation as Britain's saviour, which few senior naval officers doubted, and on the other side by the general good humoured tolerance, sense and resilience of the admirals who served him. The proof is to be found in what they achieved together, not in the price paid by their mistakes.

11
'A true affection . . .'

With the entry of the United States into the war on 7 December 1941 there opened a new phase in the relations between Churchill and Roosevelt, bringing them together into a unique personal alliance. In December 1941 Britain was like a hardened, veteran warrior, blessedly thankful for the support of this new ally, sympathetic to this ally's early set-backs, eager to pass on the lessons he has learned. The language of this time reflects the authority of Britain, no longer wheedling, no longer begging; instead now laying down policies and practices. It is the 'we must' period – 'we must be ready to send considerable forces . . .', 'we must face here the usual clash . . .', 'we have, therefore, to prepare for the liberation . . .'. Brisk and firm.

As a British Chiefs of Staff meeting was told by Churchill when a member presumed that the 'softly-softly' treatment of America would continue: 'Oh! that is the way we talked to her while we were wooing her; now that she is in the harem, we talk to her quite differently.'

But not for long. By 1943 American industry and American military effort were into their stride. Britain, and Churchill, were having to yield points on a host of subjects – the nomination of commanders, priority of supplies and so on. Old suspicions and prejudices re-emerge, not only as married relations tend to become more friable in easier times, but because dominance, and with it influence, had switched to the younger member of the team. Even in an alliance of friendship, an alliance of survival, the weight of argument is measured in metal and explosive.

In one respect relations between Roosevelt and Churchill became less intense after Pearl Harbor. Until America came into the war, the Former Naval Person and the C-in-C of the US Navy were deeply and more or less continuously concerned with naval matters because the co-operation was closer and more overt than with the other two arms. Since the beginning of 1941 the two navies had been working together, with increasing intimacy. In 1942 co-operation was total for all three services; and therefore just as Churchill's day-to-day involvement in the Royal Navy was diluted after he became Premier, so the

American and British navies now became one subject in a world-wide agenda involving every item concerned with the conduct of the war.

However, minutes of the meetings of the chiefs of staff – at all levels – official reports and histories, published and unpublished memoirs, and above all the direct exchanges between President and Premier, all confirm their undiminished interest in naval affairs.

Less than a week after Pearl Harbor Churchill is hurrying across the Atlantic again, this time in the *Prince of Wales*'s sister ship the *Duke of York*. On this passage there were fewer films and no backgammon. As Roosevelt had telegraphed on the day the *Prince of Wales* and *Repulse* went down, 'Naval situation and other matters of strategy require discussion.' It was a businesslike crossing just as it was a businesslike meeting. *En route* Churchill drew up a long memorandum on the state of the war and plans for 1942.

Then to the White House, arriving in Washington by air on the evening of 22 December 1941 where Roosevelt awaited Churchill. 'There was the President waiting in his car. I clasped his strong hand with comfort and pleasure,' Churchill wrote of the occasion. 'I formed a very strong affection, which grew with our years of comradeship, for this formidable politician who had imposed his will for nearly ten years upon the American scene, and whose heart seemed to respond to many of the impulses that stirred my own.'

The formal discussions and private conversations in the evenings at the White House ranged widely over the naval scene. Coral Sea and Midway had still to be fought, and neither of the war leaders, or their staff for that matter, had any conception of the revolution that was taking place in sea fighting. While Admiral Nagumo's all-conquering carriers, unaccompanied by a single battleship, ranged freely across the Pacific and Indian Oceans, naval strategy in Washington was still built about the battle fleet. 'The Allies will not have for some time the power to fight a general fleet engagement . . .' The last general fleet engagement had been fought at Jutland in 1916, and even those proceedings were dominated by fear of the destroyers' torpedoes.

Following his three-weeks stay in the US and Canada Churchill returned to face the multitude of troubles created by Japanese advances on every front. The fate of Singapore was only one of the agonies. But three days before the city fell (15 February 1942) the Royal Navy suffered another humiliation as close to home as the English Channel when the repaired battle-cruisers *Scharnhorst* and *Gneisenau*, with the heavy cruiser *Prinz Eugen*, raced home from France. 'We are out after them with everything we have,' Churchill signalled Roosevelt. But it was not enough, and with the umbrella assistance of a strong fighter force they got through the Straits of Dover and made their way home, although both big ships were damaged by mines.

When Roosevelt learned that the three German men o'war had passed through the Channel without being sunk he characteristically des-patched a telegram of cheer – 'I hope you will be of good heart' – and judged that in fact it had been a British tactical victory: 'I am more and more convinced that the location of all the German ships in Germany makes our joint North Atlantic naval problem more simple.'

In order to help the Royal Navy to contain the substantial German force of surface raiders now that they were concentrated, Roosevelt proposed to send two new battleships to reinforce the British Home Fleet, although in the event only one battleship, a carrier and two heavy cruisers were finally sent.

But it was the U-boat and its remorseless and unremitting war on Atlantic shipping that concerned the two war leaders more than any other subject in their communications. In March 1942 Roosevelt asked if the RAF could concentrate some of its resources on bombing U-boat bases and building and repair yards, and within a few days Churchill was able to report that 250 bombers had attacked 'U-boat nests' at Lubeck – 'Results are said to be the best ever.' (In fact, no concrete U-boat shelter was ever penetrated by a bomb.)

In March–April 1942 the subject of Malta was a prime consideration of the two war leaders. The Germans and Italians had unleashed an unprecedented air assault on the island where a surviving force of twenty-five fighters faced an enemy force of some 600 fighters and bombers. Churchill proposed the use of the American carrier *Wasp* for taking fighter reinforcements to within 600 miles of the island, and flying them off. Would Roosevelt agree to this dangerous mission? Admiral King, as usual, was suspicious of British motives. He worked out that HMS *Furious*, once a Fisher-inspired 18-inch-gunned battle-cruiser now converted into a carrier, had the capacity for the job and thought that Churchill was again trying to commit American ships to do the work the British could do themselves. Roosevelt overruled King and made the *Wasp* available. With further fighters aboard the British carrier *Eagle* this desperately needed supply probably saved the island, which was at its last gasp. The *Wasp* made a second delivery of some fifty fighters and Churchill telegraphed Roosevelt his thanks 'for allow-ing *Wasp* to have another good sting ...'; and to the captain of the carrier, 'Who said a wasp couldn't sting twice?'

If King failed to deprive Churchill of this carrier for the Mediterranean for the succour of Malta, he succeeded in torpedoing Churchill's plans for American reinforcement on the other side of the world. April 1942 was the month when Admiral Nagumo was creating havoc in the Indian Ocean and Churchill begged for a modern battleship and carrier from the US Pacific Fleet to reinforce British forces, already badly hammered in that area. 'It is my personal thought', Roosevelt concluded a long message (16 April 1942), 'that your Fleet in Indian Ocean can well be safeguarded during next few weeks without fighting major engagement . . .'

In the midst of all these naval crises, in the Mediterranean and Indian Ocean, General Douglas MacArthur, C-in-C Far East, asked the British directly for a carrier and more shipping to support his operations. Where did he think this was to be found? The only British carrier in Indian waters, the little *Hermes*, had just been sent to the bottom. Churchill was stupefied: 'I should be glad to know whether these requirements have been approved by you,' he asked the President, 'and whether General MacArthur has any authority from the United States for taking such a line.' They had not been so approved.

In the early summer of 1942 the naval situation was as critical in the far Arctic north as in the mellow Mediterranean and tropical Indian Ocean. Here the Murmansk–Archangel convoys were suffering acute and finally unacceptable losses, assailed by destroyers, torpedo and bombing planes and U-boats, while the giant battleship *Tirpitz* lay in its Norwegian lair, threatening to strike at any time. The two leaders agreed on the political as well as military necessity of getting supplies to Russia, but it was Britain that was bearing the main burden of the losses. Roosevelt suggested that convoy escorts in the Atlantic should be diverted to the Murmansk run. Churchill replied (1 May 1942): 'With very great respect what you suggest is beyond our power to fulfil . . . difficulty of Russian convoys cannot be solved merely by anti-submarine craft. Enemy heavy ships and destroyers may at any time strike.' Churchill then listed recent losses. 'I beg you not to press us beyond our judgement in this operation which we have studied most intently . . . . I can assure [you] Mr President we are absolutely extended . . .'

Appealed to in these terms, Roosevelt always accepted Churchill's judgement, and as a compromise suggested that supplies to Russia should be cut and that Stalin should be told that the reason for this was that the war supplies and the shipping were needed for the invasion of the Continent – actually still more than two years away.

This desolate picture from every naval quarter was at last relieved by the news of Admirals Spruance and Fletcher's dramatic victory at the Battle of Midway. 'Delighted to hear your good news . . .' Churchill signalled.

The high summer weeks of 1942 marked the U-boats' 'happy days' (as the crews called them) in the Caribbean and along the east coast of the United States too, when shipping sailed unescorted and the

U-boats worked with the added advantage of un-blacked-out American cities as silhouette illumination. It was like a turkey shoot. The reversal of roles allowed Churchill to pay back some of the assistance generously given by the US Navy a year earlier. Now he proposed that the numerous patrol craft being built in American yards for the British Navy should be placed in a common pool and drawn upon by the US Navy as well as the Royal Navy as required. Two flotillas of British anti-submarine escorts were sent to strengthen the American escorts and instruct them in the tactics of convoy protection. Closer collaboration could hardly be imagined : this was total unity of action. Roosevelt agreed at once (24 July 1942) and suggested that the allocation of patrol craft should be decided by the Combined Chiefs of Staff.

While the Battle of the Atlantic continued to rage at high intensity through that summer of 1942 – almost a million tons of shipping were lost in May – the Allies were completing their preparations for their first major offensive in the west. This was Operation 'Torch', the invasion of North Africa following upon a major attack from Egypt. Torch required the closest Anglo–American naval co-operation and this worked so smoothly and cordially that the two leaders were rarely brought into the detail of arrangements. Meanwhile, Eleanor Roosevelt made her first wartime visit to Britain and correspondence was for a while on a mutually affectionate domestic note.

At the turn of the year 1942–3 the Churchill–Roosevelt naval alliance was put under strain again as a result of inter-service discord. Admiral King had always wanted to fight the Pacific war first, contrary to the Allied commitment that Hitler must be beaten as first priority, and relentlessly tried to reverse this decision. As well, King wanted to beat the Japanese Navy without British support ; he would have preferred to dispense with Australian support too, but this was clearly impossible. General Marshall on the other hand was in favour of attacking Germany as soon as practicable and with an invasion of the mainland of Europe.

But after a year of war in the south Pacific, King was down to a single, damaged carrier and was obliged to sink his pride and ask for a loan from the Royal Navy. Churchill offered to send two fast modern fleet carriers in exchange for a small American carrier to support the Home Fleet. This conformed with the principle of integration so abhorred by Admiral King. 'I am much in favour of sending you two carriers rather than one if this can be managed,' Churchill suggested to Roosevelt, 'as this will not only give you increased strength but would allow the two ships to work as a tactical unit . . .' Such a force would also demonstrate to Australia and New Zealand that the Mother Country was deeply concerned for their safety and that it was not only America upon whom they were dependent. King disliked what he regarded as a gesture of imperialism as much as he disliked the idea of a separate British task force working with the Pacific Fleet rather than a single carrier being absorbed into Admiral Nimitz's command. There was for a time a good deal of unpleasantness at command level. But the two leaders damped down the fires, and the fast armoured carrier *Victorious* was sent to Pearl Harbor, to be warmly welcomed by Admiral Nimitz.

Once again, in March 1943, the burning topic between the two leaders was the U-boat menace. 'I am extremely anxious about shipping situation,' Churchill signalled on 24 March, and wrote in detail of 'its extreme gravity'. For Germany and Italy the shipping problem scarcely existed – North Africa was the only front supplied by sea – but for the Allies the shipping burden was almost crushingly heavy and must, so it seemed, increase with the build-up towards the invasion of Europe.

The Battle of the Atlantic, then, remained the key contest, cruel, unremitting, stretching to the utmost both the science of destruction and human indomitability. No single weapon of war brought Churchill closer to despair than the German submarine. Its final defeat was brought about by a combination of weapons. As in the Pacific, the code-breakers played a critical part and by 1943 the Enigma code-breaking machine was reading virtually all the signals between U-boats and orders from headquarters.

Because full knowledge of Enigma has become available only in the past decade, perhaps too much emphasis has recently been placed on the near-magical wonders of the Bletchley code-breaking organization and its machines, tremendous though these were. Peter Kemp, who worked in the Admiralty Intelligence Centre throughout the war, believes today that the battle against the U-boat would have been won in the end anyway. 'It would have taken a little longer. The crucial things were centimetric radar, shipborne HFDF [High Frequency Detecting and Finding], and continuous air cover – they would have beaten them without Enigma, and we were very conscious that if we overplayed Enigma they would know and change the whole damn lot.'

Of all the changes of fortune in the Battle of the Atlantic, none was clearer than that brought about by 'closing the gap' in air cover in May 1943, which led to round-the-clock air surveillance over the entire Atlantic only weeks after Churchill's *cri de coeur*. While Churchill and Roosevelt were in session together at the Trident Conference in Washington (12–25 May 1943) air crews of long-range aircraft, sailors of escort vessels and the Bletchley code-breakers were turning the tide at last. From almost 700,000 tons of shipping losses in March, these combined forces brought the figure down to less than half this frightening total in May, and except for July 1943 kept the figure below

160,000 tons for the remainder of the year. For the Allied Powers, including Russia, it was as great a victory as Stalingrad. Admiral King refrained from offering congratulations, and instead asked Roosevelt to question Royal Navy figures of successful attacks on U-boats. Were they too good to be true? In some embarrassment, Roosevelt did as he was asked. Yes, they were all confirmed, proven 'kills', he was told.

The Trident Conference was the third meeting between the leaders and had become essential to settle future strategy following the winter successes in North Africa and the Mediterranean. Churchill sailed for America in the *Queen Mary* again along with a large party, and 500 German prisoners of war as a token of success on the field of battle. The security surrounding this voyage was even more elaborate than for the original 'fishing party', and included the setting up of ramps all over the ship to indicate falsely that Roosevelt would be sailing back to Britain to continue the conference. For the last leg of the voyage a strong presence of American men o'war closed about the liner. 'Since yesterday we have been surrounded by US Navy and we all greatly appreciate high value you evidently set upon our continued survival,' Churchill signalled his host.

Churchill crossed the (now much safer) Atlantic yet again in August 1943 – 'a most swift and agreeable journey' – in the *Queen Mary*, the first meeting this time at Quebec. The agenda included the invasion of Europe, Operation Overlord, in approximately nine months' time, the greatest amphibious operation in history and by the same definition the greatest naval operation in history. Conference agendas this time were concerned almost entirely with offensives – counter attacks in Russia, new advances in the Pacific, the invasion and defeat of Italy, the destruction of U-boats – one a day average over the past few months – mighty Anglo–American bombing offensives over Germany. And finally, and in the deepest confidence, the most epochal offensive subject of all – 'Tube Alloys', atomic energy research which was the topic of a joint agreement of the highest importance.

Churchill returned to Britain on 19 September 1943 to be met by renewed demands from Russia to reinstitute the Arctic supply convoys which proved so crushingly expensive in the past. One of the threats to these convoys was temporarily removed by a daring attack on the *Tirpitz* in her elaborately protected Norwegian anchorage. For security reasons, Churchill confined his message reporting this success to, 'We believe we have damaged the *Tirpitz* and that she will have to go back to Germany for docking.' In fact a force of miniature submarines had succeeded in penetrating the defences surrounding the giant battleship and two 2-ton bombs had been detonated beneath her hull. The resulting explosions put all her engines out of action and damaged her steering gear. Although it could not be known at the time, she was never to be made operational again. Now Admiral Fraser could face passing through the Russian convoys that winter with greater equanimity. Better still, not only did the supply armadas get through almost without loss, but when threatened by Germany's only surviving operational heavy ship, the *Scharnhorst*, Bruce Fraser sank her. For Churchill it was a Christmas evening tonic. 'The sinking of the *Scharnhorst* has been great news to us all,' signalled Roosevelt.

Naval communications between the two leaders during the winter of 1943-4 were mostly concerned with the build-up to D-Day, interspersed with vehement complaints from Churchill on the offensive and non-co-operative attitude of Russia, and less vehement complaints from Roosevelt, who increasingly saw himself as peacemaker between the socialist Stalin and the imperialist Churchill. In spite of the growing suspicion between Britain and Russia, Churchill never allowed this to affect his original pledge that he would do all in his power to support the Russian cause, and even agreed to lend the Russian Navy a battleship and a cruiser. It offended against his deepest instincts to do so, especially as the battleship was one which he had laid down during his first term of office as First Lord and carried the regal name *Royal Sovereign*.

Russia was also fed more frequently than ever with convoys during the spring of 1944, with negligible losses and heavy destruction of U-boats. 'You will be glad to hear', Churchill signalled (9 March 1944), 'that the latest Russian convoy has now got safe home, and that four U-boats out of the pack that attacked were certainly sunk ...' Since Admiral King's earlier doubts, Churchill had found it necessary to add the confirmatory 'certainly'.

It was in this same month of March 1944 that the subject of British participation on a relatively large scale in the Pacific came up again for discussion, this time on a more urgent and pressing basis. After the invasion of France in June – the date was now set – and with the surrender of the Italian Fleet and elimination of Germany's surface Fleet, the Royal Navy would have a surplus of strength, especially of fleet carriers, battleships and cruisers.

After the Combined Chiefs of Staff had approved in principle the presence of a British Fleet in the Pacific at the end of 1943, Admiral King had reluctantly agreed to accept a British and Commonwealth task force but would not put a date to it. 'I am, in the upshot, left in doubt whether we are really needed this year,' Churchill telegraphed with just a trace of asperity, on 10 March 1944. He continued :

Accordingly I should be very grateful if you could let me know whether there is any specific American operation in the Pacific

(A) Before the end of 1944 or
(B) Before the summer of 1945
which would be hindered or prevented by the absence of a British Fleet
Detachment

A British naval mission had been in Washington since February in
order to study the logistics of American task forces, with their huge
fleet trains, and reached the conclusion that any future British Fleet
must follow the American organization which had proved so successful. The British Pacific Fleet came into formal being on 22 November
1944, consisting of two fast modern battleships, four fleet carriers with
a total complement of about 250 aircraft, five cruisers and eleven
destroyers. Admiral Fraser was the C-in-C, and its base was Sydney,
Australia.

Although largely a political force – the Americans had quite adequate
forces of their own to deal the final blows at Japan, just as the British
Grand Fleet had had sufficient strength to cope with the German Fleet
in 1917 – Admiral Fraser brought the Fleet to a high pitch of efficiency,
and the American Command was much impressed. The British carriers
had stoutly armoured flight decks, and withstood bombing much better
than their American counterparts.

Admiral King had determined that this Fleet should not operate with
Admiral Nimitz's main central Pacific thrust but instead attach itself
to General MacArthur's American–Australian command and assist in
the recapture of the Straits of Malacca and Singapore. But Churchill
would have none of this. He wanted the Fleet to be in the main front
line, and in at the eventual and inevitable surrender of Japan. Roosevelt
agreed and told King to make the necessary arrangements.

Admiral Nimitz warmly welcomed Task Force 57, as the British Fleet
had now become. 'The British force will greatly increase our striking
power and demonstrate our unity of purpose against Japan,' he signalled. 'The United States Pacific Fleet welcomes you.'

Churchill had always been most punctilious in sending com-
miserations or congratulations to Roosevelt on events in the Pacific
war. 'I was delighted to read of your success . . .' and 'Your operations
in the Pacific assume every day a more vehement and compulsive
course,' were typical. After the six-day Leyte Gulf battle, which cost
the Japanese Navy twenty-four warships, including four carriers and
three battleships, Churchill signalled:

Pray accept my most sincere congratulations which I tender on behalf of His
Majesty's Government on the brilliant and massive victory gained by the sea
and air forces of the United States over the Japanese in the recent heavy
battles.

We are very glad to know that one of His Majesty's Australian cruiser squadrons had the honour of sharing in this memorable event.

In his turn, Roosevelt was quick to congratulate Churchill on the bombing of the *Tirpitz* : 'The end of the *Tirpitz* is great news,' adding with a typical waggish touch, 'We must help the Germans by never letting them build anything like it again, thus putting the German Treasury on its feet.'

With the military advance across France and Belgium in the summer of 1944 and the even swifter progress of the American naval forces in the Pacific, exchanges between Premier and President became more and more concerned with grand strategy during the closing stages of hostilities and the world-wide political problems which were already beginning to loom – sometimes ominously – through the fog of war.

At the end of 1944, as Churchill was to write :

The whole shape and structure of post-war Europe clamoured for review. When the Nazis were beaten how was Germany to be treated ? What aid could we expect from the Soviet Union in the final overthrow of Japan ? And once military aims were achieved what measures and what organization could the three great Allies provide for the future peace and good governance of the world ?

Above all, the fate of the Polish people, which had triggered this second great German war, was again causing as much anxiety as it had five years earlier, even if the grasping fists reached out this time from the east and from an ally.

It was hoped in Washington that, to spare Roosevelt, this proposed new meeting of 'the big three' war leaders could take place somewhere half-way to Moscow. But Stalin would not leave the borders of his country for health reasons, he said, and Yalta on the Black Sea was eventually fixed as the meeting place.

The travel arrangements involved many inter-naval exchanges, including the decision to send warships to stand off Yalta as a floating headquarters and in case of need of accommodation. Churchill was anxious to rendezvous with Roosevelt at Malta for preliminary conversations and in order that 'our military men should get together for a few days before we arrive at Yalta'. But Roosevelt was anxious not to give the ever-suspicious Russians the impression that there was pre-conference collusion between the Western allies, and to present the United States in neutral guise for the delicate and complex negotiations that lay ahead.

However, Roosevelt could not refuse all discussion in view of the rendezvous, but he arranged his itinerary so that there would be time for only the briefest meeting. He therefore crossed the Atlantic in the 13,600-ton heavy cruiser *Quincy*, arriving in Valetta harbour, with all its evidence of the long siege and savage bombing, less than twenty-four hours before the outward journey to Russia.

Roosevelt was a sick man. Normally, such was his love for the sea and for sailing with his navy that 'no matter how tired and worn he might appear when he started off on a cruise, he emerged from it looking healthy and hearty and acting that way'. But when Admiral King went on board the cruiser to greet his President, 'he was alarmed by the state of his health', noting deterioration rather than improvement.

Churchill had already arrived by air direct from Britain in one of three aircraft accommodating his party. One of the planes crashed *en route*, with few survivors – 'such are the strange ways of fate', as he commented.

The USS *Quincy* arrived under a cloudless blue sky on the morning of 2 February. It was just three and a half years since the leaders' first wartime meeting. Now it was like the Newfoundland 'fishing party' in reverse, Churchill the host on the deck of the cruiser HMS *Orion*: two elderly men who had led the free Western world to the brink of victory in the greatest war in history.

'As the American cruiser steamed slowly past us towards her berth alongside the quay wall,' Churchill recalled, 'I could see the figure of the President seated on the bridge, and we waved to each other. With the escort of Spitfires overhead [at Placentia Bay it had been seaplanes], the salutes, and the bands of the ships' companies in the harbour playing "The Star-spangled Banner" it was a splendid scene.'

Churchill transferred to the *Quincy* for lunch, and they were able to hold one brief meeting that evening with their staffs. Then, all through that night, the aerial armada, carrying the total entourage of some 700 people, took off at ten-minute intervals for the gruelling, and cold, flight of 1,400 miles.

Churchill was asleep when the big Globemaster plane flew over the Dardanelles, the scene of the disasters of exactly thirty years earlier which had crippled, and almost destroyed, his political career. Then the intention had been to support and open up communications with the hard-pressed Russian armies, which had eventually succumbed in 1917 in the face of the German onslaught. Now everywhere the Germans were in retreat on the Russian fronts, in spite of the Dardanelles remaining closed.

Under international treaty no warships could pass through the Dardanelles and the Sea of Marmara without prior permission of the Turkish

Government. Although the Turks had been mainly sympathetic – if non-belligerent – to the German cause in this war, there was no need for a bombardment before sending through the men o'war – past the once blood-stained Gallipoli shores, over the sunken wrecks of 1915.

'Should we not tell President Inonu [of Turkey] about them at the latest possible moment,' Churchill suggested to Roosevelt, 'for his own strictly personal information, and ask him to give all the orders necessary to ensure that the ships shall pass through unquestioned except by formality?' This time the Turks were in no position to bar the way; but there was an element of irony in the fact that Churchill thought it diplomatic to make the request at all.

After Yalta, Roosevelt flew to Egypt and returned home in the *Quincy*, through the Mediterranean, to Newport News, arriving on 27 March 1945. 'It is good to be home,' Roosevelt was telling the cheering House of Representatives two days later. 'It has been a long journey.' Everyone could see the price that Roosevelt had paid, and his speech was slurred in delivery and often repetitious, the vintage rhetoric faded.

Far away in the Pacific, Roosevelt's navy was still heavily in action. Admiral Spruance led a carrier task force to within twenty minutes' flying from Tokyo and launched a scorching bomber attack on the Japanese capital. Seven battleships with cruisers and destroyers in support opened a bombardment of 22,000 rounds of shells on the small but strategically vital island of Iwo Jima – an assault of high explosive that made the Dardanelles bombardment in 1915 seem like a volley from an air rifle. Carrier bombing planes followed this assault.

In four months' time, Roosevelt was informed, the first atomic bomb would be tested.

From the haven of Warm Springs in early 1945 Roosevelt wrote to Josephus Daniels, urging that the Philippines should be given their independence at the earliest possible time after complete liberation. It might cause 'Uncle Ted' to turn in his grave, it might run counter to Roosevelt's own boyhood delight when the USA annexed the islands; but it conformed with his more recent principle of anti-colonialism, and would give a good example to the imperialist British, French and Dutch who gave every sign of wanting to hold on to *their* old possessions.

'I do wish you could have been in my office the other day,' Roosevelt added in his letter to Daniels, referring to his son Jonathan's inauguration as his Press Secretary. 'He is a grand person . . .'

It was Roosevelt's last letter to his one-time chief. A few days later, on 12 April 1945, he died swiftly and without warning.

'When I received these tidings early in the morning of Friday, the 13th, I felt as if I had been struck a physical blow,' Churchill wrote.

My relations with this shining personality had played so large a part in the long, terrible years we had worked together. Now they had come to an end, and I was overpowered by a sense of deep and irreparable loss. I went down to the House of Commons, which met at 11 o'clock, and in a few sentences proposed that we should pay our respects to the memory of our great friend by immediately adjourning. This unprecedented step on the occasion of the death of the head of a foreign State was in accordance with the unanimous wish of the Members, who filed slowly out of the chamber after a sitting which had lasted only eight minutes.

Later that day Churchill composed a letter to the man who, more than anyone else, brought into being this unique personal alliance, and held it tight for three and a half tumultuous years, Harry Hopkins:

I understand how deep your feelings of grief must be. I feel with you that we have lost one of our greatest friends and one of the most valiant champions of the causes for which we fight. I feel a very painful personal loss, quite apart from the ties of public action which bound us so closely together. I had a true affection for Franklin.

Roosevelt fully understood the nature of Churchill's relations with the Royal Navy and recognized the sharp difference with his own less mercurial and interventionist policy. The President's admiration for what Churchill did for the Royal Navy when Roosevelt was a young Assistant Secretary remained unchanged, and if he was critical of the Royal Navy's performance from time to time, notably off Norway in 1940, he was as worried as Churchill about the fate of the French Fleet in 1940. And he did not add his voice to the critics of Churchill's decision to intervene in Greece in 1941. On the contrary, while he deplored the savage naval losses at the hands of the Luftwaffe, he greatly admired Churchill's courage and principle in going to the rescue of an ally in distress, and many people believe that it led Roosevelt to put pressure on Congress to legislate Lend-Lease.

In their wartime relationship there were many points of dispute, sometimes serious and prolonged dispute, between the Premier and the President. Roosevelt was high-handed about the disposal of the Italian Fleet, about certain military appointments, and about his relations with the Soviet Union. The Yalta Conference, in which Churchill's voice was perforce muted, was in its consequences for the Western world an utter and irretrievable disaster, with 'the fast-failing President' coming to the meeting 'determined to establish a world republic of independent liberal nations and who believed that, unlike Churchill and the British "colonialists", Stalin was ready to underwrite such a world ...' On the other hand Churchill *was* excessively imperial-minded in 1944–5 and had no intention of advancing the Indian cause for independence after the fighting was over. They even quarrelled about the Argentine, Roosevelt wanting Britain to cut off diplomatic relations because of that republic's pro-Nazi intransigence, while Churchill knew Britain needed the meat.

But personal relations never seriously suffered and to talk of a crumbling alliance in personal terms is the height of nonsense. The two men were different in so many ways: sense of humour, attitude to women, taste in drinking even – Roosevelt being a restrained but ritualistic cocktail man, Churchill a steady champagne, brandy and whisky drinker. They both liked to put on a show and both were megalomaniacs, but their styles were quite different. No sense of insecurity ever tormented Roosevelt, but both men were physically tough and courageous. By a wide margin, Roosevelt was the greater politician, in part because his judgement of his fellow men was sounder and because he was possessed of massive guile. When members of the joint American Houses of Congress and Representatives heard Churchill suggest that he might be there as President of the United States if an accident of birth had given him an American father and a British mother instead of the other way round, they could be forgiven if they had all discreetly raised an eyebrow while they laughed. Churchill would not have got to the White House in a thousand years.

When it is suggested that the close alliance would never have been formed but for the exigencies of war, it is not only hypothetical; it also reflects the greatest credit on both men, whose sense of duty and the demands of survival made the alliance work to save Western civilization *and* showed the world that personal friendship makes a politico-military alliance happier and more effective.

No two people had better opportunity for observing the two war leaders together, nor better qualifications for making a judgement on the relationship than Robert E. Sherwood and General Ismay, two of the small group of lieutenants at the top who ran the war and made the alliance work. Roosevelt's speech-writer has written:

It is a matter of sacred tradition that when an American statesman and a British statesman meet the former will be plain, blunt, down-to-earth, ingenuous to a fault, while the latter will be sly, subtle, devious, and eventually triumphant. In the cases of Roosevelt and Churchill this formula became somewhat confused. If either of them could be called a student of Machiavelli, it was Roosevelt; if either was a bull in a china shop, it was Churchill. The Prime Minister quickly learned that he confronted in the President a man of infinite subtlety and obscurity – an artful dodger who could not readily be pinned down on specific points, nor hustled or wheedled into definite commitments against his judgement or his will or his instinct. And Roosevelt soon learned how pertinacious the Prime Minister could be in pursuance of a purpose. Churchill's admirers could call him 'tenacious, indomitable', and his detractors could describe him as 'obstinate, obdurate, dogged, mulish, pigheaded'. Probably both factions could agree on the word 'stubborn', which may be flattering or derogatory. In any case, it was this quality which at times made him extremely tiresome to deal with and at other times – and especially times of most awful adversity – made him great.

Roosevelt and Churchill certainly had the capacity to annoy each other, but the record of their tremendous association with one another contains a minimum of evidences of waspishness or indeed of anything less than the most amiable and most courteous consideration. For they had a large and wonderful capacity to stimulate and refresh each other. In one of the darkest hours of the war Roosevelt concluded a long, serious cable to Churchill with the words : 'It is fun to be in the same decade with you.'

General Ismay as Churchill's Chief of Staff, privy to every detail and every nuance of the relationship and present at all but the most private *tête-à-têtes*, chose 'a remarkable episode' in Washington after the first Quebec Conference in 1943 to signify the depth of affection and confidence between the two men.

The President had to go to Hyde Park before Churchill had finished all that he wanted to do. On leaving, he said, in so many words, 'Winston, please treat the White House as your home. Invite anyone you like to any meals, and do not hesitate to summon any of my advisers with whom you wish to confer at any time you wish. Please break your journey to Halifax at Hyde Park and tell me all about it.' Churchill took advantage of this offer, and presided over a top level meeting on 11 September. The Americans were represented by Admiral Leahy, General Marshall, Admiral King, General Arnold, Mr Harry Hopkins, Mr Averell Harriman and Mr Lewis Douglas. On the British side there were Field Marshal Dill, Admiral Noble, Air Marshal Sir William Welsh, Lieutenant-General Macready and myself. It was like a family gathering, and every sort of problem was discussed with complete frankness. I wonder if, in all history, there has ever existed between the war leaders of two allied nations, a relationship so intimate as that revealed by this episode. The affection and trust which Churchill had inspired in Roosevelt was not the least of his services to the Allied cause.

The same must be said of the war-winning value of the affection and trust inspired in Churchill by Franklin Roosevelt. It is hard to believe that the Grand Alliance – the special relationship – which destroyed tyranny in 1945 could have endured through eight subsequent presidents and nine prime ministers and preserved the world from nuclear conflict if the foundations had not been laid with such precision and strength almost half a century ago.

Appendix A

Letter from George VI to President Roosevelt delivered by Churchill's hand, Placentia Bay, 9 August 1941

My dear President Roosevelt,
   This is just a note to bring you my best wishes, and to say how glad I am that you have an opportunity at last of getting to know my Prime Minister. I am sure that you will agree that he is a very remarkable man, and I have no doubt that your meeting will prove of great benefit to our two countries in the pursuit of our common goal.
Yours sincerely,
George R.I.

Longhand letter from President Roosevelt to George VI dated 11 August 1941

ABOARD USS Augusta

My dear King George:
   We are at anchor in this Newfoundland harbor close to HMS *Prince of Wales* and I have had three delightful and useful days with Mr Churchill and the heads of your three services. It has been a privilege to come to know Mr Churchill in this way and I am very confident that our minds travel together, and that our talks are bearing practical fruit for both nations.
   I wish that you could have been with us at Divine Service yesterday on the quarterdeck of your latest battleship. I shall never forget it. Your officers and men were mingled with about three hundred of ours, spread over the turrets and superstructure – I hope you will see the movies of it.
   Will you be good enough to tell the Queen that her radio address yesterday was really perfect in every way and that it will do a great amount of good.
   We think of you both often and wish we could be of more help – But we are daily gaining in confidence in the outcome – We know you will keep up the good work.
   With my very warm regards,
Sincerely yours,
Franklin D. Roosevelt

Appendix B
The Atlantic Charter

THE PRESIDENT of the United States [of America] and the Prime Minister, Mr Churchill, representing His Majesty's Government in the United Kingdom, being met together, deem it right to make known certain common principles in the national policies of their respective countries on which they base their hopes for a better future for the world.

FIRST, their countries seek no aggrandisement, territorial or other.

SECOND, they desire to see no territorial changes that do not accord with the freely expressed wishes of the people concerned.

THIRD, they respect the right of all people to choose the form of government under which they will live ; and they wish to see sovereign rights and self-government restored to those who have been forcibly deprived of them.

FOURTH, they will endeavour, with due respect for their existing obligations, to further enjoyment of all States, great or small, victor or vanquished, of access, on equal terms, to the trade and to the raw materials of the world which are needed for their economic prosperity.

FIFTH, they desire to bring about the fullest collaboration between all nations in the economic field, with the object of securing for all improved labour standards, economic advancement, and social security.

SIXTH, after the final destruction of [the] Nazi tyranny, they hope to see established a peace which will afford to all nations the means of dwelling in safety within their own boundaries, and which will afford assurance that all the men in all the lands may live out their lives in freedom from fear and want.

SEVENTH, such a peace should enable all men to traverse the high seas and oceans without hindrance.

EIGHTH, they believe [that] all of the nations of the world, for realistic as well as spiritual reasons, must come to the abandonment of the use of force. Since no future peace can be maintained if land, sea or air armaments continue to be employed by nations which threaten, or may threaten, aggression outside of their frontiers, they believe, pending the establishment of a wider and permanent system of general security, that the disarmament of such nations is essential. They will likewise aid and encourage all other practicable measures which will lighten for peace-loving peoples the crushing burden of armaments.

Source References

A full entry is given at the first reference to a book's title; subsequent references are abbreviated: e.g. A.J.Marder, *The Dreadnought to Scapa Flow*, Vol. 1 (1960), p. 96, becomes Marder, *Dreadnought*, 1, p. 96.

The Churchill titles most frequently quoted are, first, the official biography in (so far) six volumes, the first two by his son, Randolph Churchill, the remaining by Martin Gilbert. All but Volume VI have accompanying Companion volumes of related papers. These last are abbreviated thus: *Churchill* II *Companion* III, p. 1875. Second, Churchill's own history of the First World War, *The World Crisis*, in seven volumes; and lastly, Churchill's own history of the Second World War in six volumes. The references to these are abbreviated thus: WSC, *World Crisis*, III, p. 29 and WSC, *Second World War*, I, p. 343.

Acknowledgements are due to William Heinemann for the use of extracts from the official biography of Winston Churchill by Randolph Churchill and Martin Gilbert; to Odhams Press for the use of extracts from Churchill's *The World Crisis* and *My Early Life;* to Cassells for the use of extracts from Churchill's *The Second World War;* and to The Oxford University Press for extracts from *H.H.Asquith: Letters to Venetia Stanley,* selected and edited by Michael and Eleanor Brock.

The Fishing Party (pp. 1–12)

Page	*Line*	
I	16	M.Gilbert, *Finest Hour: Winston S.Churchill 1939–41*, Vol. VI (1983), p. 1155
3	26	H.V.Morton, *Atlantic Meeting* (1943), p. 83
3	37	S.E.Morison, *The European Discovery of America: The Northern Voyages* (1971), p. 181
4	8	Morton, p. 84
4	17	J.P.Lash, *Roosevelt & Churchill 1939–1941* (1977), p. 393
5	21	*Time* magazine, 11 August 1941
5	43	Franklin D.Roosevelt Library (FDRL), OF 200–J–R
7	43	A.Averell Harriman and Elie Abel, *Special Envoy to Churchill and Stalin 1941–46* (1975), p. 75
8	21	A.Cadogan, *Diaries* (1972), p. 398
8	25	E.Roosevelt, *As He Saw It* (1946), p. 29
9	3	S.E.Morison, *History of U.S. Naval Operations in World War 2*, Vol. I (1948), p. 70n
9	28	W.S.Churchill, *The Second World War*, Vol. III: *The Grand Alliance* (1950), p. 384
9	34	R.E.Sherwood, *The White House Papers of Harry L.Hopkins*, Vol. I (1948), p. 354
9	40	WSC, *Second World War*, III, p. 385
11	8	*Time* magazine, 25 August 1941
11	11	*New York Times*, 18 August 1941
11	32	Morton, p. 125
11	39	B.Brooke, *Alarm Starboard* (1982), p. 85

1: 'Kitchener the blackguard . . .' (pp. 13–23)

Page	*Line*	
13	3	R.S.Churchill, *Winston S.Churchill*, Vol. I (1966), p. 362
13	6	*Ibid.*, p. 363
13	9	*Ibid.*, p. 43
13	28	*Ibid.*, p. 126
14	5	*Ibid.*, p. 116
14	18	W.S.Churchill, *My Early Life* (1930), p. 28
14	26	*Ibid.*, p. 207
15	43	*Ibid.*, p. 62
16	9	*Churchill*, I, p. 349
16	26	*My Early Life*, p. 269
19	7	*Ibid.*, p. 161
19	31	*Churchill*, I, p. 407
20	3	*My Early Life*, p. 191
20	22	*Churchill*, I, p. 415
20	40	*Ibid.*, p. 424
21	21	*Churchill* II *Companion* I (1969), p. 445n
22	9	T.Morgan, *Churchill 1874–1915* (1983), paperback edition (1984), p. 278
22	17	Quoted in E.Longford, *A Pilgrimage of Passion* (1979), p. 388

2: Scottish Tryst (pp. 24–41)

Page	Line	
24	30	A.J.Marder (ed.), *Fear God and Dread Nought: The Correspondence of Admiral of the Fleet Lord Fisher of Kilverstone*, Vol. II (1956), p. 310
25	38	*Ibid.*, p. 419
26	23	W.S.Churchill, *The World Crisis*, Vol. I (1923), p. 73
26	38	*Fear God*, II, p. 155
27	20	3 March 1910. Fisher Papers, Churchill College, Cambridge
28	22	*Fear God*, II, p. 200
29	24	WSC, *World Crisis*, I, p. 37
29	29	*Fear God*, II, p. 232
29	34	*Ibid.*, p. 226
30	20	WSC, *World Crisis*, I, pp. 50–51
30	36	*Fear God*, II, p. 380
31	13	Churchill to Lloyd George: F.Owen, *Tempestuous Journey: Lloyd George, His Life & Times* (1954), p. 213
32	4	A.J.Marder, *From Dreadnought to Scapa Flow*, Vol. I (1961), p. 245
32	23	McKenna Papers. Quoted in Marder, *Dreadnought*, I, p. 249
33	14	V.Bonham-Carter, *Winston Churchill as I Knew Him* (1965), pp. 235–6
33	25	R.B.S.Haldane, *An Autobiography* (1929), p. 236
33	29	*Churchill as I Knew Him*, p. 235
34	3	Haldane, p. 236
34	11	*Churchill as I Knew Him*, p. 237
34	29	Marder, *Dreadnought*, I, p. 253
35	7	*Spectator*, 28 October 1911
35	13	*The Times*, 27 October 1911
35	34	*Fear God*, II, p. 401
36	16	WSC, *World Crisis*, I, p. 84
37	29	*Ibid.*, p. 38
38	1	*Ibid.*, pp. 118–19
38	22	Kilverstone Papers (in possession of Lord Fisher of Kilverstone)
39	10	*Ibid.*
39	38	R.S.Churchill, *Churchill*, Vol. II (1967), p. 648
40	4	*Ibid.*, p. 649
40	11	*Ibid.*, p. 652

3: Recalcitrant Admirals (pp. 42–52)

Page	Line	
42	25	Hopwood to Churchill, 24 October 1912. Quoted in *Churchill* II *Companion* III (1969), p. 1657
43	10	*Churchill*, II, p. 629
43	29	*Ibid.*, p. 630
44	7	*Churchill* II *Companion* III, p. 1678
44	11	*Ibid.*, p. 1679
44	29	*Churchill*, II, p. 633
45	24	W.Wemyss, *The Life & Letters of Lord Wester Wemyss* (1935), p. 141
46	23	R.Bacon, *The Life of John Rushworth, Earl Jellicoe* (1936), p. 183
46	40	*Churchill* II *Companion* II, p. 1798
47	25	*Ibid.*, p. 1801
47	39	*Ibid.*, p. 1754
48	17	*Fear God*, II, p. 436
49	2	Bacon, *Jellicoe*, pp. 181–2

Page	Line	
49	26	Marder, *Dreadnought*, I, p. 254
50	3	J.A.Fisher, *Records* (1919), p. 184
50	10	Kilverstone Papers
50	29	*Churchill* II *Companion* III, p. 1875

4: Indignant Turks (pp. 53-77)

Page	Line	
53	24	WSC, *World Crisis*, I, p. 189
54	19	*Ibid.*, p. 190
54	24	*Ibid.*, p. 191
55	39	*Churchill* II *Companion* III, pp. 1987-8
56	30	WSC, *World Crisis*, I, p. 197
57	10	R.Hough, *Louis and Victoria* (1974), p. 281
57	7	WSC, *World Crisis*, I, p. 198
58	15	*Churchill* II *Companion* III, p. 1993
59	32	M. and E.Brock (eds), *H.H.Asquith Letters to Venetia Stanley* (1982), pp. 150-1
60	8	J.Corbett, *History of the Great War: Naval Operations*, Vol. I (1920), p. 177
60	34	Keyes MSS (Churchill College, Cambridge)
61	1	R.Hough, *The Great War at Sea 1914-18* (1983), p. 195
61	5	Jellicoe MSS(British Library), 30 September 1914
61	40	*Asquith-Stanley Letters*, p. 260
62	5	M.Gilbert, *Churchill*, Vol. III (1971), p. 109
62	12	*Ibid.*, p. 113
62	22	*Asquith-Stanley Letters*, p. 260
62	32	*The Morning Post*, 19 October 1914
63	1	*Churchill*, III, p. 133
63	4	*Ibid.*
63	6	*Ibid.*
63	41	*Churchill* III *Companion* I (1972), p. 250
64	21	*Asquith-Stanley Letters*, p. 290
64	29	Hough, *Louis and Victoria*, p. 305
64	39	WSC, *World Crisis*, I, p. 401
65	2	*Ibid.*
65	17	1 May 1916. Copy in Marder Papers (University of California, Santa Barbara)
65	26	*Asquith-Stanley Letters*, p. 290
66	1	K.Rose, *King George V* (1983), p. 187
66	11	Marder, *Dreadnought*, Vol. II (1965), p. 91
67	14	WSC, *World Crisis*, I, p. 452
68	11	*The Times*, 25 January 1915
69	4	*Churchill*, II, p. 526
69	21	A.Balfour to E.Marsh, 8 September 1911. Balfour MSS (British Library)
69	39	R.Bacon, *Lord Fisher*, Vol. II (1929), p. 181
70	17	Hough, *Great War at Sea*, p. 148
71	29	*Churchill*, II, p. 95
72	19	P.Magnus, *Kitchener: Portrait of an Imperialist* (1958), p. 279
73	14	*Churchill*, III, p. 35
73	18	*Ibid.*, p. 36
73	27	*Ibid.*, p. 61
73	36	*Ibid.*, p. 81
74	2	*Ibid.*, p. 92

Page	Line	
75	8	*Churchill* III *Companion* I, pp. 298–9
75	24	*Churchill*, III, p. 165
75	39	*Asquith—Stanley Letters*, p. 329
76	2	*Churchill as I Knew Him*, p. 270
76	9	*Churchill*, III, p. 165
76	18	*Ibid.*, p. 166
76	38	*Churchill* III *Companion* I, p. 315
77	5	*Ibid.*, p. 841
77	5	*Churchill*, III, p. 167

5: The Bombardment (pp. 78–96)

Page	Line	
78	21	*Asquith–Stanley Letters*, p. 394
79	20	*Churchill* III *Companion* I, pp. 367–8
80	4	Churchill to Fisher, 23 December 1914. Kilverstone Papers
80	26	Marder, *Dreadnought*, II, p. 205
80	27	H. H. Asquith, *Memories and Reflections*, Vol. II (1928), p. 63
80	33	10 February 1915. Balfour MSS
80	40	*Fear God*, Vol. III (1959), p. 85
81	6	W. James, *The Eyes of the Navy* (1955), p. 81
81	17	*Ibid.*
81	25	*The War Memoirs of David Lloyd George*, Vol. I (1936), p. 395
81	31	A. J. Marder, *Portrait of an Admiral* (1952), p. 140
81	37	*Ibid.*, p. 141
82	14	*Churchill* II *Companion* I, pp. 405–6
82	29	M. Hankey, *The Supreme Command 1914–1918*, Vol. I (1961), pp. 265–6
83	5	*Churchill*, II, p. 111
83	12	*Ibid.*, p. 103
83	17	*Fear God*, III, pp. 128–9
83	30	*Ibid.*, p. 133
83	41	*Churchill* III *Companion* I, p. 462
84	9	*Ibid.*, p. 460
84	17	*Churchill*, III, p. 260
84	40	Dardanelles Commission report
85	13	*Churchill* III *Companion* I, p. 471
85	16	*Fear God*, III, pp. 149–50
85	24	*Churchill* III *Companion* I, p. 471
86	5	*Churchill*, III, p. 290
86	12	*Ibid.*, p. 289
86	20	Asquith, *Memories*, p. 63
86	23	*Churchill*, III, p. 289
86	27	*Ibid.*
86	34	*Ibid.*
87	13	*Ibid.*, p. 29
87	28	WSC, *World Crisis*, II, p. 184
87	38	Asquith, *Memories*, p. 64
88	7	*Churchill* III *Companion* I, p. 586
88	15	*Ibid.*, p. 587
88	25	Asquith, *Memories*, p. 96
89	22	Dardanelles Commission report
89	27	A. J. P. Taylor, *The First World War* (1963), p. 61
89	35	WSC, *World Crisis*, p. 182
90	14	Marder, *Dreadnought*, II, p. 236
90	23	A. J. P. Taylor, p. 61

Page	Line	
91	9	Unpublished memoirs of Group Captain H.A.Williamson. Marder Papers
92	1	Norman Macleod to A.J.Marder, 26 March 1966. Marder Papers
92	30	Pipon to Marder, 18 October 1965. Marder Papers
93	29	Hough, *Great War at Sea*, p. 161
93	34	Asquith, *Memories*, II, p. 65
93	35	*Ibid.*, p. 68
94	16	Dewar Papers. K.G.B.Dewar. Copy Marder Papers
94	28	Marder, *Dreadnought*, II, p. 243
94	36	Keyes, *Memoirs*, I, p. 105
95	7	*Churchill* III *Companion* I, p. 729
95	26	WSC, *World Crisis*, II, p. 235
95	32	*Churchill* III *Companion* I, pp. 731–2
96	3	WSC, *World Crisis*, II, p. 253

6: 'My regiment is awaiting me' (pp. 97–124)

Page	Line	
97	12	*Fear God*, III, p. 183
97	30	*Ibid.*, p. 193
98	5	*Ibid.*, p. 194
98	10	WSC, *World Crisis*, II, p. 306
98	35	*Churchill*, III, p. 371
99	18	*Ibid.*, p. 373
99	29	*Ibid.*, p. 383
100	4	*Ibid.*, p. 386
100	18	*Ibid.*, p. 387
100	23	*Churchill* III *Companion* I, p. 316
100	32	*Churchill*, III, p. 394
101	30	*Ibid.*, p. 387
101	32	*Ibid.*, p. 389
102	7	*Ibid.*, p. 398 WSC, *World Crisis*, II, p. 316
102	25	B.H.Liddell Hart, *History of the First World War* (1930), (1970 edn) p. 233
103	2	*Churchill* III *Companion* II, p. 852
103	39	*Fear God*, III, p. 217
104	2	*Ibid.*, p. 219
104	34	WSC, *World Crisis*, II, p. 346
105	17	*The Times*, 14 May 1915
105	41	*Churchill*, III, p. 423
106	31	*Ibid.*, p. 433
107	2	WSC, *World Crisis*, II, p. 354
107	17	*Asquith–Stanley Letters*, p. 596
108	9	Group Captain H.A.Williamson to A.J.Marder, 31 July 1968. Marder Papers
108	15	*Churchill*, III, pp. 435–6
108	27	Marder, *Dreadnought*, II, p. 278
109	39	*Lloyd George*, I, p. 225
110	18	*Ibid.*
111	1	WSC, *World Crisis*, II, p. 360
111	24	*Fear God*, II, p. 231
111	35	Quoted in R.Hough, *First Sea Lord* (1969), p. 343
113	14	*Asquith—Stanley Letters*, p. 601
113	28	WSC, *World Crisis*, II, p. 365

Page	*Line*	
114	29	*Ibid.*, p. 369
115	23	*Churchill*, III, p. 456
116	14	*Ibid.*, pp. 457–8
116	30	*Ibid.*, p. 459
116	42	*Ibid.*, p. 400
117	13	*Ibid.*, p. 464
117	26	*Observer*, 23 May 1915
117	31	S.Roskill, *Admiral of the Fleet Earl Beatty* (1980), p. 127
117	35	Marder, *Dreadnought*, II, p. 288
118	3	*Churchill*, III, p. 468
118	10	*Fear God*, II, p. 251
118	14	*Ibid.*, pp. 237–8
118	22	WSC, *World Crisis*, II, pp. 374–5
118	34	*Ibid.*, p. 373
119	10	*Ibid.*, p. 371
119	20	Longford, *Pilgrimage of Passion*, p. 409
119	30	*Churchill*, III, p. 472
120	1	*Ibid.*, p. 473
120	6	Marder, *Dreadnought*, II, p. 289
120	35	*Portrait of an Admiral*, p. 203
121	3	*Churchill* III *Companion* I, p. 284

7: 'Disentangled from the ruins . . .' (pp. 124–46)

Page	*Line*	
124	8	*Churchill*, III, p. 658
125	3	Hankey diary, 5 June 1916. Hankey Papers
125	9	*Churchill*, Vol. IV (1975), p. 13
126	6	*Ibid.*, pp. 179–80
127	7	Quoted in S.Roskill, *Churchill and the Admirals* (1977), p. 74
128	8	*Churchill*, Vol. V (1976), pp. 75–6
128	19	Kemp to author, 17 September 1984
128	29	Churchill V *Companion* I (1979), p. 243
128	41	*Churchill*, V, p. 104
129	10	Beatty Papers. Quoted in Roskill, p. 78
130	42	Conversation with Admiral Grantham, 11 July 1984
131	8	Conversation with Sir Clifford Jarrett, 25 June 1984
131	35	W.S.Churchill, *The Second World War*, Vol. I (1949), p. 325
132	32	S.King-Hall, *My Naval Life* (1952), pp. 97–8
133	18	WSC, *Second World War*, I, p. 321
134	16	Quoted in Roskill, *Churchill*, p. 95
137	16	*Churchill*, Vol. VI (1983), p. 7
139	26	*Ibid.*, pp. 188–9
140	21	WSC, *Second World War*, I, p. 465
141	12	*Churchill*, VI, p. 219
141	15	Conversation with Jarrett, 25 June 1984
142	20	*Hansard*, 11 April 1940
142	28	*Churchill*, VI, p. 235
142	39	WSC, *Second World War*, I, p. 474
143	6	*Hansard*, 11 April 1940
143	26	Conversation with Martin Gilbert, 1 August 1984
143	30	*Churchill*, VI, p. 257
145	24	WSC, *Second World War*, I, p. 460
146	17	H.Macmillan, *The Blast of War* (1967), p. 72
146	21	Leo Amery, *Hansard*, 7 May 1940

8: 'As naval people . . .' (pp. 147–77)

Page	Line	
148	23	Morison, I, p. xxxiv
149	2	*Ibid.*, p. xlviii
150	I	J. MacGregor Burns, *Roosevelt: The Soldier of Freedom* (1971), p. 149
150	4	Franklin D. Roosevelt Library (FDRL), PPF166: 2 March 1933
150	12	*Ibid.*, 22 June 1933
150	41	FDRL, PSF 83: Swanson to Roosevelt, 11 June 1934
151	2	FDRL. Swanson Papers: 30 June 1937
151	7	FDRL. Roosevelt to Captain Daniel Callaghan, 10 May 1939
151	31	*Ibid.*
151	36	FDRL 166, 17 March 1939
154	5	FDRL. HPP Raeder War Diary, 11 September 1939
155	17	WSC, *Second World War*, I, p. 435
156	I	J. R. M. Butler, *Lord Lothian* (1960), p. 271
156	14	Lash, p. 97
156	19	Henry Morgenthau, quoted in Lash, p. 265
158	9	*Lord Lothian*, p. 265
158	12	*Ibid.*, p. 287
158	28	FDRL. HPP US Naval Attaché's Diary, 24 September 1939
158	31	Roskill, *Churchill*, p. 108
158	35	*Churchill*, VI, p. 410
159	42	W. F. Kimball (ed.), *Churchill & Roosevelt: The Complete Correspondence*, Vol. I (1984), p. 139
159	43	Lash, p. 130
160	3	*Ibid.*, p. 156
161	14	FDRL. HPP Frank Knox, PSF 82
161	28	WSC, *Second World War*, Vol. II (1949), p. 357
161	39	Lash, p. 209
162	31	*Churchill*, VI, p. 733
162	36	Lash, p. 134
162	43	*The Times*, 14 October 1940
165	14	WSC, *Second World War*, II, p. 211
168	35	Morison, I, p. 27
169	7	*Churchill*, VI, p. 691
169	28	Roosevelt to Leahy, 26 June 1941: E. Roosevelt (ed.), *The Letters of Franklin D. Roosevelt*, Vol. III (1949), p. 377
170	21	Morison, I, p. 50
171	3	*Churchill*, VI, pp. 999–1000
172	12	W. A. Harriman and E. Abel, *Special Envoy to Churchill and Stalin 1941–1946* (1975), pp. 33–4
172	29	*Churchill*, VI, p. 1095
175	17	*The Memoirs of Lord Ismay* (1960), pp. 269–70
176	24	*Churchill*, VI, pp. 972–3

9: Day of Infamy (pp. 178–92)

Page	Line	
178	2	Sherwood, I, p. 435
179	25	WSC, *Second World War*, III, p. 539
180	7	Frances Perkins, Oral History Project, Columbia University. Quoted in Lash, p. 488
180	32	FDRL. PPF 166: Stark to Roosevelt, 23 October 1941
181	32	D. Macintyre, *The Battle for the Pacific* (1966), p. 30
182	2	Sherwood, I, p. 165

Page	Line	
182	8	*Ibid.*, p. 365
182	22	*The Times*, 26 June 1956
182	31	*Daily Telegraph*, 28 May 1981
183	4	A. Bryant (ed.), *The Alanbrooke War Diaries 1939–1943: The Turn of the Tide* (1957), p. 289 (paperback edition)
183	20	*The Times*, 22 February 1966
183	26	*Ibid.*,
183	29	S. E. Morison *The Ocean Two-Ocean War* (1963), p. 581
183	40	FDRL. PPF 8541
184	1	*Two-Ocean War*, p. 581
184	13	S. E. Morison, *History of U. S. Naval Operations in World War II*, Vol. IV (1953), p. 82
184	18	*The Times*, 16 December 1969
184	30	*Two-Ocean War*, p. 582
185	27	Kimball, III, p. 118
185	36	R. G. Albion and R. H. Connery, *Forrestal & the Navy* (1962), p. 127 FDRL. John L. McCrea file, 24 February 1942
186	3	Samuel John Stone, *Lyra Fidelium* (1866)

10: Premier's Team (pp. 193–205)

Page	Line	
193	19	Conversation with Sir Clifford Jarrett, 25 June 1984
193	21	Conversation with Admiral Sir Guy Grantham, 11 July 1984
193	30	*Churchill*, VI, p. 849
195	20	A. J. Marder, ' "Winston is Back": Churchill at the Admiralty 1939–40', *English Historical Review*
196	8	Bryant, *Alanbrooke*, I, p. 215
196	12	*Ibid.*
196	18	FDRL. PPF 8552
197	1	WSC, *Second World War*, Vol. III (1950), p. 551
198	2	*The Times*, 27 December 1945
198	9	R. R. James (ed.), *Chips: the Diaries of Sir Henry Channon* (1967), p. 190 (paperback edition)
198	18	*Sunday Telegraph*, 23 September 1984
198	23	Conversation with Captain John Litchfield RN, 21 June 1984
198	34	Conversation with Peter Kemp, 21 April 1984
199	13	Jarrett to Marder, 9 September 1973
199	13	Kemp to author, 9 December 1984
200	4	*Ibid.*
200	12	*Ibid.*
200	16	*Ibid.*
200	25	A. Bryant (ed.), *The Alanbrooke War Diaries 1943–46: Triumph in the West*, Vol. II (1959), p. 56 (paperback edition)
201	1	Admiral of the Fleet Viscount Cunningham of Hyndhope, *A Sailor's Odyssey* (1951), p. 641
201	21	*The Times*, 30 June 1963
201	30	Admiral Grantham to author, 21 December 1984
202	16	WSC, *Second World War*, Vol. VI (1954), p. 12
202	41	R. Hough, *Mountbatten: Hero of our Time* (1980), p. 165
203	5	Kemp to author, 9 December 1984
203	10	Marder, 'Churchill at the Admiralty'
203	27	Conversation with Admiral Grantham, 11 July 1984
203	31	P. Ziegler, *Mountbatten* (1985), p. 227
204	10	J. Wheeler-Bennett (ed.), *Action this Day* (1968), p. 160

Page	Line	
204	39	*Sailor's Odyssey*, p. 250
205	6	WSC, *Second World War*, III, pp. 591–2
205	10	Conversation with Martin Gilbert, 1 August 1984

11: 'A true affection ...' (pp. 206–21)

Page	Line	
206	14	*Turn of Tide*, p. 282
207	11	Kimball, I, p. 286
207	16	WSC, *Second World War*, III, pp. 587–8
207	30	Kimball, I, p. 304
207	40	*Ibid.*, p. 360
208	4	*Ibid.*, p. 363
208	18	*Ibid.*, p. 424
208	36	*Ibid.*, p. 477
209	2	*Ibid.*, p. 456
209	10	*Ibid.*, p. 478
209	25	*Ibid.*, p. 482
211	9	*Ibid.*, p. 167
211	29	Conversation with Kemp, 21 April 1984
212	6	Kimball, II, p. 501
212	16	WSC, *Second World War*, VI, p. 212
212	21	*Ibid.*, p. 382
213	38	Kimball, III, p. 38
214	33	*Ibid.*, p. 195
214	38	*Ibid.*, p. 376
215	4	*Ibid.*, p. 388
215	15	WSC, *Second World War*, VI, p. 289
215	34	*Ibid.*, p. 297
216	11	Sherwood, II, p. 41
216	15	WSC, *Second World War*, VI, p. 299
216	23	*Ibid.*
217	37	F.D.R., *Letters*, III, p. 520
218	1	WSC, *Second World War*, VI, p. 412
218	13	*Ibid.*, p. 413
218	37	*Triumph in the West*, p. 319 (paperback edition)
219	35	Sherwood, II, p. 365
220	22	Ismay, pp. 319–20

Index
by Douglas Matthews